MONTGOMERY COUNTY MARYLAND

DEED BOOKS

LIBERS L-M-N

Abstracts
1803–1807

Abstracted by
Patricia Abelard Andersen

Land Records Read from: Microfilm, and the Maryland State Archives Land Records website

HERITAGE BOOKS
2020

HERITAGE BOOKS

AN IMPRINT OF HERITAGE BOOKS, INC.

Books, CDs, and more—Worldwide

For our listing of thousands of titles see our website
at
www.HeritageBooks.com

Published 2020 by
HERITAGE BOOKS, INC.
Publishing Division
5810 Ruatan Street
Berwyn Heights, Md. 20740

INTRODUCTION

Land Record Abstracts for Montgomery County, for Libers A-E, were done by Mary Gordon Malloy and are available in manuscript form at the Jane C. Sween Library of the Montgomery County Historical Society in Rockville, MD. Their web site is www.montgomeryhistory.org

The author of this volume has also compiled two prior volumes of land records for Montgomery County. One includes selected records pertaining to slaves in Libers A-E, and reread those entries to include more information, and also included all records from Libers F, and F-7, a small volume done by Thomas Munro, who served as Clerk of Court for a brief period after the death of Brooke Beall, and before Upton Beall assumed the post in Liber G. A second volume of land records for Montgomery County, Libers H -I/J-K has also been published.

The deeds are indexed in the general indexes and are also available online from the Maryland State Archives web site: www.mdlandrec.net. Once you have identified deeds of interest, you may wish to go online and print out the original deeds to obtain the full metes and bounds describing the property. The Montgomery County Historical Society has a set of overlays identifying the location of many of the original land tracts in Montgomery County.

The "land record books" include many non land items however. You will find information about slave sales and manumissions in these volumes, as well as mortgages of both real and personal (or chattel) property. Occasionally other documents are also recorded. When the official indexes were compiled these records were often omitted, since they did not pertain to current needs for records for the county clerks, so it is only in abstracts that you will often find these interesting aspects of your ancestor's lives.

Although some of the individual libers do possess indexes either at the beginning or end of the book, it can be time consuming to locate and use them, and due to aging and missing pages, some of these indexes are incomplete or missing. To find these original indexes, online, go to page 1 of volume, hit the previous page button, and you may find the original index, if they digitized those pages. Not all of the books have these indexes digitized, unfortunately.

In this volume, the names of the witnesses, when they appear to have been court officials, or justices of the peace, are often omitted to save space. When it appears that they are family members, as is frequently the case in bills of sale, they are included. Often you will then have two sets of witnesses in deeds. When deeds were witnessed by other than the Justices of the Peace, they would then be acknowledged before the Justices of the Peace, as was required.

Also in this volume, there are a few deeds for District of Columbia property, but generally they were now being recorded in the District.

List of Some Terms and Abbreviations Used in the Abstracts

£	Pounds – the common currency used during the colonial and early federal period. Usage here is £10..10..10 read as 10 pounds, 10 shillings 10 pence. However in 1803, dollars $ are becoming the more frequently used currency. You will however, see occasional reference to other forms of currency, including, Tobacco, still being used.
AAC	Anne Arundel County
ack	Acknowledgment of the deed by the grantor.
afd/afs'd	aforesaid
dower rights:	A wife or a widow's right to 1/3 of all her husband's real property during her lifetime. This right had to be released whenever he sold property. If not done at the time the deed was made, the widow could come back later and exercise a claim against the property, and sometimes later dower releases were recorded.
draught/draft:	One of the upper branches of a river or creek.
FC	Frederick County
Indenture:	Any written contract. "Indentured servants" comes from this
M&B	Metes and bounds - description of real estate boundaries.
PGC	Prince George's County
rsy/rsy'd	resurvey/resurveyed
SMC	St. Mary's County

Maryland Deed Records Abstracts

Montgomery County Deeds, Liber L, Liber M and Liber N

Liber L:1. Barton Harris to William Orr, recorded 2 August 1803 for £75, bill of sale for Negro boy, Charles, 12 years of age. Wit: Richard Turner.

L:1-2. Richard Ayton recorded 3 August 1803, I Jane Ayton for love and affection, and for the better maintenance of my son, Richard grant to him, all my claim to tract *Charles and Benjamin,* conveyed to me by Jeremiah Berry 3d. 9 April 1803. Signed before Jno Thomas 3d, John Adamson. Acknowledged.

L:2-5. Thomas Scott Sr., recorded 4 August 1803, from Thomas J. Beatty of Georgetown. Whereas in August 1790 he made bond to said Scott Sr. For tract called *Outlett,* 204 acres and second tract *Strong Beer,* 6 1/4 acres for £1576..17..6 in part conveyed by Rebecca Smith to Nathaniel Offutt.

L:5-6. Joseph N. Chiswell recorded 4 August 1803 made 2 April from Raphael Knott and Catherine Knott his wife of Nelson county, Kentucky, for £44..5 assigns tract *Fortune* undivided 1/4 part.

L:7-8. William Brewer recorded 4 August 1803 from Joseph Newton Chiswell, undivided 1/4 part of tract called *Fortune,* for £54..5. Eleanor Chiswell released dower.

L:8. Jesse Wilcoxon recorded bill of sale 6 August 1809. I Nicholas Gray for consideration of debt, for £25 conveys all house and kitchen furniture. Signed by mark.

L:8-11. Joseph Harris, son of Joseph Harris deceased recorded 6 August 1803, made 15 July from Jesse Harris, administrator of his father, Joseph Harris. Signed. Dorcas Harris wife of Jesse released dower rights.

L:11-13. John Kender recorded 9 August 1803, from Joseph Aud of Frederick County for £328 part of *Conclusion,* resurveyed for William Deakins. Ann Aud released dower rights.

L:13-14. John H. Boswell recorded bond 9 August 1803 as constable. Signed by Sam Lane and Richard Turner, securities.

L:14. William Hempstone recorded bill of sale 10 August 1803. I Archibald Brown for £98..5, sells crops (incl. Tobacco), hogs, cattle, mare, geese, farm tools listed. Signed by mark.

L:15-16. Benjamin Waters recorded mortgage 11 August 1803, from Walter Mitchell and Lucretia his wife. Whereas Edward Browning, father to Lucretia did by his will devise tract called *Brownings Folly.*

L:16-19. Upton Beall recorded contract 11 August 1803, among children of Brooke Beall, who died intestate, late of Georgetown, for the support of Margaret Beall their mother. Signed by Margaret Beall, Upton Beall, Elisha O. Williams, Harriett Williams, B. Mackall, Christina Mackall, Kitty Mackall, Aquilla Beall, Wm Steuart, Hellen Steuart, Lewis Beall.

L:19-21. Peter Kemp and James Willson Perry recorded 12 August 1803 from Upton Beall. Whereas Walter Beall of Bairds Town, Nelson County, Kentucky, appointed Upton his lawfull atorney to sell tract called *Harding's Choice,* for £600 sells 100 acres.

L:22. Power of attorney recorded for Walter Beall made 13 March 1798.

L:23-25. William Hawker recorded 13 August 1803, made 5 May between Joseph N. Burch of Prince George's County for £47..5, two tracts called *Slipe,* and *Small Purchase.* 14 ½ acres. To 10th line of *Resurvey on John's Delight,* adjacent to tract *Elizabeth.* Eleanor wife of Joseph Newton Burch released dower rights.

L:25-26. Kinsey Gittings recorded 15 August 1803, between John Hewitt of Washington D.C. trustee for sale of real estate of heirs of Richard Ober for *Drane's Final Conclusion, Dranes Luck.*

L:27. Francis Fish, Henry Lansdale, Benjamin Perry recorded constables bond, 15 August 1803

L:27-28. James Ray recorded 22 August 1803, made on 13 March 1773. John Waters Jr. Late of Prince Georges County, conveyed to his son Samuel Waters of Prince George's County, recorded in Liber P:666-667 of Frederick County, parts of *Bear Neck,* and *Maiden's Fancy,* 6 acres. Original boundary marker has been lost, and this date agreement made to mark spot, between Thomas Waters and James Ray.

L:28-29. Leonard Hays recorded 23 August 1803, from Samuel Hepburn of Prince George's County, for £300. *Resurvey on Hanover.* Jane Hepburn released dower.

L:30-31. Solomon Holland, Benjamin Ricketts and Zachariah Gatton, recorded bond for £452 as Justice of Levy Court, 23 August 1803.

L:31-33. James Dunlop recorded 26 August 1803 from Doctor John Carroll of the City of Baltimore, part of *Joseph's Park,* on line of Philip Barton Key's land.

33-34. Weathers Smith, now of Kentucky, from Charles Rogers recorded 27 August 1803 for valuable consideration, transfers Negro woman Charlot 17 years of age. If Charles Rogers pays before 20th instant, £25..16..3, then bill of sale is void. Signed before William Culver.

L:34 Lydia & Susan Smith recorded 27 August 1803, from Charles Rogers, for love and affection I bear to my sisters-in law of Bourbon Co., Kentucky, grants them all furniture contained in two small trunks together with their sister's wearing apparel, being in my house in Clarksburg. Signed 11 August 1803 before Wm Culver.

L:35-36. James Lackland recorded 29 August 1803 from Thomas Beall of George, tract called *Belvedere* for 123 acres. Nancy Beall his wife released dower

L:36-37. Josias Fendall Beall and James Alexander Beall of Montgomery County, and Ann Fendall Beall of Prince George's County, recorded 5 September 1803 deed from Benjamin Bradley Beall for 5 shillings, all his right to tract *Layhill Beall's Reserve,* late the property of Josias Beall deceased. Signed before Wm Marshall, Francis Dyer, J.P's, Prince Georges Co. Mary Beall, wife of Benjamin B. Beall, released dower.

L:37-39. Frederick Duvall recorded 6 September 1803 from Richard Morgan for £200 lot #44in town of Williamsburgh, now called Rockville.. Eleanor Morgan released dower rights.

L:39-40. James Day recorded 12 September 1803 from Peter Boyer for 5 shillings, part of *Henry and Elizabeth Enlarged,* and part of *Flag Patch.* Mary Boyer wife of Peter released dower.

L:41. Nathan Harris recorded bill of sale 9 September 1803 from William Hurley. For £15, one grey mare and colt, two cows, other household goods. Signed by mark before Richard Beall.

L:42-43 William Hilton recorded 14 September 1803 deed made 12 August 1803 from Joseph Harris (son of John) for £5. Part of a tract of land called *Mount Zion,* beginning at a stone and fixed at the end of 17 ½ perches on the 11th line of a tract called *It May Be Good in Time,* containing 3/4 of an acre. Signed Joseph Harris Jr before Lenox Martin, Richard Beall.

L:43-44 Joseph Harris from William Hilton Recorded 14 September 1803, made 12 August 1803. £5. Sells part of *It May Be Good in Time,* containing 5/8 acre. Signed before Richard Beall, Lenox Martin.

L:44 Thomas Morton to Negroes John & Rose, manumission recorded 14 September 1803. Black man John Miles to be free at expiration of 9 years from 27 March; Rose Brown to be free 3 years from 6th December next. Signed 13 September 1803. Witnesses Mary Camden, Lenox Martin.

L:44-47. Samuel Robertson 3d, recorded 14 September 1803, from Edward Crow, Sr., part of *Benjamins Square and Pigman's Purchase.* On the second line of a deed from the heirs of Lodowick Davis to Ignatius Pigman, adjacent to *Fertile Meadows.* Tract includes waters of mill dam, 150 acres. Signed before Wm Smith, Archibald A. Beall. Acknowledged.

L:47-49. Samuel Howard recorded deed 14 September 1803, from Samuel Robertson for £1000 one half of following tracts*: Land of Goshen,* and *Pigmans Purchase,* and part of *Resurvey on Benjamin Square.* Signed. Rachel wife of Samuel Robertson released dower rights.

L:49-50. James P. Soper recorded deed 15 September 1803, made 1 April, from Joshua Aldridge of Garrett County in the State of Kentucky, for $1762. Part of tract called *Moore's Rest,* 75 acres, together with 150 acres added. Signed before William Culver, Jno Thomas 3rd.

L:50-52. Zachariah Downes recorded 15 September 1803, made 24 June between James Soper of Anne Arundel Co., and Joseph, Charles, Barton and Eater Soper of Montgomery County, for one pound 4 shillings, sell parcel called *Lady Day,* beginning at 35th line of *Deer Park,* containing 3 3/8 acres. Signed by the five parties. Receipt. Acknowledgment.

L:52-53. James Soper and others [Joseph, Charles, Barton and Ester Soper] recorded deed 15 September 1803, from Zachariah Downes for £17..10 part of tract called *Deer Park,* containing 8 4/10 acres. Receipt. Acknowledgment.

L:53-54. James Lawson recorded 15 September 1803, from Nicholas Bailey, bill of sale for £50, 5 head of black cattle, 3 head of sheep, 7 head of hogs, one wagon and gears, 4 horses, and all my household furniture and plantation utensils, Signed before Edward Burgess.

L:54-56 Lenox Martin from Thomas Moreton, recorded 19 September 1803, pursuant to a writing deed of bargain made 15 June 1793 for part of *Bealls Good Will,* 251 acres. Adjacent to Part of Peter Klem's land, called *Rays Venture,* and the 4th line of William Norris's land called *Pretty Spring,* and the given line of John Tannehill's land, containing 10 ½ acres, together with all mills, etc. Signed, acknowledged, Susanna, wife of Thomas Moreton examined apart, released dower rights.

L:56-58. Agreement between Ignatius Davis recorded 19 September 1803 from Lenox Martin, for £200 he assigns ½ part of the grist and saw mills in the use and occupation of the said Ignatius Davis, Thomas Morton with free ingress and egress to in and from the said mills, extending from the 2nd line *Bealls Good Will*, regarding mills on north side of road near mouth of Monocacy. Elizabeth wife of Lenox Martin examined apart and released any dower rights.

L:58-60. Thomas Morton recorded 19 September 1803, from Lenox Martin, for 5 shillings agreements as above for ½ part of the grist and saw mills, as above. Elizabeth wife of Lenox Martin examined apart and released any dower rights.

L:60-62. William Cash and others recorded deed 20 September 1803, from Philip Hammond Hopkins for part of parcel called *Labyrinth,* said William Cash being etitled to 1/5 part of aforesaid parcel; Rezin Cash to 1/5 part; Jonathan Cash to 2/5 part, Isaiah Cash to 1/5 part, which in consideration of these premises, Philip Hammond Hopkins is willing to convey same, tract described adjacent to *Pascalham,* containing 15 1/4 acres more or less.

L:62-64. John Willson Jr. recorded deed 20 September 1803, from William Cash and Rezin Cash, and Johnathan Cash their undivided shares in parcel for £359..8 At same time, Keziah, wife of William Cash; Sarah wife of Jonathan Cash released their dower rights. Acknowledged before Lenox Martin, Wm Smith.

L:64-65. Negroes Harry and Suck recorded 20 September 1803, they to be immediately free, and Negro Jacob to be free from 1 January 1809 and Negro Sam from 1 January 1815, Hez. from 1 Jan. 1821; John from 1 January 1823; Mary, Suky and Sarah, from 1 January 1820 and Betty from 1 January 1823. Any children born to these slaves, will be free at 25 for males and 21 for females. Signed by George Washington Haymon before Richard West, Alexander Adams.

L:65. Benjamin Duvall recorded certificate of qualification as deputy sheriff, 18 September 1803.

L:65-67. Ignatius Waters recorded deed 23 September 1803, made 7 May from George Ellicott of Baltimore County, for $213. 1/3 tract of land called *George and Elizabeth,* granted 12 April 1796, which contains for variation less than half the quantity of 53 acres. Elizabeth Ellicott released dower rights.

L:68-69. Christopher Hussey recorded 24 September 1803 from Thomas Wright of Baltimore County for £500. Part of tract *Charley Forrest.,* now called by the name of *Pigman's Inheritance,* laid out for 50 acres. Signed before Ozias Offutt, Richard West.

L:69 Thomas Wright recorded release 24 September 1803, from Caleb Bentley. Whereas Thomas Wright in 1799 recorded mortgage of tract called *Pigman's Inheritance,* and that is now fully paid. Signed 23rd day 9th month, 1803. Signed Caleb Bentley.

L:69-72. Pierre Legus Belisle recorded 24 September 1803 power of attorney before Philippe Bellenger, Notary public for the Department of Calvados Arrondissement of Falaise resident of the Commonality of Clay, undersigned on the fourteenth Germinal, 10th year of the French Republic, at the borough of Clay were present citizens Jacques and Teau de Caindry, brothers of Charles and Anne Solier deceased, Jacques Fortin and Francoise DeCaindry, his wife; likewise all of them living in the commonalty of Clay in the disrtrict of Thevey Harcourt, Arrondissement of Falaise in the department of Calvados, as sole and presumptive heirs of Charles DeCaindry, their brother and brother-in-law, deceased in Montgomery County in the month of September of the year 1800; and they have jointly appointed citizen Pierre LeGris Belisle, inhabitant of Norfolk in Virginia for their general and special attorney, to sell property of their deceased brother. Translated by John H. Shruber of the City, attested to by Samuel Serett Not. Public Baltimore.

L:72-74. Peter Bowie recorded release 24 September 1803 from Pierre Legre Belisle, of Norfolk, Virginia, lawful attorney for James deCaindry, John deCaindry, James Fortin and Francis DeCaindry his wife, Piere de Leact and Mary DeCaindry his wife all of the commonalty of Clay, in the district of Thevey Harcourt, circle of Falaise, department of Calvados in the French Republic; the lawful brothers and sisters of Charles DeCaindry late of Montgomery County, Maryland. The sum of $1063.37, equal to 5582. Seares, on account, makes indenture

L:74 Thomas Offutt recorded a list of Negroes imported from Virginia, 3 October 1803, called London, Fanny and Mary. Signed before Upton Beall.

L:75. Benjamin Ray Jr., recorded 3 October 1803, bill of sale from Samuel Middleton , for £5, grants Negroes Charles 34, Rachel 35, Sal 16, Nan 12 and Ben 15 years old. Signed before Richard Turner, as a J.P.

L:75-76. Benjamin Ray Jr. Recorded bill of sale 3 Oct 1803 from William O'Neale Jr., grants five Negroes, Frank 40, James 21, Fan 18, Monica 14, Nan 13 years old. Signed.

L:76-77. John Ward of Clark Co., Kentucky, recorded bill of sale 3 Oct. 1803 from John Poole of Montgomery County, a Negro woman Nancy, and her child Sarah for £130. Witness Lenox Martin.

L:77-78. Peter Bayer recorded deed 7 October 1803, from James Day, for 5 shillings, part of tracts *Henry and Elizabeth* and *Flag Patch*. Containing 160 1/4 acres. Sarah Day released dower.

L:78-80. Richard Andrews and others [Charles Andrews, Edward Andrews and Jonathan Andrews] recorded deed 17 September 1803 from Thomas Sprigg for £150 sells tracts of land called *Rich Land,* and tract called *Round Bottom,* containing 120 acres in whole. Signed by Thomas Sprigg before Lewis Duvall, Greenbury Howard.

L:80. Sheriff of Montgomery County recorded schedule from John Green 18 September 1803 includes walnut furniture and accounts against James Stewart and Griffith Davis.

L:80-81. Sheriff of Montgomery County recorded schedule of James Bolton before Ozias Offutt

L:81-82. John Gartrell recorded deed 11 Oct. 1803, from Philemon Plummer, Jr., for $500, tracts adjoining Nicholas Worthington, Benjamin Gartrell, and Obed Leeke, tract called *Gray's Delight,* and *Gray's Lot,* signed. No dower release.

L:82-84. Lloyd Dorsey, son of Michael, of Anne Arundel County, recorded 11 October 1803, deed from John Gartrell for $797.50 part of *Addition to Brooke Grove,* and *Gray's Lot,* adjacent to *Leeke's Lot,* 72 ½ acres. Lucresy, wife of John Gartrell released dower.

L:84-86. Lloyd Dorsey of Anne Arundel County, blacksmith, recorded deed 11 October 1803, from Richard Green, executor of Basil Mullican. Basil Mullikin in his lifetime was possessed of a parcel called *Gittings Hah Hah,* on west side of fork roads above Greens Bridge, Rachel Mullican, widow of Basil released dower right, and Margaret Riney, two of the legatees of said Basil Mullican deceased, voluntarily relinquished dower rights.

L:86-87. John Poole Jr., recorded bill of sale 11 Oct. 1803 from Christopher Miller for a certain sum of money, paid on behalf of me to my creditors, three head of horses, three head of cattle, all my household and kitchen furniture.

L:87-88. Edward Crow Senior recorded deed 14 October 1803, from Thomas Kelly for £1..7 part of *Resurvey on Younger Brother,* adjacent to tract *Oronoke,* 3 ½ acres of land. Signed by mark. Hannah wife of Thomas Kelly released dower.

L:89-90. Thomas Plater recorded deed 14 October 1803 from Thomas Fletchall for 5 shillings, assigns parts of the following tracts, part of *Brightwell's Hunting Quarters, Sugar Bottom, Blantyre, Cors Basket,* and *Prevention* containing 144 acres. Sarah Fletchall released dower.

L:91-92. Thomas Plater recorded deed 14 Oct. 1803 from Thomas Fletchall for 5 shillings, grants tract called *Three Springs,* next to *Cider and Ginger,* conveyed by William Hickman of Stephen to William Hickman of Arthur, containing 50 acres. Sarah Fletchall released dower rights.

L:92-94. John Letton recorded deed 15 Oct. 1803, from Thomas Nicholls of Simon. Whereas in a judgment by Thomas Nicholls against John Hayman Nicholls, the Sheriff by writ of fi fa took tract of land called *Prevention,* containing 331 acres and also tract called *Exeter,* containing 220 acres, and one other tract called *Hermitage,* containing 274 ½ acres Cassandra Nicholls released dower rights.

L:94-95. Charles Perry of Robert recorded bill of sale 15 Oct. 1803, from Robert Perry for 3000 lbs. Crop tobacco and £51..10 assigns one grey mare, 15 years old, one roan mare colt about 6 months; one cow and calf and 14 pigs, 10 small shoats, two feather beds and furniture, one cyder mill, and three cyder casks, 20 barrels corn and 1000 lbs. Transfer tobacco, 10 head of sheep, two barshear plows, one shovel plows.

L:95-97. Kinsey Beall recorded deed 17 October 1803, from George Culp Junr for £414..10 tracts called *Culps Desire, and Thompson's Pasture,* containing 50 9/10 acres. And 22 acres. Eleanor wife to said George released dower rights.

L:97-98. John Austin recorded deed 17 October 1803, from Robert Ferguson of Charles County, for £175..14, sells tract containing 240 acres conveyed to him and Alexander Hamilton as joint tenants, 27 August 1794, called *Inclusion.* Acknowledgment.

L:98-99. George Hussey and John Fisher recorded deed of trust 19 October 1803 from Christopher Hussey. Mortgage on tracts *Charley's Forest* and *Pigman's Inheritance,* to secure debts to firm of Hussey and Fisher of Baltimore. Lydia wife of Christopher Hussey released dower.

L:100-101. Thomas Peter of Washington, D.C., recorded deed 20 October 1803, from Henry O'Neale for £237..7..6 tract of land called *Beall's Design,* on road which leads from Seneca Mills to the Sugar Lands, to line which divides O'Neale's land from the property of Joseph Ward the elder, deceased, now the property of Joseph Ward the younger, deceased, containing 24 acres, also tract called *Hazard,* containing 2 4/10 acres; Margaret, wife of Henry O'Neale released dower rights.

L:101-103. Mary Maccubbin recorded 20 October 1803 from Solomon Holland sheriff. Whereas Elizabeth Lanham and [Walter Lanham] executors of Aaron Lanham obtained judgement in general court in October Term 17– against Zachariah Maccubbin for sum of money, a writ of fi fa, was issued against a tract of land called *Huntington,* and was sold to highest bidder.

L:103-104. Benjamin Bacon of the City of Washington recorded bill of sale 21 October 1803, from Benjamin Owens for $650. Household stuff, furniture and one Negro man, Harry about 32 years of age, one bay mare, 2 cows, one yearling 6 sheep, 16 hogs, 3 beds, one bay mare, three beds, bedsteads and furniture, 2 chests, 5 chairs, one walnut table, 2 gunds, crop of corn in ground 3 plows, four horses, 16 turkeys, 14 geese, 14 ducks, sundry dung hill fowls.

L:104. William O'Neale Jr. recorded bill of sale 22 October 1803. from Benjamin Ray Jr. Five following Negroes: Frank, 40 years; James 21; Fan about 18 years; Monica about 14 years and Ned about 13 years old. Signed before Richard Turner, associate justice.

L:104-105. Samuel Middleton recorded 23 October 1803, bill of sale from Benjamin Ray Jr., for £5, Negroes Charles 34, Rachel 35, Sal 16, Nan 12 and Ben 15 years old. Signed before Richard Turner, as a J.P.

L:105-107. Samuel Middleton, recorded 22 October 1803, deed from William O'Neal for 5 shillings, lots 71, 72 & 73 in Rockville, adjacent to lot sold to Evan Jones. Wit: Wm Smith, Richard West. Sarah, wife of William O'Neale released dower rights.

L:107-109. William Rickerds recorded deed 27 October 1803, from George Ellicott and Elizabeth his wife, for $564.66 tract called *The Great Meadows,* on 5th line of *Resurvey on Hartley's Lot,* Signed before Gerard Brooke, John Ellicott.

L:110. William Duley recorded manumission 28 October 1803 for Negro Cass and her increase, from this date. Signed before Elemelech Swearingen, Basil Beall.

L:110-111. Henry Taylor recorded schedule 29 October 1803, to the Sheriff of Montgomery County: 2 blankets, 1 ax, 1 mattox. Signed by mark.

L:111-112. Zachariah Linthicum recorded on 29 October 1803 marriage agreement with Ann Clagett, widow Whereas each of them hold property separately, her property to be free of claim from the said Zachariah Linthicum. Agreement made 24 October 1803.

L:112-114. Nathaniel and David Crawford, executors of David Crawford, deceased, recorded mortgage bond from William Thornton of Washington City, D.C., on bond made 9 June 1800 Thornton gave security assigns Negro slaves, man Daniel 30 years, Lucy, wife of Daniel 22 years and their children, a girl Bet 4 years and William between 1 & 2 years old; and a Negro man Joe, about 22 years old. Signed William Thornton before Ozias Offutt.

L:114-117. John Benson recorded 1 November 1803 from Nathan Harding and Rebecca Harding his wife of Brooke Co., Virginia, tracts *Forest,* and *Two Brothers,* formerly conveyed to Elias Harden.

L:117. John M. Reed, recorded bill of sale 1 November 1803 from William Didenhover for £110, sells Negro woman Charity, age 23 years. Wit: Greenberry Howard.

L:117-118. Richard Harwood recorded 2 November 1803, from Samuel S. Harwood of Loudon Co., Va. for $100 his right to land which his father Samuel Harwood died seized of. Signed before Lenox Martin, Richard Belt.

L:118-119. William S. Belt recorded 2 November 1803, from Samuel S. Harwood, for £50 Virginia currency, sells Negro girl Elsey. Signed before Elemelech Swearingen, Richard Harwood, Thomas N. Harwood.

L:119. Richard Harwood recorded bill of sale 2 November 1803 for three Negroes, Heze about 40 years, Priss about 38 and Nelly 10 months old.

L:119-120. John Thompson recorded schedule 2nd November 1803 to the Sheriff of Montgomery County.

L:120-121. William Prather recorded 4 November 1803, from Thomas Prather for $375. transfers claim to land Aaron Prather conveyed to them jointly. Jane Prather released dower rights.

L:121-122. Solomon Simpson recorded deed 7 November 1803, from William Young of Loudoun County, Virginia, for £159..7 assigns an undivided 6th part of a tract called *Willson's Delay,* which contains 42 ½ acres

L:122-123. Solomon Simpson recorded deed 7 November 1803, from Mauduit Young of City of Washington, D.C., for £159..7 assigns undivided 6th part of a tract called *Willson's Delay,* which contains 42 ½ acres.

L:123-125. Solomon Simpson recorded deed 7 November 1803 from Jonathan Tucker for £741..16..6 sells part of *Flints Grove.* Signed by mark. Betsy Tucker released dower rights.

L:125-126. Walter MacCattee, recorded bill of sale 7 November 1803 from Stephen Joy of Prince Georges County for £100 current money, Negro girl Henny, 16 years. Signed by mark before Samuel Hepburn.

L:126-127. Robert Brown recorded deed recorded 8 November 1803 from Vachel Gaither of Anne Arundel County for £103 his interest in a tract in Montgomery County called *Benjamin's Lot,* containing 39 acres; Signed before Richard Green, John Burgess.

127-129. Peter Bowie recorded release of mortgage 8 November 1803, from Peter Daniel Decandry

L:129. Ephraim Warfield of Anne Arundel County, recorded deed of bargain and sale 8 November 1803, from Joshua Pigman Sr. For £300 tract called *Advice,* 59 1/4 acres. And a tract called *Hillsborough,* 45 acres. Jemima, wife of Joshua Pigman released dower.

L:130-134. John Poole Junr and Priscilla his wife recorded deed 8 November 1803 from Henry Camden and Mary his wife. Whereas Frederick Sprigg, late of Montgomery County deceased, father of Mary B. Camden and Priscilla Poole, died seized in part of tract formerly called *Happy Choice,* and now called, *Happy Choice Fortified,* intestate, without male issue, and Deborah Sprigg is also since deceased, land descended to his three daughters, Mary Camden, Margaret Jarrett, and Priscilla

Poole, and whereas Henry Camden and Mary Camden, Daniel Jarrett and Margaret Jarrett, and Joshua Pierce then guardian of Priscilla Sprigg (now Poole), have heretofore made a division of the land on 27 March 1798. This is deed signed by Henry Camden, Mary B. Camden released dower.

L:134-135. Jesse Phillips recorded deed 9 November 1803 from Saml Hardy of Mason County, Kentucky, Henry Wheeler and Rebecca Wheeler his wife, and Norris Reid and Elizabeth Reid, his wife, of Montgomery County, heirs of Samuel Hardy deceased, for 5 shillings sell all their interest in tract, *Hard to Get.*

L:135-138. Ann Shaw recorded deed of trust November 9, 1803. Made 25th of August between Ann McKay and Margery Read both of the City of Washington and Mary Boyd of Frederick County, which said Ann, Margery and Mary are three of the devisees in fee named in the will of William McKay of Montgomery County; and Ann Shaw of City of Washington, the remaining devisee. Devised to Ann McKay, Margery Read then Margery Gun, Mary Boyd and Ann Shaw, tracts called *Willsons Discovery* and *McKay's Chance.*

L:138-139. Stephen Anderson Junr. recorded deed November 1803, from Philemon Plummer Sr. For £200, tract of land called *Bordley's Choice,* Sarah wife of Philemon Plummer released dower.

L:139-141. Joseph Harris son of John, from Jesse Harris, administrator of his father Joseph Harris, deceased who on 4 August 1786 surveyed *Mount Zion,* and in his will bequeath part to his grandson, Joseph, containing 150 acres. Metes and bounds given for property.

L:141-142. Blandford Sewell recorded bill of sale 10 November 1803 from Evan Trunnell, for £60 bay horse, sorrel horse, personal property.

L:142-143. Leonard Hays recorded deed 10 November 1803, from Joseph Harris of John, for £518..11 adjacent to land that was conveyed to Jacob Stier Junr. 1 1/4 acres; to part conveyed to William Hilton 3/4 acre; containing 110 acres of land. Signed Joseph Harris, son of John. Mary, wife of Joseph released dower rights.

L:143-145. Leonard Hays recorded deed 10 November 1803, from James Barnes for £200, sells part of *Resurvey on Jerremiah's Park,* 2 acres on the main road leading from Mouth of Monocacy, to Green's Bridge. Ann wife of James Barnes released dower. Acknowledged before Richard Beall, Lenox Martin

L:145-146. Henry Winemiller of Frederick County, recorded deed 10 November 1803, from Aaron Freeman for £297. Tract called the *Square,* on Aldridge's Road, containing 50 acres, and part of *Moneysworth,* containing together 100 acres more or less. Signed by mark. Sarah Freeman released dower rights.

L:146. Richard Ricketts recorded deed 10 November 1803, from Edward Crow, for 5 shillings, part of tract called *Peckerton,* for 23 ½ acres; and also a second part of tract containing 3 ½ acres.

L:147-149. Solomon Veatch recorded deed of release 12 November 1803. from Anacletus Dyer, indenture dated 19 September 1800 for 380 pounds of tobacco paid by Annecletus Dyer, part of tract called *Progress,* and also part of tract formerly called *Narrow Lane,* if said Solomon should pay the quantity of 3980 lbs tobacco with legal interest, sale should be void. Said quantity paid to him by the hands of John Thompson Veatch, receipt whereof here acknowledges, discharges the mortgage.

L:149-151. John Thompson Veatch recorded deed 12 November 1803, from Solomon Veatch, in consideration of 41 1/8 acres of land, lying in Hardy County, Virginia, and the further quantity of 4000 lbs of inspected tobacco, assigns to him to tracts of land by name of *Progress,* and *Narrow Lane,* but being since resurveyed and known as *The Three Tracts,* metes and bounds given, to the center of a spring formerly used in common by John and Solomon Veatch, to the given line of a part of *Progress,* formerly conveyed to Ninian Veatch, for 75 acres; to *Narrow Lane,* to the bank of the Potomac, in two parts one 6 7/8 acres one 34 1/4 acres. Signed by mark. Mary, wife of Solomon Veatch released dower.

L:151-152. Ann Belt recorded deed 12 November 1803 from John Thompson Veatch for £205, assigns part of two tracts *Progress,* and part as conveyed by Solomon Veatch to Carlton Belt for about 3 1/4 acres, and part called *Narrow Lane,* 34 acres, the whole 41 1/8 acres (same as deed above). Signed John T. Veatch, before Richard Beall, Lenox Martin. Mary, wife of John T. Veatch released dower.

L:153-154. Ann Belt recorded deed 12 November 1803, from John Veatch for £45, sells part of tract called *The Three Tracts,* containing 12 1/4 acres. The same day came Nancy, wife of John Veatch and released her right of dower.

L:154-155. Joshua Sear recorded deed 12 November 1803, from Ann Belt for £10..11..2, part called *Three Tracts,* [same tract as conveyed above by John and Nancy.]

L:155-156. Ann Belt recorded deed 12 November 1803, from Joshua Sear for £4..6..2 ½ assigns part of tract called *Rich Bottom,* beginning at end of tract of land called *Progress.* Containing 1 3/8 acres.

L:156. Samuel Busey recorded bill of sale 15 November 1803, from Adam Robb, Henry Lansdale and Catherine Lansdale, for love and affection which we have for the children of John Busey, and for 5 shillings paid by Eleanor, Charles, Joshua, Thomas Jefferson and Samuel Busey, the children of said John Busey, grant one Negro girl, called Charity, formerly sold by John Busey to Adam Robb, and her increase.

L:157-158. Thomas Cramphen recorded deed of trust, 17 November 1803 from Benjamin Nicholls for £44..13 assigns two feather beds and furniture and following Negro slaves: Jack, 16, Margery 18, Simers 4 years, Cass 2 years of age; nevertheless if sum is paid, then trust deed is void.

L:159-160. Solomon Holland recorded 18 November 1803, mortgage from Henry Lansdale for debt due to the firm of Thomas Linstead and Solomon Holland for £121..5..3, to secure the same, mortgages Negro slaves, Lucy 55; Richard 34; Jude 55; Winny 34; David 8 years and Mary 3 years old. Signed before Elemelech Swearingen.

L:160. Robert Bowie of Prince George's County, recorded bill of sale 19 May 1803, from John Baden of Robert, for £160, for one Negro woman named Anakey, boy Harry and child Poll, four head of sheep, a sorrel mare and yearling colt, my share of crop of hogs and tobacco. Signed by mark.

L:161. Joseph Elgar recorded deed 22 November 1803 from Gerard Brooke for £40 lots #12 and #13 in Town of Brookeville, bounded by Market Street on the south, by High Street on the west, by lots belonging to Richard Thomas Jr. on the north, and by lots sold to John Leeke containing 1/4 acre each. Acknowledged before Wm Culver, Jno Thomas 3d.

L:161-162. William Harding of Frederick County and Elias Harding of Montgomery County, recorded release 22 November 1803 from Rezen Harding. For £100 tract called *The Hermitage*, 257 ½ acres, during my mother, Eleanor Harding's natural life, also the following Negro woman named Cloe and boys named Frank, Tom and Jacob. No other rights conveyed.

L:162.-163. Joseph Elgar Junior recorded deed 22 November 1803 from John Leeke for £50 two lots in Brookeville, #10 and #11, containing 1/4 acre each. Signed by John Leeke, Cassandra Leeke.

L:163-165 Thomas Fletchall recorded deed 28 November 1803 from Thomas Plater for 5 shillings, assigns part of *Brightwell's Hunting Quarters*, 143 7/8 acres. Martha Plater released dower.

L:165-166. Benjamin Burditt recorded deed 28 November 1803 from William Leakens of Frederick County, made 20 August 1803, for 7000 lbs. Tobacco, , part of *Resurvey on Locust Bottom* containing 100 acres. Signed before Greenberry Howard, Edward Burgess Jr., Martha Leakins released dower.

L:166-167. Brice Selby recorded bill of sale 28 November 1803 from Richard Groomes for £22..10, furniture. 167. Top of page missing. Brice Selby recorded November 28th 1803 for $50 paid to Richard Groomes, goods and chattels. Acknowledged before John Adamson.

L:167-168. Asher Leaton recorded deed 29 November 1803 from Jacob Proctor of Frederick County, for £17..10, part of a lot ?. Ragged edges to pages. Elizabeth Proctor released dower.

L:168-169. Hannah Briggs recorded deed 14 Feb. 1804, deed of bargain and sale from Richard Thomas Junr. And Deborah Thomas for $24. Two lots in town of Brookeville.

L:169-172. Charles Gassaway and Mary Gaither, relict of Johnsey Gaither, two of the executors, recorded deed 30 November 1803 from Jane Threlkeld. Whereas Jane Threlkeld gave her bond of obligation for parcel called *Ebenezer*, to said Johnsey Gaither, he to pay annually during her life time, a quantity of bushels of wheat for said land,

L:173 to approx 188. Plot & certificate of town of Rockville – very poor shape, all pages are loose, and edges are frayed, but microfilm from Hall of Records is quite good copy.

"An act entitled to erect a Town in Montgomery County and for other purposes passed at November Session 1801."

... "Whereas it is represented to the General Assembly by the petition of sundry inhabitants of Montgomery County that Thomas O. Williams, Elisha O. Williams, William P. Williams and Edward O. Williams did lay off a parcel of their land adjacent tot he court house of the said county in lots a great part of which have since been purchased and considerable improvements made thereon and there being no record of the same, the titles of the properties there of are precarious and uncertain and it is prayed that the same may be conveyed marked and bounded and erected into a town. Therefore: Be it enacted by the General Assembly of Maryland that John Adamson, Josias

11

Hanson McPherson, William Holmes, Benjamin W. Jones and Thomas Linsted be and they are hereby appointed commissioners who shall on or before the first day of August next at the court house aforesaid and having so met, the said commissioners or any two of them shall have power and authority to direct the surveyor of Montgomery County or any person whom they may think proper to appoint to survey the said Town and the several lots thereon and make and erect plot thereof and shall ascertain and limit the extent of the lots streets and lanes thereof most agreeably to their original locations according to the best evidence that can be obtained and the said lots set out shall by them be number one two three and so on for distinguishing each lot from another and shall cause the said streets and lanes to be named by certain names and the said commissioners or a majority of them shall have power to adjourn from day to day till the duties imposed by this act are fully performed.

L:189-190. Richard Ricketts recorded mortgage 1 December 1803, from Archibald Trail, for 5 shillings, and in consideration of him signing a note as security for $82.60 with interest in favor of Saml Lane, administrator of Hardage Lane, parts of tracts called *Rockhead*, 3/4 acre, *Pleasant Fields*, and *Younger Brother*, 27 acres.

L:190. Joshua Pearce recorded bill of sale 2 Dec 1803 from Benjamin Owens, for tobacco to cover security for debt to Francis Mantz, merchant of Frederick. Ack. Before Greenberry Howard.

L:191. Thomas West recorded deed 23 July 1803 from William O'Neale. Part of lot #71, 72, 73 in town of Rockville. Sarah, wife of William O'Neale released dower.

L:191-192. Evan Jones recorded deed 23 July 1803 from William O'Neale for 10 shillings, part of lots #71, 72, and 73 in Rockville, adjacent to lots sold this day to Richard West. Sarah, wife of William O'Neale released dower.

L:192. Richard West recorded deed from William O'Neale for 5 shillings, part of lots #71, 72 & 73 in Rockville, adjacent to part conveyed to Thomas West.

L:192-193. William O'Neale Jr. recorded deed from William O'Neale, part of lots 71, 72 and 73 in Rockville. Sarah O'Neale released dower.

L:194-195. Laurence O'Neale recorded deed 27 July 1803, from Samuel Hepburn of Prince George's County, for 5 shillings, part of tract called *Resurvey on Hanover,* adjacent to Joseph Newton Chiswell's land, and a line of Christian Townley Hempstone's, containing 200 1/4 acres. Jane Hepburn released dower.

L:195-196. Jane Threlkeld recorded deed 6 December 1803, from Archabald Orme for $275. Parcel of land, on south side of road leading from Mr. John Orme's plantation to Thos Beall of Georgetown. Tract called *Ebenezer*. Elizabeth, wife of Archabald Orme released dower.

L:196-197. Nancy Threlkeld and Jane Threlkeld recorded receipt and agreement, received by the hand of Samuel Williams, from Mrs. Jane Threlkeld, for tract called *Ebenezer,* except for 65 3/4 acres sold to Nancy Threlkeld ... signed Charles Gassaway, executors of Johnsey Gaither. Mary Gaither. August 22nd 1803.

L:197. Benjamin Reeder imported a Negro girl from Virginia, 8 December 1803, named Luce, given to Ann Reeder by her father, Charles Hungerford of Loudon Co., Virginia. The deed of gift recorded here was signed by him, and witnessed by Patty Hungerford and Charlotte Hungerford.

L:197-199. William Jones recorded deed 9 December 1803, from David O'Neale for £5..5 tract called *Partnership,* in two parts, and *Resurvey on Wheel of Fortune,* containing together 51/8 acres.

L:199. Hammutal Welsh recorded manumission, 12 December 1803, granted to Negro man named Harry Jones, aged about 43 years, from this date. Signed by mark before Richard D. Green.

L:199-201. Thomas Rhoades of Prince George's County, recorded deed 12 December 1803 from Basil Lucas of Harrison County, Virginia. Whereas in 1801 he made over to Rhodes, tract called *Hard Struggle,* 27 7/8 acre, to rectify errors in deed.

L:201-202. Greenbury Howard recorded deed of trust 12 December 1803, from Jonathan Browning and John L. Browning, for 5 shillings, lot #3 in Clarksburgh.

L:202-204. Doctor Samuel Lukens recorded deed 13 December 1803, made 20th of October, from Benjamin Berry of Baltimore County. Whereas Josias Beall on 3 Dec 1761 conveyed to John Berry, the father of the said Benjuamin Berry, tract *Drumelda,* 225 acres and Clement Williams sold John Berry, parts of *Snowden's Manor Enlarged,* parts containing 8 acres, [bottom corner of page torn off] and 125 1/4 acres, and one other tract of 16 1/4 acres, were devised by his will to Benjamin Berry, for £2217..12 sells the aforesaid tracts. Land borders Samuel Bonifant and Henry Culver. Signed before Owen Dorsey and Wm Russell, Justices of the Peace for Baltimore County. Elizabeth wife of Benjamin Berry released dower.

L:204-205. Jacob Swanley recorded deed 13 December 1803, From Thomas Plater for £30, lot on which Baltis Fulks lives, adjoining the tanyard where said Swanly lives, containing 1 3/4 acres.

L:205-206. Jonathan Fry recorded deed 13 Dec. 1803 from Bernard Gilpin and Sarah Gilpin his wife for $40, part of *Resurvey on Mount Radner,* at southeast corner of Elisha Etchison's lot, to third line of Nicholas Watkin's lot, containing 10 1/4 acres.

L:207-208. John Thomas 3d, grandson of Richard Thomas Senior, recorded deed 13 December 1803 from Richard Thomas Sr. for natural love and affection, assigns tract *Snowden's Manor Enlarged,* beginning at 24th line of *Charles and Benjamin,* as made by William Dent, to tract *Addition to Charley Forest,* containing 33 acres. Signed and acknowledged.

L:208-209. Joseph Clagett recorded deed of bargain and sale, 13 December 1803, from William Benson, Allen Simpson and Sarah Simpson his wife. Whereas the above named William Benson, Sarah Simpson his sister, and Allen Simpson in consequence of his marriage with said Sarah, and Ninian Benson, a brother to the said William and Sarah are entitled to the two following tracts of land, *The Retrospect,* containing 10 acres, and *The Critical Review,* containing 5 3/4 acres, which parcel a certain Nicholas Pegno, guardian to the said Wiliam, Sarah and Ninian during their minority, sold to the above Joseph Clagett for a valuable consideration, and entered into a bond for the deed's conveyance, and whereas the said William and Sarah have come of age (and Ninian is still a minor) for 5 shillings they acknowledge deed. Sarah Simpson, and Sarah wife of William Benson released dower rights.

209-210. Zachariah Knott recorded deed 17 December 1803, from John Belt for £120 assigns tract called *Liberty,* on first line of *Friendship,* for 42 3/4 acres, Signed before Wm Smith, Richard Beall.

L:210-211. Rachel Mullican recorded manumission, 19 December 1803, to Negro Henry Butler and Lydia Butler his wife, signed before Richard Green and Basil Griffith.

L:211-212. George Beall Magruder recorded deed 20 Dec. 1803, from Edward Talbott of Frederick County, Virginia, for £218..5, tract, *Ravenspring,* surveyed for William Bates Willson in 1787, for 50 ½ acres.

L:212-213. George Beall Magruder recorded deed 20 Dec. 1803, from Samuel Brewer Magruder for $395. Part of *Bealls and Magruder's Honesty,* adjacent to part of Robert Peters, and to part conveyed by John B. Magruder to Ninian Magruder, containing 39 ½ acres, as laid down by Archibald Orme in 1803.

L:213-214. Thomas Fletchall recorded deed 22 December 1803, from Thomas Hickman, for £225 part of tract called *Three Springs,* and *Cider and Ginger,* lands which fell to him in division of the lands of his father William Hickman as conveyed by William Hickman of Stephen to William Hickman of Arthur. Peggy, wife of Thomas Hickman released dower rights.

L:215. Benjamin Ray Jr. recorded bill of sale 24 December 1803 from Hezekiah Veirs for £200 sells Negroes, Hannah, Toby and Sook

L:215-216. John Hodges recorded bill of sale 24 December 1803 from John Baden for £37 sells one black mare.

L:216-217. Upton Beall and Aquilla Beall recorded deed 24 Dec. 1803 from Lewis Beall, Elisha O. Williams and Harriett his wife, Benjamin Mackall and Christina his wife, Leonard Mackall and Catharine his wife, William Stewart and Helen his wife, heirs of Brooke Beall deceased, in order to divide real estate and for $1, assigns *Beall Mount,* 1590 acres, also part of *Pine Grove,* 300 acres; *Long Acre,* along the Potomac River adjoining John Brackenridge, and *Montrose,* 49 acres, now in possession of Archibald Orme. Signed by all parties.

L:217-218. Frederick Linthicum recorded bill of sale 24 December 1803, from William Magrath for £150, one Negro man, Samuel, about 22 years old.

L:218. Joseph Forrest recorded bill of sale 29 December 1803 from Samuel Etchison in consideration of rent due Joseph Forrest, and further amount of $1. Assigns one old cow, 4 pigs and one sow, other farm equipment and furniture.

L:218-219. Samuel Etchison recorded schedule of property 30 December 1803, to Sheriff of Montgomery County, one drawing knife, one old hoe, hatchet, parcel of old iron, old pewter dishes. Signed by mark.

L:219. Caleb Bentley and David Newlen recorded bill of sale from Michael Sipe for £12..9 sells six chairs, one painted poplar table, other housewares. Signed by mark.

L:220. Commission of the Justices of the Levy Court 2 January 1804: Henry Brookes, Edward Burgess Jr., Richard West, Thomas B. Evans, Ozias Offutt, Thomas Linsted and George Riley.

L:220. Commission of the Justices of the Peace 2 January 1804: William Smith, Lawrence O'Neale, Richard Green, Henry Brookes, Greenbury Howard, Edward Burgess Jr., Elemelech Swearingen, Benjamin Gaither, James Lackland, Archibald O. Beall, Lewis Duvall of Hyatts town, Ozias Offutt, John Thomas, John Burgess, William Culver, Thomas Simpson, Lenox Martin, Richard West, Thomas B. Evans, John Adamson, Robt Bowie, Camden Riley, Warren Magruder, Richard Beall, John Belt and Gassaway Howard, all of Montgomery County.

L:220-221. Susannah Sanders recorded bill of sale 3 January 1804, from Ann Sanders for £50, sells Negro woman Rachel and boy Sam. Witnesses James Bowie Brookes.

L:221-222. John Read recorded deed 5 January 1804, from John Gardner for $90 sells lot #7 of ground in Clarksburgh, conveyed to John Gardner by William Duncan of Baltimore City, containing 5/8 of an acre. Cassandra, wife of John Gardner released dower.

L:222-224. Joseph Browning of Washington, District of Columbia, recorded deed 6 January 1804, from Jeremiah Browning Sen. of Frederick County, Maryland, for $24 one undivided fifth part of lands lying in Montgomery County, the *Resurvey on Red Oak Slipe,* metes and bounds given for 104 acres and tract *Fancy,* lying on a draught of Middle Bennet Creek, called Dumpling Creek, containing 30 acres; tract called *No Name,* containing 14 acres; which lands came to Jeremiah from his father Edward Browning. Signed by Jeremiah Browning, before Michael Boyer, Lewis Browning. The wife of Jeremiah (no name inserted), came and examined apart released dower.

L:224-226. Barton Duly recorded 6 January 1804. James Doull died seized of *Coronat Oput,* although he did convey or intend to convey the same to James Offutt, late of said county. James Offutt on 3 November 1789 contract with Philip Shoall for sale and passed a bond for its conveyance but said Shoall never paid the purchase money. James Offutt by his will of 20 July 1802, devised money too wife and certain children and grand children. Because the original deed was questioned, the court confirmed in November 1802, the sale and proceeds for $1,291.73 between Rebecca Offutt widow of the deceased James Offutt, and Mordecai Burgess Offutt and Jane his wife; Charles Beatty and Verlinda his wife; James Offutt of William and Rebecca his wife, the said Jane, Verlinda and Rebecca were daughters of James Offutt, deceased; and William Wade and Cassandra his wife, Charles Offutt Jones and William Edmonston and Elizabeth his wife; the said Cassandra, Charles Offutt Jones and Elizabeth were grandchildren of James Offut deceased, the children of his daughter, the late Elizabeth Jones.

L:226-227. John Shook recorded deed 7 January 1804, from Charles Porter for 5 shillings sells tract, part of *Brandy Hall* and a second tract conveyed to Porter by Charles Perry, for about 14 acres. Mary, wife of Charles released dower rights.

L:227. Meshack Browning recorded qualification as magistrate 13 January 1804. He took the oaths appinted by law for that purpose before Edward Burgess Junr.

L:228. Hanberry Jones recorded bill of sale 13 January 1804. I Robert Fish for £20 sell Negro girl Delila, aged 6 years old. Signed before John Fleming.

L:228-229. Lenox Martin to Ignatius Davis, agreement. Recorded 11 January 1804, a bond dated 15 July 1793. Davis agrees to purchase ½ of grist and saw mills from Martin, lying in Montgomery

County on Little Monocacy for £500; and Martin a bond from Mr. Taber at the glassworks for £100 more with interest. Schedule of payments made, land adjoining neighbor Harris. Thomas Morton, a common friend shall judge any deficiency. Signed before Philip Sengstack, Daniel Ragan. On back of the agreement, endorsements August 10, 1793, received of Mr. Ignatius Davis £352 including a note of hand assigned to me from Messrs Amelung and Tabers at the glassworks, part of the purchase money of my part of the mills within mentioned. Lenox Martin. On 30 June 1800, agreed with Mr. Martin to take what there may be of the land herein described with what he may hold on the other side of the mill and on the same side of the road near the preaching house in lieu of the 5 acres herein described which assignment to before James Crofford in that respect the conveyance made on the 20th August 1803 is satisfactory. Signed 9 January 1804, Ig Davis.

L:229-230. Zadock Offutt recorded 14 January 1804, from Jesse Wade for £140. Negro woman Sal and Negro Basil. Signed before Ozias Offutt.

L:230-231. Richard Groomes recorded schedule 14 January 1804 to the Sheriff of Montgomery County, 1 parcel of shoemakers tools, razors, tea kettle.

L:231-232. Edward Iglehart, late of Frederick County, but now of Anne Arundel County, recorded deed 14 January 1804, from George Chandlee, late of Montgomery County, but now a resident of Pennsylvania, for £561, part of tracts called *Pembroke,* and part of *Resurvey on Mount Radnor,* 114 1/4 acres. Signed before Wm Culver, Jno Thomas 3d.

L:232-233. Henry O'Neale recorded deed 17 January 1804, from Thomas Beall of George of Washington County, Territory of Columbia, for £1570..1 shilling; sells part of land heretofore assigned to Ann Dorsey, the wife of William H. Dorsey, for her part of the real estate of her deceased grandfather, James Brooke, which said part was on 9 October 1799 conveyed to Thomas Beall of George by William H. Dorsey and Ann his wife, recorded in Liber H:667-668, being part of *Addition to Brooke Grove.* Containing 323 ½ acres, being separated by the new road aforesaid from the lands heretofore conveyed by the said William H. Dorsey and Ann Dorsey to a certain Joseph Barnes. Nancy, wife of Thomas Beall released dower.

L:234. Brice Letton recorded bill of sale 18 January 1804 from Benjamin Thompson for £25 sells one gray mare, furniture, farm equipment.

L:234. Richard Morgan recorded schedule of property 22 January 1804 to the Sheriff of Montgomery County lists credits due Hezekiah Viers, Felix Hilair, Simon Carney, Simon Carver, pot hook, 2 flour barrels, looking glass, 1 spit.

L:235. Joseph Clagett recorded deed 26 January 1804, from Hannah Kelly, the widow of Thomas Kelly, late of Montgomery County and Thomas Kelly and Benjamin Kelly. Whereas she is desirous of advancing the interests of her sons, the above named Joseph, Benjamin and Thomas Kelly by selling all the real estate of her deceased husband, and dividing the money arising from such sale amongst them, desirous of dividing estate between.. Joseph, Benjamin and Thomas Kelly. Sells part of *Resurvey on Younger Brother,* adjacent to *Resurvey on William and John,* 124 acres; also part of *Gibson's Choice,* 33 ½ acres. Hannah Kelly signed by mark; Thomas Kelly of Thos and Benjamin Kelly signed. Mary, wife of Thomas Kelly released dower.

L:237-238. Evan Jones recorded deed 30 January 1804, from Samuel Riggs for $2000 sells tract called *Williams Range,* and *Williams Lot Resurveyed.* Amelia Riggs, wife of Samuel released dower.

L:238-239. Benjamin Ray Jr. Recorded Sheriff's bond 31 Jan. 1804, to the State of Maryland. With bondsmen Joseph Slater, William McGrath, Thomas Fletchall, Joseph N. Chiswell, Thomas West, Archibald A. Beall and John Belt.

L:239-240. Solomon Holland recorded 31 January 1804, from Hannah Dickerson her 1/5 share of part of brother Arnold Holland's estate in tract *Charles and Benjamin.*

L:240-241. Solomon Holland from Sarah Holland, recorded 31 January 1804, her 1/5 share of part of brother Arnold Holland's estate in tract *Charles and Benjamin.*

L:241-243. Solomon Holland from Nathan Holland, Sr., recorded 31 January 1804, his 1/5 share of part of brother Arnold Holland's estate in tract *Charles and Benjamin.*

L:243. Recorded at the request of Elisha Beall 6 February 1804. I Samuel Beall for £7..10, and also for the natural love and affection I bear to the said Elisha Beall, assign forever a Negro girl named Tavey[1], aged 4 years. Signed by Samuel Beall 6 February 1804 before Elemelech Swearingen, John Thomas.

L:243-244. Laurence Conner delivered schedule of personal property to sheriff, 7 February 1804. Signed by his mark.

L:244-245. Elisha Howard recorded deed 8 February 1804, from Charles Howard for £189, part of tract called *Hopewell,* containing 63 acres. Ann, wife of Charles released dower rights.

L:245-246. Benjamin Higgins and Thomas Nicholls of Simon recorded bill of sale 10 Feb. 1804 from Brice Letton of Montgomery County, as guardian to Lewis Wilcoxon and Higgins and Nicholls are security to indemnify them from damage, therefore assigns Negroes Jenny, Anna, Warnold, Leathe and Joe. Sale is void, if estate administered.

L:246-248. John Threlkeld recorded deed 13 February 1804, from Thomas Beall of George of Washington County, District of Columbia, for $1520, grants plantations, part of Middle Plantation, and part of *Thomas's Discovery Fortified,* near east end of Seneca Bridge, for 39 acres, excepting one acre belonging to the heirs of Capt Richard Johns. Nancy wife of Thomas Beall released dower.

L:248-250. John Glasses and Thomas Robertson recorded lease 13 Feb 1804, from Thomas A. Brooke. Part of *Resurvey on Jacob's Part,* adjacent to Potomac Company land, for the express purpose of constructing a mill with one or two pair of mill stones for purpose of grinding wheat and plaster, and a ditch on said stream of water called the Falls Branch, for term of 15 years; after 7 years to pay sum of $200. Emptying into the canal. And a saw mill of the best construction. A little below Thomas S. Lee's meadow. Signed by all three parties.

---

[1]In his will in 1825, Samuel Beall gives to his son Elisha, a Negro girl Henrietta, in lieu of Negro girl Octavia, granted him by deed. From other records it would appear that Elisha was a child himself when he was given this deed to a slave girl.

L:250-252. Zadock Magruder recorded deed 14 Feb. 1804, from Basil Dyson for £375, part of *Resurvey on Non Eaten,* beginning at part formerly conveyed by Daniel Veirs to George Dyson, for 150 acres. Sarah, wife of Basil Dyson released dower.

L:252. Levi Wilcoxon imported slaves from Loudon County, Virginia, Hercules 12; Henry 9; Sarah 20 years; Miles 2 ½; Amy 1 ½; the first two from his marriage to Letha Trundle, the last three a gift from his mother, Martha Wilcoxon. Dated 12 February 1804.

L:252-253. John Howes Sr. recorded deed 14 February 1804, from John Merryman for £100, part of tract *Philemenia and Sarah,* containing 20 acres more or less. Ann, wife of John Merryman released dower.

L:253-254. Caleb Bentley recorded deed 14 February 1804, from Thomas Moore and Mary, his wife, for $47. Lots in town of Brookeville.

L:255-256. Hannah Briggs recorded deed 14 February 1804, from Richard Thomas Jr. and Deborah Thomas, his wife for $24, lots #42 and #43 in Town of Brookeville.

L:256-257. Caleb Bentley recorded deed 14 February 1804, from Richard Thomas Junr & Deborah Thomas, his wife, for $30 lots #47 and 50 in town of Brookeville, Signed before Jno Thomas 3d, John Burgess.

L:257-258. Margaret Brooke recorded deed 14 February 1804, for $12 from Deborah Phillips lot #41 in town of Brookeville.

L:258-259. Jesse Wilcoxon recorded deed 14 February 1804, from Caleb Bentley for $2195, sells part of *Addition to Brooke Grove, part of the Resurvey on Brooke Park,* part of *Fair Hill*, and part of *Sure Bind, Sure Find*, Sarah Bentley, wife of Caleb released dower rights.

L:259-260. Archibald Mason recorded deed 18 February 1804, from Bernard Gilpin and Sarah Gilpin his wife, for $400, part of *Resurvey on Mount Radner,* granted Richard Brooke by patent February 1766, containing 125 acres.

L:261-263. John Henderson and Marsham Waring recorded deed of trust 27 February 1804, from James McCubbin Lingan of Washington County, District of Columbia, indebted to bank of Columbia for large sums of money, assigns tracts on Seneca Creek, with mills, purchased of a certain Abraham Faws, and resurveyed under the name of *Middlebrooke,* containing 250 acres. And 50 acres more or less bought of a certain George King, with improvements.

L:263. William B. Hungerford and George Ray, recorded certificates of qualification as deputy sheriffs. 29 February 1804.

L:264. Richard Thomas Sr. recorded bill of sale 1 March 1804 from Charles Rogers one sorrel horse, saddle and bridle.

L:264. John Henry Jr. resident of Loudoun Co., Va., recorded certificate of Negroes 5 March 1804, he brought Anthony 7 years old to Maryland, came to me by deed of gift.

L:265. Negro Betty & others, recorded manumissions 5 March 1804, from Samuel Nicholls of Samuel. Negroes Betty, age 20 to be free 25 December 1809; Cyrus 15 years to be free 25 December

1814; Maria 3 years old to be free 25 December 1822; Hannah aged 3 to be free 25 December 1822; any issue born to them while in slavery to be free at 25 years of age. Signed before Wm Smith, Nathaniel E. Magruder.

L:265-267. Charles Saffell recorded deed 5 March 1804, from Carlton Belt for £170..17, tract of land formerly called *Money's worth,* but now called *Woodport,* containing 101 1/4 acres. Elizabeth, wife of Carlton Belt released dower.

L:267-268. William Bennett recorded deed 6 March 1804, from James Barnes for £15, part of *Resurvey on Jeremiah's Park,* adjacent to part conveyed by Vachel Hall to John Summers for about 1 acre, metes and bounds for 1 ½ acres. Ann, wife of James Barnes released dower. Deed acknowledged before Lenox Martin, Richard Beall.

L:268-269. James Hawkins recorded deed 6 March 1804, from Thomas Browning for £13..2..6, a half acre parcel or lot in Clarksburg. Signed by mark before Lewis Duvall, M. Browning.

L:269-270. Recognizance recorded 6 March 1804 by John Reed, John Kinder and Shadrock Cheney. Acknowledged bond for £52..10, the condition is that whereas Ann Nicholson made oath that John Reed was the father of her illegitimate child, he posts bond to keep the same from being chargeable to the county.

L:270-271. Benjamin G. Orr recorded deed 6 March 1804, from Walter Mackall of Calvert County, for $1727 and a half dollars, assigns tract called *Bradford's Rest,* and *Resurvey on Batchelor's Forest,* which was heretofore conveyed by David Lynn to William Bayly and recorded in Liber G:680 of land records of Montgomery County; and adjacent to Mr. Williams' lease and to the beginning of Thomas Swearingen's lease, which are a part of *Bradford's Rest,* to corner lot of George Robertson's land, then with said land containing 363 1/4 acres.

L:271-272. Zachariah Thompson recorded bill of sale 7 March 1804 from Frances Perry for £62..18, Negro woman, Hum, 24 years; and her 2 year old child. Sale void if sum paid with interest.

L:272-273. Thomas Webb recorded deed 7 March 1804, from Thomas Jones for £75 tract called *Providence,* being adjacent to tract called *Rockingham,* adjacent to *Refuse,* and the *Swamp,* on 2nd line of a tract of land called *Joseph's Park.* 12 ½ acres more or less, attested to by Thomas Jones, 10 May 1794.

L:273-274. James W. Ward recorded bill of sale 7 March 1804 from Augustus Easton for $80 sell one red and white cow, one red and white yearling, assorted furniture including looking glass, signed by mark before John Adamson.

L:274. Lewis Harding of Frederick Co., recorded bill of sale 7 March 1804 from Thomas Swearingen of Montgomery County for £300. Negro Peg, 23 years old; Negro Jacob 4 years and Cass, 1 year old.

L:274-276. Henry Griffith Junr. Recorded deed 8 March 1804, from Hezekiah Thomas for £425, tract called *Samuel's Chance,* being at the head of Hollands River, which Hezekiah Thomas purchased of Aquilla Johns, containing 175 acres. Jean Smith Thomas, wife of Hezekiah Thomas, released dower.

L:276-277. James Hilton recorded deed 8 March 1804, from Jesse Harris for 5 shillings, all his right to tract called *Mount Zion*, resurveyed for Joseph Harris 24 August ------, containing about 78 acres more or less and devised to Elizabeth Harris by his father, the afsd Joseph, and by the said Elizabeth Harris devised to the said Jesse and her two sisters Mary and Sarah Harris; also one other tract of land adjoining said land called *Basils L----*, beginning at bounded red oak on hill of spring that falls into Little Monocacy, purchased by the aforesaid Elizabeth Harris from Rachel Ennis and John Ennis, [page has ragged edges, some text missing] Dorcas arris released dower rights.

L:277-279. Mary Harris recorded deed 8 March 1804 from Jesse Harris, administrator of his father, Joseph Harris, late of Montgomery County. Said Joseph Harris had on or about 24 August 1781 surveyed a tract called *Resurvey on Mount Zion,* for 1217 3/4 acres and in his will bequeath to his daughter, Mary lot #5 of said tract to contain 100 acres on north side of Cabin Branch. Metes and bounds for 96 1/8 acres. Dorcas, wife of Jesse Harris released dower.

L: 279-282. Thomas Moore, Caleb Bentley and William Stabler, trustees for the Sandy Spring Boarding School Co., recorded deed March 1804, from Richard Thomas, for $2250. Assigns tract near Sandy Spring Meeting House, land is the same he received from his father Richard Thomas, 125 3/4 acre part of *Addition to Charley Forrest,* on east side of the road from the meeting house to Brookeville.

L:282-283. Jacob Smith recorded deed 8 March 1804, made 13 September 1803, from Jesse Hyatt for £6, lots #17 and 71 in Town of Hyattstown. Signed before Edw Burgess Jr., Lewis Duvall.

L:283-285. Anthony Reintzel recorded deed 11 March 1804, from John Hewitt, trustee appointed in chancery case of Charles Lowndes, Francis Lowndes, John Suter, Valentine Reintzel and George King, complainants of Richard Ober's heirs, defendants, passed February term 1801. Anthony Reintzel was high bidder on real estate, consisting of 104 ½ acres of *Drane's Final Conclusion,* and *Dranes Luck,* about 10 1/4 acres. And whereas, afterwards Reintzel sold all but six acres to Henry Gittings on 6th June last. This deed is for 6 acres beginning at 2nd line of tract called *Outlet.*

L:285-286. Philip Nicklin and Robert E. Griffith of Philadelphia, Pennsylvania, merchants, recorded deed 15 March 1804 from John Oliver of Baltimore, merchant, for $5assigns tract in Montgomery County, part of *Addition to part of Conclusion,* containing 236 acres. Signed before justices of Baltimore County.

287. Charles Gassaway and others recorded bond 15 March 1804, as coroner to State of Maryland

L:287-288. John Douglass recorded bill of sale from Charles Douglass of Loudon Co., VA for £14..14. For one bay mare and other livestock.

L:288-290. Thomas Watkins recorded deed 17 March 1804 from John B. Magruder for $200 land willed to me by my father, Joseph Magruder, 1/10 part of the lands, *Addition to Hansley*, Forrest, *Trouble Enough*, 1/10 part of *Bedfordshire Carrier*. Signed before Ozias Offutt and Richard West.

290. Conrad Shafer recorded deposition 17 March 1804, taken at the house of Thomas Morton.

L:290-291. Susanna Morton, for John Booth, et.al. made a deposition 15 March 1804 at the house of Thomas Morton. Susannah Morton, 57 years old, states she knew John, otherwise called John

Booth when he was a small boy. He was reputed to be a son of Cate; she was a daughter of Esther, who was a daughter of Jaffa, reputed to be a daughter of Cate Booth who she knew personally. Her father, David Weems gave the first mentioned Cate and her son John, to this deponents sister, Williamina who was wife to a certain Doctor Mudd. Further, when she knew Cate Booth, parent to all the above Negroes she was very old and passed as a free woman. She did not know if she was born free or was set free by her master, King Harrison, but she remembers her father David Weems at the time, held a number of the descendants of said Cate Booth as slaves and further saith not. Sworn before Lenox Martin, J.P.

L:291-292. Walter Griffith recorded deed 17 March 1804, From Samuel Griffith Sr., for $500, tracts called *Griffith's Chance* and *Water's Discovery,* containing 104 acres. Signed before Archibald A. Beall, John Belt. Ruth Griffith, wife of Samuel released dower rights.

L:292-293. Hezekiah Thomas recorded deed 17 March 1804, from Walter Griffith for $1000, his right to tracts *Griffith's Chance* and *Water's Discovery,* containing 104 acres. Signed before Archibald A. Beall, John Belt. Sarah Griffith, wife of Walter released dower rights.

L:293. Joseph Forrest recorded certificate of Negroes 21 March 1804, Selena 20, Nanny 50, Milly 18 years old from Washington, D.C. Peter, 14, Sarah 13, given to Mrs. Elizabeth Forrest by her mother, Mrs. Eliza Dulaney of Virginia.

L:294. Thomas C. Nicholls recorded qualification 21 March 1804, as deputy sheriff.

L:294-295. Nathan Browning of Nathan, recorded deed 23 March 1804, from Verlinda Browning for £20, one lot, part of *Moneysworth,* in Clarksburg, containing one acre.

L:295-296. Caleb Pancoast of Frederick County, recorded deed 24 March 1804, from Richard Thomas Jr. and Deborah Thomas (his wife) for $35, two lots #17 and #16 in Brookeville.

L:296. John Vinson recorded deed of gift 27 March 1804 from Charles Hungerford in Loudoun County, to his nephew, John Vinson, a Negro girl named Henny.

L:296-297. Edward Crow recorded deed 27 March 1804, from Richard Ricketts, made 5 November 1803, for 5 shillings, tract called *Quince Orchard,* containing 23 ½ acres. Signed by mark. Elizabeth, wife of said Richard released dower.

L:298-299. Edward Crow Jr recorded deed 27 March 1804 from Edward Crow for 5 shillings tract called *Rich Meadow,* containing 11 acres. Acknowledged before William Smith, Jno Thomas 3d

L:299-300. Thomas Knott recorded deed 27 April 1804, from Philip Edelin of Montgomery County, for £101 sells one tract, part of *Constables Range*, and part of a tract called *Conclusion*, beginning at end of ten perches on fourth line of a deed for part of land formerly conveyed to Barton Wathen for 200 acres, to end of 7th line of tract formerly conveyed to Thomas Knott for 43 acres, to end of 57 perches on 8th line of *Addition to Constables Range*, to beginning containing 46 ½ acres. Signed by Philip Edelin before Greenbury Howard, M. Browning. Receipt, acknowledgment.

L:300-302. Philip Edelin, gentleman, recorded deed 27 April 1804 from Francis Edelin, Edward Edelin, Richard Edelin, Arnold Edelin and Leonard Edelin of Charles County, Maryland, gentlemen for £300 parts of *Constables Range*, and part of *Addition to Constables Range*, part of a tract called

Conclusion, and *Resurvey on Conclusion*, beginning at the end of 1ˢᵗ line of *Constables Range*, except for 43 acres for Thomas Knott, containing 157 acres

L:302-303. John Whalen recorded 31 March 1804, from William Magrath for £127..10, sells three Negroes: Betty, Zadock and Betty's young daughter (not named).

L:303-304. Jesse Phillips recorded bill of sale 2 April 1804 from Norriss Read for £40 for furniture and livestock.

L:304. Belt Brashears and Elie Brashears recorded deed 4 April 1804, from Jesse Hyatt for £12 sells lots #33, #34, #87 and #88 in Hyattstown. Signed.

L:304-306. Robert Ferguson recorded deed 4 April 1804 from Solomon Holland, trustee appointed in suit brought before Alexander Hanson, Chancellor of Maryland, between John Gordon, Henry Riddle, John Campbell, John Campbell Jr., Alexander Lowe and William Ingram, surviving partners of John Glasford & Co., complainants against Rachel Oden, widow of David John Oden and Gerard, Nathan, Jesse, Elizabeth, Darky, Mary and Rebecca Oden, and Samuel Carter and Tabitha his wife, and Ann and Lydia Oden, heirs of David John Oden, deceased. Sold at auction, tracts in Montgomery County, *Boy's Lot,* 100 acres and part of *Fellowship,* 51 ½ acres, and Robert Ferguson by Henry McPherson his agent was high bidder at £249..19..6.

L:306-308. Director Smallwood recorded deed 5 April 1804, from Sampson Trammel. Whereas a conveyance found in 1793 was found to be defective, so for £5 paid by said Director Smallwood, this deed is to make provision for her and for the children of her by the said Trammell, begotten, sells all that island in the River Potomac called *Darby Island,* opposite the mouth of Watts Branch, containing 100 acres; which I bought of Pritchett's heirs, and of John Hopkins and John Thompson; also one other island called *Long Island,* which I bought of McDonald, containing 80 acres; also *Short Island,* at lower end of *Darby Island,* containing 4 acres; and island two miles above Seneca called *Merrick's Delight,* bought of William Hickman, and island by name of *Trammels,* 4 ½ acres, and another island, *Trammels Walk,* and a parcel called *Addition to Weaver's Den,* purchased of Galworth, containing 9 3/4 acres, and all the Negroes and personal property: Simon, James, Amy, Hannah and Judah, Sias, Moll, Dapney and Peter, George and Ludea, Betty, Ned, Jacob, man, Becky, Rose, Charles, Bill, Patty, Patt, Easter, Isaac, Jacob, Rachel, Hannah Rose, Sarah and also all the goods and chattels belonging to the said Sampson Trammel, to the said Director Smallwood for the support of herself, the said Sampson Trammell and her four children until her youngest daughter Betty Trammell Smallwood arrives at age 21, then land to be equally divided between the two sons Sampson Trammell Smallwood and William Trammel Smallwood; and the Negroes divided between the two sons and Susannah P. Cloud to have for her part Negroes Ned, Jacob the son of Nan, his mother, James, Becky and Rose, the mother of Becky; Betty T. Smallwood is to have Negroes Charles, Bill, Isaac with the two Patts, Hannah, Judah and her sister Hannah, Easter, and the whole stock is to be divided among the four children, the children giving sufficient bond to provide support for the parents. Signed before Ozias Offutt, Richard West.

L:308-310. Ephraim Gaither of Montgomery County, and Hugh Anderson, now of New Market, Frederick County, recorded articles of agreement regarding leasing of property to Hugh Anderson for 5 years, assigns all the ground adjoining "my red painted dwelling house which in present year has been tended in corn, together with said dwelling, kitchen, smoke house, stable and other houses, the ground at the north end sufficient for a commodious wagon yard, the gardens now enclosed containing nearly one acre in front of Henry Counselman's lot, where the said Hugh Anderson, may thick a suitable place for a brick yard, agrees to build a stable within one year, and to have water available and a pump; and to manufacture bricks and provide Gaither with 100,000 merchantable bricks. Gaither is to haul one wagon full of Hugh Anderson's belonging from his present location. Signed by Hugh Anderson, Ephraim Gaither.

L:310-311. John Henry recorded bill of sale 7 April 1804 from William Howington, a dun mare, and gun, jack plane, hand saw other items.

L:311-313. Samuel Willson recorded deed 9 April 1804, from William Willson, Benjamin W. Jones and Margaret Jones his wife, George Magruder and Charity Magruder his wife, and Martha Willson, all of Montgomery County for £500, sell all their right to two parcels, *Susanna* and *Resurvey on William and John,* 207 ½ acres. Signed by all parties. Rebecca Willson, wife of William Willson released dower rights.

L:313-316. Henry Camden and Mary his wife recorded deed 10 April 1804, from John Poole Jr. and Priscilla his wife. Whereas Frederick Sprigg, late of Montgomery County, father of the said Mary Camden and Priscilla Poole, died intestate without male issue, seized in fee simple of a tract formerly called *Happy Choice,* but resurveyed as *Happy Choice Fortified,* and he had three daughters, Mary B. Camden, Margaret Jarrett (married to Daniel Jarrett) and Priscilla Sprigg, who by her guardian Joshua Pearce, made deed, but now married to John Poole Jr.; makes deed for 207 1/4 acres, laid off for Mary and Henry Camden, metes and bounds given adjacent to Daniel Jarrett and Margaret his wife's part.

L:317. Thomas Offutt Jr recorded certificate 10 April 1804, for Negro named George, about 18 years of age, brought from Virginia and acquired by marriage with Miss Minor of Virginia.

L:317-318. Elijah Viers recorded deed 11 April 1804, from Maddox Dyson and Jane his wife of South Carolina, York District, for $100, all their right of dower in parcel of land on Seneca, *Resurvey on Day Spring, Swan's Good Luck,* and *New Year's gift,* property of John Swan deceased. Aquilla Dyson was present as a witness.

L:318-319. Hezekiah Viers recorded deed 11 April 1804, from Edward Viers for $550, tract called *Mary,* 4 3/4 acres, and also all tracts in Huntington County, Pennsylvania.

L:320. Basil Darby recorded deed 13 April 1804, from Talbott Alnutt, grants one fifth of an undivided tract of land, called *Thomas's Discovery,* part conveyed to the said Talbott Allnutt by George Coones and Sarah Coones his wife, and confirmed by a decree from the Chancellor of Maryland; signed before George Howard, John Belt.

L:320-321. Negro Cloe recorded manumission 16 April 1804 from Levi Hayes, who signed by mark before Lenox Martin and John Sprigg.

L:321-322. Joshua Pigman recorded letter of attorney 16 April 1804, from William Stevens and Anne, his wife of the Commonwealth of Kentucky, Ohio County District, appoint attorney to make over unto Philemon Duvall of Montgomery County all right of dower of the said Anne in parcel called *Franklin.*

L:322-324.   Philemon Duvall recorded deed 16 April 1804, from Joshua Pigman attorney for William Stevens and Anne, for $100 assigns their interest in tract *Franklin.* Metes and bounds given adjacent to 9th line of *Resurvey on Star's Fancy,* containing 47 acres.

L:324-325.   Commission to Levy Court Justices, pursuant to Act of Assembly, recorded 17 April 1804 to Henry Brookes, Edward Burgess Jr., Richard West, Thomas B. Evans, Ozias Offutt, George Riley and Warren Magruder, of Montgomery County.

L:325-326.   Henry B. Horrell recorded mortgage 23 April 1804, from Joseph Cahill for $221.20 tract called *Deakin's Lot,* containing about 80 acres.

L:326-327.   Thomas Rawlins recorded deed 24 April 1804, from Joseph Clagett for £11..2 part of tract called *Resurvey on Younger Brother* beginning at 3rd line of tract called *Oronoko* thence to end of 9th line of *Resurvey on William and John ,* containing 7 and 4/10 acres. Susannah, wife of Joseph released dower.

L:327-328.   Thomas Rawlins recorded deed 24 April 1804, from Hannah Kelly, widow of Thomas Kelly deceased, and Thomas Kelly and Benjamin Kelly, of the one part; by his will he decreed that the said Hannah Kelly and Thomas Kelly were to be his executors, and after her death, the property to be sold by surviving executor and divided among his three sons, Joseph, Benjamin and Thomas Kelly.   Signed by marks by Hannah Kelly and Thomas Kelly of Thomas, and Benjamin Kelly. Mary, wife of Thomas Kelly released dower rights.

L:329-330.   Thomas Rawlins recorded deed 24 April 1804, from Hannah Kelly for 5 shillings, part of *Resurvey on William and John,* signed by mark by Hannah Kelly.

L:330-331.   Benjamin Owens recorded bond under insolvent act, 26 April 1804, from Honore Martin, Richard Beall and Solomon Holland, bound in sum of £50. Whereas the above Benjamin Owen is now confined to prison in Montgomery County, and has petitioned Elemeck Swearingen, John Belt and John Fleming for his discharge according to the Act of Assembly for the relief of Insolvent Debtors; that the said Owen had indirectly sold and lessened and disposed interest and concealed some part of his goods, stock, securities, contracts and estate whereby to secure the same and to accrue or expect some profit and advantage thereof, now the condition is that the above bound Honore Martin, shall well and truly pay or satisfy all damages which the said Benjamin Owen shall sustain, in Honore Martin's objecting against the said Owen's discharge.

L:331-333. Thomas Morton recorded 2 May 1804, from Mary Morton of Charles County, Maryland for £300, tract where Thomas now lives, part of *Bealls Good Will,* also her moeity or share of grist and saw mill and Negroes James for 3 years; Ned Brown for 8 years; Ned Booth for 3 years; Susanna for 6 years and Jane for 6 years. Signed Mary Morton, before Henry A. (Arundel) Smith, and Samuel Hawkins, justices of the peace for Charles County.

L:333-334. Lewis Beall recorded deed 2 May 1804 from Richard Wooton, for love and affection, and 5 shillings, part of *Exchange and New Exchange Enlarged* conveyed to Wootton by Arthur Nelson of Frederick County in June 1784.

L:334. Hezekiah Lezear and William Warfield recorded bill of sale 3 May 1804 from John Poole of William for one black horse, two cows and yearlings.

L:334-337. Basil Brooke recorded deed 7 May 1804, from James Brooke and Esther, his wife for $5960 part of the following tracts, *Addition to Brooke Grove, Resurvey on Brooke Park, part of Dickerson's Choice, and Discovery.* Metes and bounds given for 198 acres. Signed by James Brooke, Heather Brooke before Elemelech Swearingen, Jno Thomas 3d.

L:337-338. Solomon Holland recorded mortgage 16 May 1804 from Thomas Garrott for debt due to firm of Thomas Linstead and Solomon Holland of £73..2, Negro woman Beck 42 years; mulatto boy Owen, 19 years; girl Jenny 16 years; Polly 14 years; boy Bob 8 years; girl Harriet 6 years; livestock and furniture as well.

L:338. Gassaway Watkins Harwood recorded 8 May 1804 certificate of qualification as Justice of the Peace, before Richard Beall.

L:338-339. George Hardy of Anne Arundel County, recorded bill of sale 22 May 1804, from John Boswell, for $40, for one black mare. Signed my mark, John Boxwell.

L:339-340. Syrus Bowen recorded bill of sale 22 May 1804, from James Currin for £21, one brown mare, 7 years old; one sow and 7 pigs, 6 leather bottom chairs, 6 white oak bottom chairs; one desk, one large pot, one small pot, one dutch oven, skillett, other household items.

L:340-341. Thomas Orme recorded deed 24 May 1804, from Alexander Contee Hanson, Esq., chancellor. Whereas Andrew Heugh, now deceased, purchased of Daniel St. Thomas Jenifer, tract, and John Hugh, his son, released his right to Robert Ferguson, who released his right to Thomas Orme, to tract called *Tradesmen's Value,* deed is made by the Chancellor for the premises, tract within metes and bounds, beginning at southern most part of Bennett's Creek, containing 35 acres.

L:341-342. Hugh Thompson recorded bill of sale 24 May 1804, from Perry Beall for 5000 weight crop tobacco, he assigns 3 feather beds and furniture; one table, one walnut chest, one hair trunk, other household, plantation items, crops of corn, and tobacco.

L:342-343. William Benson recorded bill of sale 24 May 1804, from Nicholas Pegno for £584 for Negro man Toby 45, Rachel 20 years; Jim 16 years; Henry 14; Isaac 3 years; and Negro man Tom 60 years; girl Nan 8 years; cattle, etc.

L:343-344. Ruth Griffith recorded deed 28 May 1804, from Sarah Gartrell, one of the daughters of Stephen Gartrell, deceased, for $1. assigns all her right to undivided lands devised by her father, in Montgomery and Anne Arundel County. Signed by mark.

L:344-345. Ruth Griffith recorded deed, 28 May 1804, from Rachel Mullican one of the daughters of Stephen Gartrell, deceased, for $1. assigns all her right to lands in Montgomery and Anne Arundel County. Signed by mark.

L:345-346. Richard McDaniel recorded bill of sale 29 May 1804, from Peter Flanagan for £60 for one cow and calf, 2 heifers, other livestock, and farm and plantation tools. Signed by mark.

L:346-347. Joseph Soper recorded deed 31 May 1804, from Isaac Aldridge of the City of Baltimore for $107, his undivided one half of *Aldridge's Discovery.* Acknowledgment.

L:347-349. Joseph Soaper recorded 31 May 1804 from Joseph Wilson son of Lancelot of Prince George's County. Whereas Joseph Wilson, did on 30 October 1775, mortgage to Cunningham, Findley and Co., merchants in Glasco, a tract then in Frederick County, called *Beall's Seat,* 100 acres of for securing payment; and he has paid no part of the claim, now with interest, amounting to £473..15..11, they mutually agreed to sell 100 acres to the highest bidder, which sold for £115.

L:349-352. Joseph Soaper recorded release 31 May 1804 from Richard Ponsonby of Bladensburg, Prince George's County, for and in behalf of, as agent for the merchants listed above, sells for £176..4..10, property as mortgaged and recorded in Frederick County deeds W:472-475.

L:352-353. Thomas Beall of George of the Territory of Columbia, recorded deed 1 June 1804, from Anthony Ricketts of Montgomery County, for $800, part of *Waters Forrest,* 86 ½ acres. Adjacent to part conveyed by Basil Waters to John House. Also a tract of land called *Goshen,* adjacent to *Water's Forrest,* containing 21 1/4 acres. Margaret wife of Anthony released dower.

L:354-356. Amon Riggs Jr. recorded deed 26 May 1804, from Amon Riggs Sr. and Ruth Riggs his wife, for £50 assigns part of tract called *Cow Pasture.*

L:356-358. William Holmes recorded deed 5 June 1804, from Gassaway Rawlings of Anne Arundel County, trustee of Richard Alexander Contee, a lunatic, deceased; and Elisabeth Gassaway Contee, widow of said Richard, of Prince George's County, for £851..19..4, sells parcel, a part of *Snowden's Manor Enlarged,* adjacent to Seth Hyatt's land, *Layhill,* and Philip Hawker's land, bounded by *Roger's Chance,* for 500 acres.

L:358-359. Commission for Justices of the Peace on 11 June 1804. To William Smith, Lawrence O'Neale, Richard Green, Henry Brookes, Greenbury Howard, Edward Burgess Junior, Elemelech Swearingen, Benjamin Gaither, James Lackland, Archibald A. Beall, Lewis Duvall of Hyattstown, Ozias Offutt, John Thomas, John Burgess, William Culver, Robt Bowie, Thomas Simpson, Lenox Martin, Richard West, Thomas B. Evans, John Adamson, Camden Riley, Warren Magruder, Richard Beall, John Fleming, Samuel Elger, Meshach Browning, John Belt, Gassaway Howard, and Walter Brooke Beall.

L:359-361. Samuel Magruder recorded deed from Kinsey Beall for £215 for two tracts, part of *Culp's Desire,* 36 acres, and part of *Hannah's Inheritance,* 6 acres. Signed before Ozias Offutt, Richard West. Charlotte released dower rights.

L:361-362. Jacob Bowman recorded bill of sale 13 June 1804, from Philip Hopkins for £30 for livestock.

L:362-364. Alexander Offutt recorded deed 22 June 1804 from Aquilla Magruder for £953..5 sells part of *Grubby Thickett.* Deed exempted 6 sq. perches where Nathaniel Magruder and his wife were buried, adjacent to Walter Magruder's part. Mary Ann Magruder, wife of Aquilla, released dower

L:365-368. William Carroll recorded deed 22 June 1804, from Rt. Rev. John Carroll of Baltimore, and Robert Brent Carroll of the District of Columbia, surviving executors of Daniel Carroll Senior.

Whereas Daniel Carroll Esq., deceased by his will named John Carroll, Notley Young and Robert Brent all his estate, to be applied to the education of his grandchildren, and to be divided as they might deem proper. For 5 shillings, paid by William Carroll, one of the grand children of the deceased, they assign part of *Joseph's Park,* formerly conveyed by Daniel Carroll Sr deceased to Daniel Carroll Junior deceased, adjacent to part of tract formerly held by Clement Beall; to 1st line of *Lost Coat,* part of *Joseph's Park,* held by Benjamin Becraft; then to a corner of the land formerly belonging to Thomas Miles; to a part formerly leased to a certain Thomas Nicholls, to 2nd line of *Joseph's Park,* then to the first beginning containing 447 3/4 acres.

L:368-370. Solomon Simpson recorded deed 23 June 1804, from John Hoggins, Elizabeth Hoggins, Aquila Cawood and Catherine Cawood his wife, Robert Edwards and Rebecca Edwards his wife; all of Montgomery County, for £175. Sell part of tract called *Henry,* containing 100 acres. Signed, acknowledged and dower releases by parties.

L:370. Clement Jarboe recorded bond recorded 26 June 1804, to State of Maryland for $250 with Gerard Jarboe the condition that he shall perform duties of constable.

L:371. Zachariah Maccubbin Jr., recorded qualification as deputy sheriff, 29 June 1804.

L:371 Negro William Gantt, 33 year old mulatto, recorded manumission 30 June 1804, from Basil Darby. Wit: Nicholas Dawson, George Dyson.

L:371-373. Benjamin Perry recorded 30 June 1804 from James Lee for £300, part of *Hermitage* beginning at first line of parcel sold by Benjamin Harris now in the possession of Allen Bowie, called *Adventure,* now containing 292 1/8 acres. Signed before Thos Simpson, Walt. B. Beall. Ruth, wife of James Lee released dower rights.

L:373-374. Thomas Jenkins recorded bill of sale 3 July 1804 from Joseph Howell of Montgomery County for $50. For feather beds, furniture, looking glass, two linen wheels, 3 iron pots.

L:374-376. Arnold Warfield recorded deed 11 July 1804, from Lawrence Snyder, lot on *Moneysworth.* Eve Snyder released dower rights.

L:376-377. Henry Winemiller recorded deed 11 July 1804, from John Belt for $100. Part of *Three Brothers.* Signed before Greenby Howard, Lewis Duvall.

L:377-380. Aquilla Beall recorded deed 12 July 1804 from Samuel Hanson Wheeler, Tilghman Hillery and Ann Hilleary his wife for £700..10, part of *Longacre,* adjacent to *Elting's Rest.* Ann Wheeler and Ann Hilleary released dower rights.

L:380-382. Thomas Perry Willson recorded bill of sale 12 July 1804 from Thomas Austin Sr. for £133..11, sells to Thomas Perry Willson, Jesse Leach and Robert Wallace, all his household goods and Negroes, to wit: boy Tom, 9 years old, John 7 years old, woman Henny, 21 years old, girl Harriett 6 years old, wagon, livestock and other furniture.

L:382-384. Samuel Wilson recorded deed from Enoch and Susanna Magruder, his wife of Jefferson County, Kentucky for £120 sells tracts called *Susanna,* and *Resurvey on William and John.*

L:384-385. John Poole Jr. Recorded bill of sale 16 July 1804 from Arthur Steele for £67..10 one sorrell mare and colt, other livestock, feather beds and furniture

L:385-387. James Wade recorded deed 17 July 1804 from George H. Offutt executor of Thomas Sparrow deceased, tract called *Hold Fast*

L:387. John Vinson recorded certificate of qualification

L:387-388. Jesse Mills recorded manumission 21 July 1801, to Negro Jane now in the poor house, who was given to me by Mr. Burwell of Queen Ann, and her two children Peggy and Nace. Signed 20 July 1803 by mark, witnessed by John Flemming.

L:388-389. Thomas Nicholls of John recorded deed 21 July 1804, from Jesse Davis for £100 for one third part of *William and John* said to contain 124 acres. Acknowledged before Elem Swearingen, Benjamin Gaither

L:389-391. Joshua Inman recorded deed 24 July 1804 from Jesse Hyatt for £7..10, lots #14 and #68 in Hyattstown. Signed before Lewis Duvall, M. Browning.

L:391-393. Gerard Brooke recorded deed 28 July 1804, from Bernard Gilpin & Sarah his wife for $880. Assigns part of *Addition to Brooke Grove,* and part of a tract of 200 acres purchased of James Brooke, metes and bounds given for 50 acres for 2nd tract 29 1/4 acres. Signed before Richard Green, Jno Thomas 3d.

L:393-396. Gerard Brooke recorded deed 28 July 1804 from Basil Brooke and Mary his wife, for $5960 conveys tract of land, 298 acres more or less. Same witnesses as above.

L:396. Jesse Phillips recorded certificate as deputy sheriff 31 July 1804.

L:396. Philip Connell recorded certificate as deputy sheriff 31 July 1804

L:396-397. Honore Martin recorded deed of mortgage, 30 July 1804, from Charles Saffle for $200 grants part of tract originally called *Moneysworth,* but by subsequent survey called *Wood Port.* Beginning at 7th line of whole tract, parcel contains 101 1/4 acres.

L:398. Walter B. Beall, recorded Certificate of Qualification as magistrate 2 August 1804

L:398. Samuel S. Harwood late of Frederick County, Virginia, and now of Montgomery County, recorded 6 August 1804, importation of a slave from Virginia, called Otho, 10 years old, acquired by marriage to Elizabeth W. Belt of Loudoun County.

L:398-399. Walter Simms recorded constables bond to State of Maryland 6 August 1804 with Catherine Simms.

L:399-401. Robert Peter of Washington, D.C., recorded deed 6 August 1804 from Samuel Brewer Magruder, surviving executor of his father, Samuel Magruder III, who did in his lifetime, 3 January 1758, by deed of gift in consideration therein expressed make over to his son, Ninian Beall Magruder, 250 acres by name of *Magruder and Beall's Honesty,* recorded in Liber F, 357-358 of Frederick County, and on 15 Nov. 1766 by deed Ninian Beall Magruder sold land to Robert Peter, recorded in Liber K:799- of Frederick County, and the said Robert Peter by a recent examination of the bounds has found a deficiency in the acreage, deeds over 39 acres, adjacent to part previously deed by Samuel Magruder to Ninian Beall Magruder. Signed before William Smith, Ozias Offutt.

L:401-402. Negro Benjamin recorded manumission 6 August 1804, from William Hilton, Benjamin to be free in 4 years from 1 January last. Signed before Lenox Martin and Sarah Camden.

L:402. Evan Belt recorded constables bond 7 August 1804.

L:402-403. Thomas C. Nicholls recorded constable's bond 7 August 1804.

L:403-404. Noah Hardy recorded deed 8 August 1804, from John Poole Junr. for £43..10 assigns part of tract called *Jeremiah's Park*, conveyed by Vachel Hall containing 5 1/4 acres. Signed John Poole Jr., Prissa W. Poole, released dower rights.

L:404-406. John Peter Junr. of Washington, District of Columbia, and John Peter Sr. of the same place, recorded trust deed 9 August 1804, from Thomas B. Evans. Whereas about 1 October 1801 Thomas B. Evans and John Peter Jr. Under the name and firm of Evans and Peter contracted sundry large debts for goods, wares and merchandise, and the said Thomas B. Evans by agreement dated 21 June 1804 confirmed contract between them, to take to himself to collect all debts due the firm and at the same time making himself responsible for all debts contracted by the firm, and to secure him from harm makes over to John Peter Sr in trust the following property, to wit: Negroes Davy, Daniel, Will, London, Priss, Sear, and Kitty. Now for $1 he makes over the third part of all the property aforesaid, signed Thos B. Evans.

L:406-407. James Austin recorded deed 11 August 1804, from John Austin for 5 shillings, part of tract called *Conclusion,* formerly conveyed by William Deakins to Simon Reeder, adjacent to parts of Francis Thomas and Richard Hoggins. Laid out for 82 2/3 acres. Signed John Austin. Charity, wife of John released dower.

L:407-408. Thomas Gatton recorded 13 August 1804, that on 8th August he imported Negro Harry, 9 years old, formerly a resident of the District of Columbia.

L:408. John Hall recorded bill of sale 14 August 1804 from Joseph Hall for $200. For Negro girl Henny, 12 years old, and one cow, yearling and furniture.

L:409. George Bowling recorded bill of sale 14 August 1804 from Shadrack Ellis for £50 for livestock, furniture, crop of tobacco.

L:409-410. Negro Jack, about 45 years old recorded manumission 14 August 1804, from Solomon Stimson for divers good causes. Signed by mark before Wm Smith, Wm Rutherford.

L:410-411. John Hose recorded bill of sale 14 August 1804, from William Hinton for £25 for gray horse, 4 hogs, furniture and plantation utensils.

L:411. Evan Belt qualification as deputy sheriff, August 1804.

L:411-413. John Plummer recorded deed 18 August 1804, from Jesse Harris for £43..2, part of *Mount Zion,* and *Harris's Loss,* containing 8 5/8 acres, beg. At Mary Harris's part. Dorcas wife of Jesse released dower rights.

L:413-414. Edward Willett recorded deed 18 August 1804. Whereas a court of chancery, on 24 March 1795, adjudged in a suit between Thomas Suter complainant and Thomas Willson by Robert Peter, his trustee, that they should convey 50 acre part of lands mentioned in suit, at request of James Suter, made over to Edward Willett, part of *Exchange and New Exchange Enlarged*, beginning at part as sold by James Dick to Barton Harris. Signed by Robert Peter and James Suter.

L:414-415. Jesse Leach and Samuel Middleton recorded instrument of writing, 20 August 1804. Leases lots 71, 72 and 73 in Rockville for 7 years; Jesse Leach to build a frame dwelling house and kitchen on said lot.

L:415-418. Henry Beggarly and others, trustees of the Methodist Church, recorded deed 21 August 1804, for 5 shillings, from Patrick Orme to Henry Baggerly, Richard Nixon, Nathan Hoskinson, Hezekiah Baggerly, Richard Lansdale and John Baggerly of Montgomery County and Richard Morsell of Prince George's County, on a lot called *Two Farms.*

L:418. William Berry 2nd recorded constables bond to State of Maryland with Robert Swails, Samuel Beall, August 1804.

L:418-419. Israel Sear recorded 23 August 1804, list of Negroes removed from Virginia: Peter 25 and woman Phany, 18.

L:419. Negro Jerry about 26 years old recorded manumission recorded 29 August 1804, made 4 July 1804, from James Lawson. Wit: Wm Browning.

L:419-421. Charles Mackelfresh et. al. (John H. Smith and Joseph Benton of Frederick County, and Samuel Hobbs and Basil Soaper of Montgomery County, trustees) recorded deed 30 August 1804 from Ely Hyatt and Mary Ann Hyatt his wife of Frederick County, Virginia; for £6 part of *The Principal,* containing ½ acre in Hyattstown, for use in building a Methodist Church.

L:422-423. Charles Mackelfresh recorded deed of trust 30 August 1804, from Jesse Hyatt for £6 lots #15 and #67 in Hyattstown.

L:423-424. William Trail recorded deed 31 August 1804, from Enoch King, for £60, deed for part of tract called *Fruitful Plains,* beginning at tract in possession of Joshua Pearce, to a line of *Resurvey on Happy Choice,* containing 20 acres Signed before Richard Turner. Barbara King released dower right.

L:425-427. William Worthington Senr. recorded deed 3 September 1804 from John Beall Magruder for £3280 assigns tract called *Granby,* beginning at a bounded black oak on the south side of a hill near the head of two valleys that falls into the forks of Rock Creek, it being the beginning of a tract called *The Robert and Sarah,* likewise of a tract called *the Ridge,* adjacent to *Addition to Turkey Thicket,* to first line of whole tract called *Magruder's Farm*, containing 445 acres. Signed before Richard Turner.

L:428. George Willson recorded constable's bond 13 September 1804, to State of Maryland

L:428. William Elson Willson recorded certificate of deputy sheriff 6 September 1804, at request of Benjamin Perry Jr., sheriff.

L:428-429. Thomas Allnutt recorded mortgage from John Adams for one sorrel mare 3 years old, one cow and yearling, one feather bed and bedstead, 4 blankets, a parcel of feathers, one chest ... 16 turkeys and some hammers and tongs. Witness John Fleming.

L:429-431. Upton Beall recorded mortgage 12 Sept. 1804, from Benjamin Ray Jr. Whereas Margaret Beall and Upton Beall administrators of Brooke Beall, did heretofore to wit at a county court held for the county on the first Monday in March 1798, recover judgment against the said Benjamin Ray Junior on his bond as Sheriff, of the county aforesaid, for the year 1796, on which said judgment the said Margaret Beall and Upton Beall, administrators as aforesaid did take out a writ of fieri facias directed to the sheriff commanding him to levy the same on the goods and chattels, lands and tenements of the said Benjamin Ray, and thereby returned the half of improved lot #23, and he assigns one Negro woman named Jenny and her three children, to wit: Betsy, Fern and Basil, provided nevertheless that if mortgage satisfied sale is void.

L:431-432. Evan Trundle recorded schedule of property to the Sheriff of Montgomery County. Old chest, table, shovel plough.

L:432-433. Zachariah Knott recorded deed 21 Sept 1804, from Henry Camden and Mary Camden, his wife for £93..10, part of *Happy Choice,* containing 22 ½ acres.

L:433-434. Charles Gassaway recorded bill of sale 22 September 1804 from Joshua Harrison for a valuable consideration, assigns one bay mare, one cow, one calf and one heifer, feather bed and furniture, one walnut chest, other items.

L:434. Benjamin Ray Jr. recorded bond as collector to State of Maryland September 1804.

L:435-436. At request of Henry Culver and Robert Edmonston deed was recorded 28 September 1804. I John Needham of Montgomery County for $150 do sell all my goods and implements of mechanics use, viz 60 molding and bench planes, 2 work benches, 9 hand and other saws, 1 hand screw, one turnkey and one other rubber stone, a dozen chisels, augers and a pair of punches, one iron bed key, 40 bed screws, 1 small chest including work patters, 15 field bedsteads partly finished, 300 ft. black walnut plank, 200 ft. cherry tree plank, 400 ft. poplar plank, and also one walking stick, and whatsoever now remaining in the possession of the said John Needham.

L:436. John Cochlin recorded schedule of property 29 Sept 1804 to Sheriff of Montgomery County consisting of 1 table, 1 chair, 1 scythe & cradle, 1 ax. Signed before Elem Swearingen, John Fleming.

L:436-437. Bennett Clements recorded constables bond 1 October 1804 to state of Maryland

L:437-438. Ely Hyatt recorded deed 4 Oct 1804 from Thomas Orme for $200 tract called *Tradesman's Value*, containing 35 acres. Conveyed to Orme by Alexander Contee Hanson.

L:438. Shadrick Cheney recorded deed 3 October 1804, from Rezin Johnson for £17..5, parcel near Clarksburg, formerly conveyed by John D. Coffee and Ann Roberts to John Clark for 151 5/8 acres; Lidda Johnson, wife of Rezin Johnson released dower.

L:439-441. William A. Needham recorded deed 3 October 1804, from Benjamin Ray Jr., sheriff. Resulting in writ of fi fa against Zachariah Maccubin, in a suit by William Woodard plaintiff. Two pieces of land herein described, tract called *the Forrest,* with two tenements occupied in one part by Edward Jance supposed to contain 250 acres and one occupied by the widow of the late John Peter Boyer, supposed to contain 65 acres more or less, lying on Rock Creek, the road from George Town to Newport Mill and William Needham was the high bidder.

L:441-442. Robert Peter recorded deed 3 October 1804, from Elisha Owen Williams of Washington County, District of Columbia, for £7..10 part of *Resurvey on William's Venture,* Harriott, wife of Williams released dower.

L:442-444. William Woodward of Anne Arundel County, recorded deed 5 October 1804, from Martha Maccubbin and William A. Needham for £195..19 two tracts, one 250 acres, Edward Janes tenant on road leading from Rockville to George Town, and the other occupied by the widow of John Peter Boyer.

L:444-445. William Benson recorded deed 8 October 1804 from Nicholas Pegno sells all that improvements and parcel of land called *Inspection* formerly the property of Weaver Barnes containing 150 acres. Signed Nicholas Pegno.

L:445-446. William Benson recorded bill of sale 8 October 1804 from Nicholas Pegno for £250 all my crop of corn, now standing in the field, supposed to contain about 200 barrells, and all my crop of tobacco now in the house.

L:446-447. Joseph Evans recorded deed 9 October 1804, from Richard Johns for £10, tract called *Piney Grove,* containing 102 acres of land. Signed before Richard Turner.

L:447-448. Elizabeth Hickman recorded bill of sale 9 October 1804 from Henry Stallings for 4500 pounds of merchantable crop tobacco, livestock, furniture.

L:448. William Roberts, with Brook Ayton, recorded certificate of qualification as deputy sheriff 9 October 1804. Beall Ayton recorded certificate, qualified same day before Benjamin Ray Jr. As Deputy Sheriff.

L:449-450. Robert Willson recorded deed 11 October 1804, from Elisha Owens Williams for £642. Part of *Resurvey on William's Venture,* and *Forrest.* Adjacent to *Wickham's Range.* Containing 214 acres with dwellings and other buildings. Signed and acknowledged, and Harriet Williams wife of Elisha Owens Williams released dower rights.

L:450-452. Hezekiah Ward recorded deed 11 October 1804 from Henry Poole for £200 part of *Ivy Reach,* on Little Bennets Creek, containing 20 ½ acres. Mrs. Emellia Poole, wife of Henry Poole released dower rights.

L:452-453. Benjamin Hersey brought into state from Virginia and recorded 12 October 1804, a list of slaves, not intended for sale, Fender age 26, Nuty age 50, Evenlinea 10, Henry 3 years old and Tom 7 months of age.

L:453. William Benson recorded 13 October 1804, a bill of sale from Nicholas Pegno, a Negro woman named Luce, and her increase, crops of corn fodder, oats, wheat and rye in the ground.

L:454. Peter Kemp recorded deed 15 October 1804, from William Marbury, trustee for the sale of the real estate of Samuel Beall, deceased, appointed by Chancery Court in June Term 1802, to sell *Snowden's Mill Land*. Sold for $500.

L:455-459. Aquila Beall of Washington County, District of Columbia, recorded deed 22 October 1804, from Upton Beall. Whereas Brooke Beall, the father of the above named Upton and Aquilla, late of Montgomery County deceased, died intestate, seized and possessed of a large estate, both real and personal lying in Montgomery and other Counties in the state, same devolved upon his widow and all his children who afterwards agreed to make divisions thereof amongst themselves, and it so fell out that the following tracts were allotted to the above named Upton and Aquila Beall, to wit: part of *Millburn*, part of *Patience, Orlando Stump's Valley, Addition, Hobson's Choice, I was Not a Thinking of it*, part of the *Dunghill*, part of *Conjurers Outdone, Beggars Benison, Cooks Carriage, Evan's Lookout, Weavers Den*, part of the *Resurvey on Boyleston's Discovery*, and part of a tract called the *Resurvey on Montross*, all contiguous to and adjoining each other, also part of a tract called *Piney Grove*, a tract called *Long Acre*, and another adjoining thereto called the variation for their part of their said father's real estate. Afterwards, on 16 Marc 1799, the said Upton and Aquila by virtue of a special warrant of resurvey and reduced into one entire tract the first above mentioned original tracts and called by the name of *Beall mont*, and returned to the land office a certificate of said resurvey, the original tracts contain clear of elder surveys 1516 ½ acres, including 14 3/4 acre part of the *Resurvey on Boyleston's Discovery*, which the said Aquila hd purchased of a certain John Chambers about the time of making the said resurvey, and further appears there were added eight pieces of contiguous vacancy containing 73 1/3 acres, making the entire tract 1590 acres. By a subsequent and more accurate measurement it is found that the original tracts contain 1567 3/4 acres. It was further agreed between them that the lands lying to the south east and south and south west of the divisional lines including the mills and their appurtenances, belonging together with the above mentioned part of *Piney Grove*, containing 281 acres should be the property and the estate of Upton Beall, and the remaining part of the said resurvey together with the two tracts called *Long Acre, and the Variation*, containing together 73 acres, as also 40 acres, part of the *Resurvey on Montross* (in the possession of Archibald Orme) not included in the above resurvey the reversion of which was in the said Brooke Beall his heirs and assigns at the death of a certain John Campbell, now living, should be the property and estate of the said Aquila Beall. Division of *Beall Mont* Follows to Aquila Beall. Metes and bounds given for division. Matilda, wife of Upton Beall released dower.

L:459-463. Upton Beall recorded deed 22 October 1804, from Aquilla Beall. Upton Beall's share of division above given in metes and bounds. Grace, wife of Aquila Beall released dower.

L:463-464. Andrew Offutt recorded deed 23 October 1804, made 1 September from Richard Thomas for all his right and title to *Thomas's Hills,* and *Thomas's Bottom,* for £211, adjacent to tracts *William and Ann, Beall's Desire,* containing 52 acres, and 1 3/4 acres. Signed and acknowledged before Wm Thomas, Wm Holmes.

___ END OF LIBER L

Montgomery County Land Records Liber M

M:1. William Benson recorded 28 October 1804 from Thomas Mockbee, for $200 bill of sale for livestock and furniture. Signed by mark before John Fleming.

M:2-3. George W. Offutt recorded deed 29 October 1804 from Thomas Burgess Offutt for love and affection and 5 shillings, two tracts, part of *Newton,* laid off in 1759 for Samuel Offutt for 310 acres; metes and bounds given for 19 acres and 48 acre parts; and one other tract called *Barren Hill* containing 41 acres. Thomas B. Offutt signed before Wm Smith and Ozias Offutt. Lydia Offutt, wife of Thomas B. Offutt released dower rights.

M:3-4. William Mullican recorded bill of sale 29 October 1804, from Bennett Smith for £30. Lists personal property with note, "as I am overseer to William Waters and cannot ascertain my part of same..." Signed by mark before John Fleming. Bennett Smith acknowledged deed.

M:4. Zachariah Downs recorded bill of sale 29 October 1804 from Mary Downs, in consideration of love and good will she has for her son, and for £3..15 sells Negro woman Sukey, about 29 years old and her four children: Rachel, Robert, Christina and Davis. Signed by mark before Wm Culver.

M:5-6. Margaret Offutt recorded 29 October 1804, deed made 24 July from George Hamilton Offutt of Woodford County, Kentucky. Whereas Edward Offutt grandfather of George did by his will devise to daughters Ruth and Mary, part of *Outlet,* for 154 acres, Ruth and her husband to have part they dwell on, and Mary married Ninian Tannyhill, who had children that died in infancy, they are also now deceased. Their part would have descended to her oldest brother then living, William Offutt, father of the above named George Hamilton Offutt, his eldest son, after death of Ninian, which part he now sells to Margaret for $500.50 containing 77 acres.

M:6-8. Lewis Browning of Frederick County, recorded mortgage 29 October 1804 from Jacob Louman for £30 tract called *Resurvey on What You Will,* on the 56th line of *Woodport,* to the second line of *Grandmother's Good Will,* containing 28 ½ acres.

M:8-9. Meshack Browning recorded bill of sale 29 October 1804 from Joseph Redman, one sorrel horse, one bay mare and one young calf.

M:9-10. Lewis Browning recorded bill of sale 29 October 1804 from Michael Tully for £20, livestock. Signed by mark before Meshack Browning.

M:10-11. Charles Perry and Anthony Perry recorded bill of sale 30 October 1804, I Robert Perry for £200 sell ten Negroes: women Ruth, Poll and Sal, girl Nell and child Luce and Harriett; boys Frank, Tom, Sandy and Ben. Signed before Benjamin Gaither.

M:11. Thomas W. Riggs, recorded schedule

M:11. William Carey's qualification as deputy sheriff, recorded 1 November 1804.

M:11. Ninian Benson's qualification as deputy sheriff, recorded 1 November 1804, dated 25 October 1804.

M:12. Stephen Adams qualification as deputy sheriff recorded 1 November 1804.

M:12-13. David Gue of Virginia recorded deed 8 Nov. 1804 rom Archibald A. Beall, for $300, assigns 205 3/4 acres; part of *Abel's Levels,* metes and bounds on 4th line of part of *Owen's Resurvey* conveyed to Samuel Crow by John Owens, for 89 1/4 acres; also part of *Phelena and Sarah,* beginning at 16th line of *Owen's Resurvey,* 15 ½ acres. Esther Beall wife of Archabald released dower.

M:13-15. Archibald A. Beall recorded mortgage from David Gue of Loudoun County, Virginia, made 2 November 1804. Mortgage on same property above. Signed by mark.

M:15-16. Samuel Hanson Wheeler, recorded deed 6 March 1804, from Tilghman Hilleary and Ann, his wife for £625 all of Ann's equal moiety to several tracts or parcels, *Concord, Esophas* and *Forrest,* 325 ½ acres, and *Frozen Levels,* 198 ½ acres devised to Ann Hilleary by her father, Clement Wheeler, late of Prince George's County, deceased. Signed before John Hilleary, Jno M. Gantt.

M:17-18. Zachariah Thompson recorded deed 6 November 1804 from Francis Perry and Hannah Perry for $34.50, tract *Point Lookout,* adjacent to *Hutchcraft's Range,* signed by Francis Perry and Hannah Perry by mark.

M:18-19. Absalom Beddo recorded deed 6 November 1804 from Peter Kemp part of tract *Snowden's Mill,* signed before Wm Culver, Thos Simpson. Sarah Kemp released dower.

M:19-21. John Shaw recorded deed 6 November 1804 from William Kirk for $305, tract *Chance,* adjacent to *Sampling Ridge,* and *Willson's Inheritance,* 50 acres. Signed by mark. Susanna Kirk released dower.

M:21-23. Leonard Williams of Prince George's County recorded deed 6 Nov. 1804 from Nathan Thompson, for $1022.50, part of *Moneysworth,* adjacent to *Benton's Lot,* 102 1/4 acres. Signed before Lewis Duvall. Mary Thomson released dower.

M:23-24. Henry Culver recorded deed 6 November 1804, from Aquilla Vinson of Prince George's County, £93..15, part of *Resurvey on the Farm,* 50 acres, signed by mark. Harriet Vinson released dower right.

M:24-26. Jesse Phillips recorded deed 7 November 1804, from John Dowden Coffee of Mason County, Kentucky as attorney in fact for Frederick A. Burnes, one of the heirs of Samuel Hardy, deceased, in right by virtue of Barbara, wife of the afsd Frederick Burnes, and daughter of Samuel Hardy, for £16..4..3, tract *Hard To Get.*

M:26-27. Jesse Phillips recorded power of attorney, from Frederick A. Burnes to John D. Coffee

M:27-28. Nathaniel Harper recorded bill of sale 1 November 1804 from John Harper, livestock and furniture. Signed by mark before William Smith.

M:28-29. George Heater recorded deed 8 November 1804 from Samuel Lane for 5 shillings sells lot that Thomas Pack formerly conveyed to said Samuel Lane for one acre on which Daniel McCarthy does now and for several years last past have resided.

M:29-31. Aquila Beall of Washington, District of Columbia, recorded deed 12 November 1804 from Archibald Orme for £116..16, tract called *Piney Grove,* adjacent to *Weavers Den, Cook's Carriage,* and to *Eleanors Green,* containing 60 1/4 acres.

M:31. Benjamin Owen or Owings, recorded schedule 12 Nov 1804 delivered to sheriff in April, includes, sow, drawing knife, jointer, iron wedges, razors, shaving box, 1 book and 1 almanack; debts due to Honore Martin, Vachel Hall, William Bennett, Lenox Martin, John Poole admr of Deborah Sprigg, Francis Mantz, John Poole.

M:31. Samuel Clapham recorded list of Negroes November 1804, brought into the state. Jacob aged 25 years, Bet about 28 years old and Jane about 12 years old. From the state of Virginia for his own use and not for sale.

M:32-33. Nathan Thompson recorded deed 15 Nov 1804, from Joseph Williams for £462..10 tract called *Saplin Ridge,* 92 acres. Wife of Joseph Williams, not named, was examined apart and released dower.

M:33-35. Solomon Holland as trustee, recorded deed 16 November 1804 from Zachariah Maccubbin. Whereas Michael Reel obtained a judgment against Zachariah Maccubin, for which Benjamin Gaither and Thomas Nicholls were security. Makes over property to indemnify said Gaither and Nicholls, Negro Poll and child, and one Negro boy named Phil about 8 years old; one sorrel horse, other livestock.

M:35. Commission to Justices of the Levy Court dated 17 November 1804 to Henry Brookes, Edward Burgess Jr, Richard West, Ozias Offutt, George Riley, Warren Magruder and Norman West.

M:35 James Redmon recorded 17 November 1804, for Jemima about 18 years old, to be free when she arrives at age of 34 years. Wit. John Fleming.

M:36. John Mauxley recorded bill of sale from John Sheats for tobacco, livestock and crops. Signed by mark before Edward Burgess.

M:37. Amos Davis recorded schedule 26 November 1804.

M:37. Zachariah Gatton recorded bill of sale 28 November 1804 from Thomas Sparrow for $53.52, livestock. Signed before Thomas West.

M:38-39. Charles Henry Waring Wharton recorded 29 November 1804 from Joseph Hall for £300 sells all Negroes, stocks, goods, acquired by marriage to my deceased wife: Negroes Nicholas, 30; Harry 20, Charity 20 and Peggy 22, child Charity 10 and boy Stephen 14, Dominick 26, Harry 10 and girl Eleanor 4 years old, boy Jesse 2, and Tom 18 months, plus livestock.

M:40. John Jennings recorded schedule 8 December 1804, a crop of corn and parcel of fodder, crop of tobacco, 1 horse, 1 cow, 1 bed and furniture, 2 ploughs, 2 pair iron traces, 2 weeding hoes, 2 grubbing hoes, 1 ax, 1 wedge, 1 pewter dish, ½ dozen plates, ½ dozen spoons, knives and forks, 4 chairs, 2 chests, 2 pots, 1 stack straw, debt Benedict Beckwith $3..50 Watson Beckwith 8/. Sworn before John Adamson, John Fleming

M:41-42. Henry W. Dorsey recorded deed 11 December 1804 from George Culp and John Culp, part of tracts *Benjamin's Square,* and *Ludwicks Range*, adjacent to part of *Davis Content*, containing 70 ½ acres land. Ann Culp, wife of John Culp relinquished dower.

M:42. Zachariah Bogely recorded bill of sale 4 December 1804 from John Chambers of H., for one black mare, 4 head of sheep, feather bed and bedding.

M:43. Thomas B. Offutt recorded deed 20 December 1804, from George W. Offutt for 5 shillings, and in consideration of another deed to him, conveys property from will of Samuel Offutt, grandfather of said Thomas and George, part of tract called *Barren Hill*. Cassandra, wife of George Washington Offutt released dower.

M:44-46. Doctor John Bowie recorded deed in trust 22 December 1804, from William Carroll. Whereas William Carroll did borrow the sum of $1800 from Mrs. Henrietta Pierce on the 1st day of May last, for which he gave his bond with Mr. Thomas Cramphin his security, to secure loan, assigns part of *Joseph's Park,* on Rock Creek, adjacent to part held by Clement Beall, to first line of tract *Lost Coat,* held by Benjamin Becraft, to corner of a tract held by Thomas Miles, to beginning of another part held by Benjamin Becraft, to a part formerly leased to Thomas Nichols, containing 447 acres. Acknowledged before Wm Culver, Walter Beall.

M:46. John Aldridge recorded bill of sale 22 December 1804, from James Gatton, livestock.

M:46-47. Thomas Perry recorded bill of sale recorded 24 December 1804 from Francis Perry for $277 Negro woman called Henn and her child called Bett; and one Negro boy called Scott. Francis Perry signed before Edward Burgess Jr.

M:47-48. Benjamin Ray and others, bond as sheriff. Signed by Ben Ray Jr., Henry O'Neale, Joseph Slater, William Magrath, Nathaniel Beall.

M:49-50. George Heeter Sr. Recorded deed 1 January 1805 from Benjamin Ray Sr. for £15 sells part of tract called *Fountain,* on main road from Montgomery Court House to Mouth of Monocacy. Signed before Richard Turner. No dower release.

M:50. Robert Perry recorded schedule on insolvent debtor, 3 January 1805. 1 straw bed, 1 walnut table, 1 pine chest, 2 iron pots, 4 chairs. Signed before John Adamson, John Fleming.

M:50. Nathan T. Pack recorded schedule as insolvent debtor, 3 January 1805. 2 cyder casks, 1 shovel plow, 1 old table. Signed before Benjamin Gaither, John Fleming.

M:50-54. Aeneas Campbell recorded deed 7 January 1805, from Solomon Davis formerly of Frederick County, now of Montgomery County, executor of Solomon Simpson, late of Montgomery County, deceased, selling his real estate to the highest bidder as directed in will. For $4541.23, sells *Simpson's Dwelling Place,* part of tracts *Johnny and Molly's Conclusion, Resurvey on Disappointment, Friendship,* and part of *Chappel's Forrest,* metes and bounds given adjacent to part Simpson sold to Richard Wootton, containing 421 acres. Signed by executor.

M:54-56 Solomon Davis recorded deed 7 January 1805 from Aeneas Campbell for $4541.23, deed for the same properties as above. Signed by Aeneas Campbell. Henrietta Campbell released dower.

M:56-59. John Willson recorded deed with power of attorney January 1805 from Isaiah Cash of Jefferson County, Ohio. For £51, 15 ½ acres part of tract *Discontent*, adjacent to *Pascalham*, and part of *Pascalham* containing 144 acres. Signed by Isaiah Cash and Mary Cash by mark, Archibald Nicholls appointed lawful attorney to execute deed, before Noah Simsly and William Cash, in Belmont Co., Ohio.

M:59-60. Ignatius Waters recorded deed 8 January 1805, from Gerard Brooke for £452..5, part of *Addition to Brooke Grove,* beginning at *Charles and Benjamin,* to dividing line between William H. Dorsey and James Brooke, on eastern side of road, laid out for 67 acres.

M:60-61. Hezekiah Beggerly recorded bill of sale 10 January 1805, from Robert Fish for £45, sells corn, fodder, crops, etc.

M:61-62. Thomas Darnold, recorded 10 January 1805 from Robert Fish bill of sale for £30 for 3 feather beds and furniture.

M:62-63. Elizabeth Offutt, wife of George Hamilton Offutt released dower rights to Margaret Offutt, recorded 11 March 1805 on tract of land called *Outlet*.

M:63-65. Benjamin Gray recorded deed 16th January 1805 from Hinton Selby Gray, lots 31, 50 & 84, part of *Exchange and New Exchange Enlarged*. In town of Rockville, alias Montgomery County Court House as conveyed by Edward Owen Williams to the said Heracles S. Gray and lot said Heracles purchased of John Gray under contract from William T. Beall.

M:65-66. Jane Ober of Montgomery County, recorded deed 16 January 1805, from Anthony Reintzel of Washington, District of Columbia, for $800 *Drane's Final Conclusion ,* 6 acres, being the same conveyed to Reintzel for the sale of certain real estate of the heirs of Richard Ober. Signed before John Mountz Jr., Robert Ober. Acknowledged before Daniel Reintzel, Mayor of the Corporation Town of Georgetown and Richard Turner, Associate Justice.

M:67. Caleb Pancoast recorded deed 10 January 1805 from Joseph Elgar Jr. for $400, Lots 10, 11, 12 & 13 in the town of Brookeville, contiguous to each other, containing 1/4 acre each. Ann Elgar released dower right.

M:67-68. Commission issued to Justices of the Peace for Montgomery County 10 January 1805: William Smith, Lawrence O'Neale, Richard Green, Henry Brookes, Greenbury Howard, Edward Burgess Jr., Elemelech Swearingen, Benjamin Gaither, James Lackland, Lewis Duvall of Hyattstown, Ozias Offutt, John Thomas, John Burgess, William Culver, Thomas Simpson, Richard West, John Adamson, Camden Riley, Warren Magruder, Richard Beall, John Fleming, Samuel Elgar, Mescheck Browning, John Belt, Gassaway Howard, Walter Brooke Beall, William Garrett and William Darne.

M:68. Commission issued to Justices of the Levy Court for Montgomery County, 15 January 1805. Henry Brookes, Edward Burgess Jr., Richard West, Ozias Offutt, George Riley, Warren Magruder and Norman West.

M:68-69. John D. Coffee recorded schedule 16 January 1805, as insolvent debtor to gain release from imprisonment, turns over to the sheriff 1 horse and 1 mare, both black, 4 cows & calves, 2 steers, 1 heifer, 20 hogs, 1 set blacksmith's tools, 1 bed and furniture, ½ doz chairs, 1 chest & trunk, some slate accounts for blacksmith's work, amount unknown, 12 sheep.

M:69-70. Thomas Linstead and Solomon Holland recorded bill of sale 21 January 1805, from Ignatius West £65..14, a Negro woman named Luce, aged about 21 years old; and a bright bay mare, if sum paid by November next, sale void.

M:70. Nicholas L. Dawson of Frederick County, recorded bill of sale 22 January 1805 from Thomas W. Riggs for one bay mare and a small colt.

M:70-72. Thomas Orme recorded deed from Peter Boyer and James Day. Mary Boyer and Sarah Day released dower rights.

M:72-75.   Thomas Orme recorded deed 26 January 1805 from Benjamin Oden and Richard Williams West of Prince George's County.

M:75-78. James Ray recorded deed 26 January 1806 from Joshua Allison executor of John Allison, who devised to his wife Elizabeth Allison all his estate for her natural life, and afterwards to all his children, viz: Joshua, John, Hezekiah, William, Thomas, Zachariah, Ruth now Ruth Prather, Ann now Ann Fields, Precious and Polly Allison. Ann and her husband William Fields and Ruth and her husband Zachariah Prather, Polly and her husband Nicholas Umpstead, Zachariah and Thomas Allison have assigned rights to said land, toPrecious with her husband John Young. Tract part of *Constant Friendship*, and *Thompson's Adventure, Clever Marsh, I am Content,* and *Pleasant Mountain*. Elizabeth Allison is since deceased, and several children have sold their undivided shares to William O'Neale and Honore Martin. Deed signed by last two and Joshua Allison, executor.

M: 78-79. Solomon Holland recorded bill of sale 28 January 1805 from Ignatius West £25.. 8 sells Negro girl Peg about 10 years old.

M:79. Charles Gassaway recorded bill of sale 28 January 1805 from Duncan Murphy, assigns furniture. Sale void if sum owing is paid.

M:79-81. Thomas Harvie Talbott recorded bill of sale 29 January 1805 from Collin Williamson, livestock, goods and chattells.

M:81. Ann Parker recorded manumission 30 January 1805, for Negro man Will, aged 32 years now in possession of Wm Willson of John, he is to be free after 14 January 1816. Signed before M. Browning.

M:81-83. Leonard Hays recorded deed 31 January 1805 from Dorcas Harris, for £37..1..2 tract called *Harris Loss,* adjacent to *Resurvey on Jeremiah's Park,* and *Beall's Good Will,* containing 17 3/8 acres. Includes plat of tract.

M:83-84. Sarah Murphy recorded 1 Feb. 1805, deed of gift for feather beds, from her father, Duncan Murphy. Wit: William Smith.

M:84-85. Thomas Linsted and Solomon Holland recorded bill of sale, 1 Feb. 1805, for Negro man Frank, from Ignatius West, mortgage for £75..3, payment due by 1 Feb. next to redeem. Wit: John Fleming.

M:85-86. Richard Lyles recorded bill of sale 2 February 1805, from Ignatius Warthen for £43..8 crop of tobacco and crop of corn, one bay horse, 2 colts, black cow, 2 hogs, 2 feather beds, Dutch oven, linen wheel, woolen wheel, desk.

M:86. Henry Lansdale recorded certificate as Deputy sheriff, 4 February 1805.

M:86-87. Henry Iglehart of Anne Arundel County recorded bill of sale 5 February 1805 from Jacob Hitechew, for $144 sells one sorrel horse, one bay horse, 3 head black cattle, all blacksmith's tools now in my shop, crops of wheat and rye in the field and crop of tobacco in the house, all my household furniture and plantation utensils. Signed in German script.

M:87 James Simpson recorded 5 February 1805, Negro man Paris to be free after 2 February 1809. Wit: Edw Burgess Jr., James Day.

M:88-89. Richard Wootton recorded deed 6 Feb 1805, from Solomon Davis, executor of Solomon Simpson, late of Montgomery County, deceased. Whereas Solomon Simpson in his lifetime sold tracts to Richard Wootton, but deed not made, this is deed for 96 ½ acres of *Willson's Delay,* for £482..10, adjacent to tract called *Saint Thomas.*

M:89. Lewis Beall recorded bill of sale 6 Feb. 1805, from William Redman for two feather beds and furniture, five splinter bottomed chairs and one walnut table. Signed by mark.

M:90. Kinsey Harrison recorded schedule 7 Feb. 1805, for 2 fish barrels, 1 pair flesh forks, 2 sheckells [sic], 1 blanket, a chair, 1 tin bucket, 1 wooden bucket. Signed by mark.

M:91. Solomon Richards recorded certificate as Justice of the Peace. 7 February 1805.

M:91. Phillip Johnson recorded bill of sale 11 February 1805 from William Bath, for $40 one bed and furniture, three split bottom chairs, one iron pot, 1 Dutch oven and four pieces wooden ware.

M:91-94. James Reid recorded deed 12 Feb. 1805, from Basil Whalen, son and heir of Daniel Whelan, late of Montgomery County, deceased, for tracts *Hickman's Discovery*, and *Mount Etna*, formerly called *Resurvey on Gatton's Good Luck,* 127 acres. Receipt for £381. Signed before Owen Dorsey, Thos B. Dorsey. Acknowledged.. Catharine, wife of Basil Whalen released dower.

M:94-95. Philip Eaglin recorded deed 12 February 1805 from Charles , Edward, Jonathan and Richard Andrews, for £45 tract of land called *Rich Land,* part of *Round Bottom,* contiguous to each other, metes and bounds given, containing 30 acres. All signed by marks. Ann, the wife of Charles; and Ann, wife of Edward Andrews, and Verlinda the wife of Jonathan Andrews, all released rights to dower before M. Browning, and Lewis Duvall.

M:96-97. Francis Jamison recorded deed 14 February 1805 from Thomas Howard, for £32..5 a tract of land called *Level,* adjacent to tracts *Appleton's Resurvey*, and *Resurvey on Hanover,* containing 10 ½ acres.

M:97-98. Margaret Tucker (wife of Jacob Tucker) and son James D. Tucker, recorded deed 16 February 1805, from Mordecai B. Offutt, for £75 for part of *Outlet.* Metes and bounds mention the spring, commonly known as the Horse Spring, and crossing the wagon road from the meeting house to Rockville. Jane Offutt wife of Mordecai B. Offutt released dower.

M:98-99. Lewis Beall recorded bill of sale 18 February 1805, from Thomas Garrett for $25, wagon, 4 collars, 4 set of gear, one grey stud horse about 9 years old. Lewis Beall agrees to let Garrett use above until November court.

M:99-100. Robert Hurdle recorded schedule 18 Feb. 1805, included two fish barrels, 1 hogshead, 3 chairs, one scythe and cradle, pair swingletree. Debts: Thomas Orme, Warren Magruder, William Giberson. Signed by mark before Ozias Offutt, John Fleming.

M:100-101. Thomas Peter of the Territory of Columbia, recorded deed 18 February 1805 from Jesse Allnutt and Ann his wife and Frances Moore and Sarah Moore his wife for $1811.60 sell *Father's Gift,* 97 1/10 acres and *Addition to Father's Gift,* containing 32 3/10 acres,

M:102-104. Thomas Reid recorded deed 20 Feb 1805, from John Howard of Jefferson County, Kentucky for $888 sells 232 acre part of *Conclusion* Power of Attorney given to Godshall Douglass of Montgomery County to make deed. Mary Howard, wife of John relinquished dower rights.

M:104-105. Zebedee Beall recorded power of attorney 20 February 1805 from Patrick Carten and Dorothy Brook Carten, his wife; Joshua Broughton and Betsey Eddy Broughton his wife and Nelly Brooke Beall of Hancock County Georgia, assign him to receive all debts and legacies from our father James Beall deceased; and to sell the property on Sligo Creek, of Thomas Beall son of Richard, deceased.

M:105-106. Thomas Clagett recorded bill of sale 22 February 1805 from Aquilla Smith for 1000 pounds of tobacco sells beds, furniture, half dozen rush bottom chairs, half dozen pewter plates, and one pot.

M:106-107. Thomas Scott Jr. Recorded deed 1 March 1805, from Thomas Scott for 5 shillings, to his son, part of *Outlet,* containing 70 acres. Margaret Scott released dower rights.

M:107-108. Mordecai Moore recorded discharge and manumission 2 March 1805, for yellow woman, Mary, 23 years old, who was left as a legacy when she was a child, to my wife by my wife's mother. Wit. H. W. Robertson, John Thomas 3rd.

M:108-111. Hezekiah Beggerly recorded deed 2 March 1805 from Robert Brent and the Right Rev. John Carroll, trustees and executors of Daniel Carroll, deceased.

M:111 Joseph Howard recorded 2 March 1805, manumission for Negro boy John, he is to be free 21 years from the date hereof. Wit. Samuel Thomas, John Thomas 3rd.

M:111-112. Benjamin Ray Jr. Recorded bill of sale recorded 4 March 1805 from Henry Butler for £3..8, 7 hogs, iron pot, ladle, plow.

M:112-113. Henry Gaither of the Territory of Columbia, recorded 4 March 1805 from William Marbury, trustee for the sale of real estate of Samuel Beall deceased, and in consequence sold at public sale, three parts or tracts of land called *Exchange* heretofore purchased by Samuel Beall of a certain Walter Beall, and other tracts devised to Narborne Beall, Matilda Beall and Harriott Beall.

M:113-116. Richard Green recorded deed from George Ellicott and Elizabeth Ellicott, his wife, tract called the *Mill Seat,* witnesses Jonathan Ellicott, John Ellicott.

M:116-118. John Lucas recorded deed 4 March 1805 from George Culp and John Culp $375.37 tract called *Glasgow,* as conveyed by George Ellicott and Elizabeth Ellicott his wife for 12 ½ acres, in February 1800, part of tract called *Resurvey on Benjamin's Square,* and part of *Lodowick's Range,* adjacent to part conveyed by Rezin Davis to Ignatious Pigman, containing 41 1/8 acres. Ann Culp, wife of John Culp released dower.

M:118 Robert Briggs recorded 6 March 1805, Negro Patt, 19 years old to be free 10 years from now; Fan, 20 years, from now, she now being 2 years old and Philip to be free 25 years from now, he is now about 6 months old. Signed before James Lackland, Wm Darne.

M:119-121. Daniel Simm recorded deed 6 March 1805, from Robert Brent of Washington, D.C., and Rev. John Carroll of the City of Baltimore, executors of the last will and testament of Daniel Carroll, deceased; assigns part of *Joseph's Park,* beginning on 2nd line, at part conveyed to James Dunlop, to Charles Jones' part. 152 3/4 acres.

M:122-124. Daniel Simm recorded deed 6 March 1805, from Robert Brent of Washington, D.C., and Rev. John Carroll of the City of Baltimore executors of the last will and testament of Daniel Carroll, deceased; assigns part of *Joseph's Park,* in payment of any money due in marriage settlement to deceased's daughter, Mary Simm.

M:124-126. Lucy Sprigg recorded deed 7 March 1805, from John Sprigg for £4..10 part of *Resurvey on Jeremiah's Park,* in Barnesville, lot #5, 1/4 acres. Elizabeth Sprigg wife of John released dower.

M:126-127. James Beall 3rd recorded deed 7 March 1805 from John Sutton Crawford for £62..10, part of *Serit,* 1/3 part. Signed before Elemelech Swearingen, John Fleming. Elizabeth, wife of John S. Crawford released dower.

M:127-128. Daniel Lee recorded deed 16 March 1805 from Robert Brent of Washington, D.C., and Rev. John Carroll of the City of Baltimore executors of the last will and testament of Daniel Carroll, for £505, part of *Joseph's Park,* from end of first line of 1st line of Leonard John's part of tract, and have appointed William Carroll and Thomas Webb of Montgomery County to act as attorney to acknowledge indenture in court.

M:129-132. Joseph E. Rowles, trustee recorded deeds 16 March 1805. Whereas Richard Johns and Leonard Holliday Johns both of Georgetown, obtained a credit form the Bank of Columbia for a large sum of money, $9629.55 to secure payment thereof, have passed a note payable to Jeremish Williams and Elisha W. Williams, joint merchants trading under the firm of Jeremiah Williams & Co. On a short order not exceeding 60 days from the date of each note, several tracts of land, two islands in the Potomac, 400 and 97 3/4 acres, the piney lands near Upton Beall's lands, about 300 acres, a part of *Pine Grove,* a tract called *Mill Seat,* 50 acres

M:132-133. George Riley recorded deed 16 March 1805, made 5 Feb. from Richard Thompson and Elizabeth, his wife for £108..5 *Wickham's Chance,* formerly the property of Colbert Pelly, 21 2/3 acres, which Richard and Elizabeth claim title to as heirs of Colbert Pelly, deceased. Witnesses Ozias Offfutt, John Flemming.

M:134-136. Samuel Pumphrey of Loudon County, Commonwealth of Virginia, recorded deed 21 March 1805, from John Wilcoxon of Montgomery County for £1688.10 assigns tracts called *The Fork,* and *Resurvey on the Fork,* containing 307 acres. Ruth Willcoxen released dower rights.

M:136-137. John Wilcoxon recorded mortgage 21 March 1805, from Samuel Pumphrey on above tract of land.

M:137-138. Lewis Beall recorded deed 22 March 1805 from Richard Wootton for love and affection and 5 shillings, assigns to him, tract called *Cuckold's Delight,* conveyed to him by Arthur Nelson.

M:138-139. Thomas Simpson recorded bill of sale 23 March 1805 from Robert Brook Beall for $300 Negro male slave named Gill, about 15 years of age.

M:139-142. Thomas Fletchall recorded deed 25 March 1805 from Thomas Hickman, Ann Ford Cross and Benjamin Cross signed deed. 21 4/10 acres of *Cider and Ginger,* adjacent to *Preston's March,* Thomas Hickman had 2/5 part of tracts and his sister Ann Cross had 3/5 part, who together with their other sisters, and their brother William Hickman the sons and daughters of William Hickman of Stephen became entitled to equal parts of 14 4/10 acres; and Elizabeth Hickman another daughter is now under age cannot convey land. Margaret wife of Thomas Hickman released dower.

M:142-143. Thomas Hickman recorded deed 25 March 1805 from Ezekial Linthicum and Mary his wife for 5 shillings, confirm tract called *Cider and Ginger,* on 83rd line of tract, *Preston's March,* containing 11 2/10 acres.

M:143-145. Doctor William Brewer recorded deed 25 March 1805, from Ezekiel Linthicum and Mary his wife. Whereas a certain William Cummens and James Edmonston, sometime in the year 1736 by this indenture leased to William Hickman about 88 acres of a tract of land called *Preston's March,* for the term of 99 years, and said William Hickman by his will devised the same to his son Stephen Hickman, who in like manner devised the same to his two sons Stephen and William Hickman to be equally divided between them, and the said Stephen, the last devisee died intestate and left issue, one daughter who has since intermarried with the above named Ezekial Linthicum, and whereas the said Cummens and Edmonstone in dividing the land belonging to them, the aforesaid part of *Prestons March* was allotted to the said Cummens who has since departed this life leaving a widow and several children, who have consented that the present possessors of the said lease might sell and dispose of the residue of the term of years to come and the said Ezekiel and Mary Linthicum have agreed to dispose of their moiety or half part to the above named Doctor William Brewer, the said Ezekial and Mary Linthicum for and in consideration of the sum of £217..10 sell same.

M:145-147. Doctor William Brewer recorded deed 25 March 1805 from Ezekial Linthicum and Mary his wife, for $640, sell tract called *Cider and Ginger,* on the 84th line of a tract of land called *Preston's March,* containing 25 acres. For second part beginning at line of lot #2 allotted to Ann F. Hickman by commission appointed to divide the lands of William Hickman of Stephen, amongst his children, containing 6 9/10 acres.

M:147-149 John Connelly recorded deed 25 March 1805 from Samuel Lazenby for $1200. Tract of land called *Girl's Gift,* containing 80 1/4 acres Sarah Lazenby, wife of Samuel released dower.

M:150. Thomas P. Ijams of Richland Township, Fairfield County, Ohio recorded bill of sale from Lewis Duvall for $360 in judgment and bonds, household furniture. John Ijams as trustee.

M:150-151. Thomas Fletchall and William Brewer recorded agreement 29 March 1805. I have no objection to Ezekiel Linthicum and Thomas Hickman assigning rights to a lease that was leased to William Hickman for part of *Preston March,* to the aforesaid Thomas and William, provided my mother, Margaret Cummings and Araminda Dorsey to agree. Signed by Mary Dorsey before Samuel Dorsey, as well as the aforesaid Margaret and Araminda before Margaret Dorsey.

M:151-153. Thomas Fletchall recorded conveyance of lease from Thomas Hickman. William Cummings and James Edmonston, did in 1736 lease to William Hickman 88 acres of *Preston March*. William by his will devised lease to his son Samuel Hickman, who in his will devised same to his two sons, Stephen and William Hickman. This William died intestate leaving five children, of which the above Thomas Hickman is one, and three sisters and one brother. Thomas Hickman bought the rights to the lease from his brother and sisters. In the division of real estate between Edmonston and Cummings, this tract went to William Cummings who has since died leaving a widow and several children. Thomas Hickman for £39..5 assigns lease.

M:153-154. James Lazenby recorded deed 1 April 1805, from Ruth Lazenby, for £97..2 sells all her interest in tracts which were the property of Henry Lazenby, deceased, viz, *Addition to Girl's Gift, Girls Gift, Addition to Lazenby's Chance, Small Purchase, the Addition to Small Purchase and Second Addition to Girl's Gift,* Signed by mark.

M:154-157. Samuel Lazenby, Cephas Lazenby and James Lazenby recorded deed of partition 1 April 1805. They have as tenants in common tracts containing 238 5/8 acres, metes and bounds given on division of tracts, *Girl's Gift,* and others. 1st part for 81 1/4 acres to Samuel 2nd part containing 67 3/4 acres to Cephas Lazenby. The remaining tracts containing 29 and 61 1/8 acres to James Lazenby's part. Sarah Lazenby, wife of Samuel and Polly wife of Cephas also signed.

M:157-158. Lewis Beall recorded bill of sale 1 April 1805 from Eleazor Stadage for £150, sells three Negroes, to wit: Peter about 30 years old, Poll about 25 years and a child, Andrew, about 7 months old. Lewis Beall agrees to release property when sum of note is paid.

M:158-159. Thomas Hickman and Walter Williams recorded bill of sale from John Scrivener Jr. One Negro man, Davey about 26 years old, and two horses for £50.

M:159-161. Erasmus Perry recorded deed 3 April 1805 from Hezekiah Baggerly for £600 part of *Joseph's Park*, beginning at 5th line of Leonard H. John's part to a corner of Benjamin Becraft's land, containing 100 acres more or less. Charlotte Baggerly released dower rights.

M:161-163. Otho Sprigg, son of Thomas Sprigg, recorded deed 10 April 1805 from Henry Camden and Mary his wife, for $1443.75 sell all their interest in parcel called *Happy Choice,* being resurveyed and now called *Happy Choice Fortified,* which according to an agreement with the said Henry Camden, Daniel Jarrett and John Poole Jr., and with the consent and approbation of Mrs. Mary Pindel and Deborah Sprigg, parties concerned allotted as the part portion and allotment unto the said Henry Camden and Mary Camden his wife, and is hereby intended to be conveyed, described as lot number 3 on plat and certificate of survey made by Hezekiah Veatch, 10 January 1801. Signed before Greenbury Howard, Lewis Duvall.

M:163-164. Jesse Steel recorded schedule 4 April 1805, of goods and chattels delivered to the sheriff.4 pair old harness, 3 pair old traces, 3 weeding hoes, 1 half gallon jug, 1 old saddle, small quantity of pewter. Signed before Elem. Swearingen, John Fleming.

M:164-166. Charles Perry recorded deed 5 April 1805, from Charles Williams, for £259..10 shillings, part of tract of land called *Hobsons Choice,* and part of tract called *The Pines,* adjacent to *Joseph and James,* and *Conclusion,* containing 115 acres, including the family burying ground. Signed Charles Williams. Ann Williams, wife of Charles, released dower.

M:166 -168. Lawrence O'Neale recorded deed 9 April 1805, from John Laird of Georgetown, for $2686.50 sells part of tract *Conclusion* on Seneca Creek, containing 560 acres; conveyed by a certain James Miller of Glasgow in Great Britain to John Laird and Thomas Dick, now deceased, and then to the survivor of them.

M:168-170. David Peter of Washington, D.C., recorded deed of trust 9 April 1805 from Richard Johns of Washington, D.C. and Leonard H. Johns, indebted for $2500 makes over and assigns 18 Negroes, to wit: Mack, Jacob, Clem, Bob, Jack, Charles, Hannah, Amey, Kitty, Letty, Patt, Sam, Nancy, Baptist, Dinah, Minty, Nancy and Jery.

M:170-172. Upton Beall recorded deed 13 April 1805 from George Beall of Prince George's county, but formerly of Washington, D.C. for £500 sells tract called *Dung Hill.* The wife of George Beall, examined apart (but not named) released dower rights.

M:172-174. James Clagett recorded deed 13 April 1805 from William Duvall for tract called *The Swamp,* to the east of *Joseph's Park,* and *Hermitage.* Sarah Duvall released dower rights.

M:174-175. Henry Baggerly recorded manumission 16 April 1805, Negro woman Rachel is to be free after 31 December 1806.

M:175-179. Stephen N. Chiswell, Enos Noland and Otho H.W. Luckett recorded plat and agreement 16 April 1805, on tracts called *Accord* and part of *Resurvey on Discord.* Plot drawn on page 178, shows boundaries of tracts for Aenes Noland, Otho H. W. Luckett and Lawson Luckett's part of *Concord.*

M:180-181. Anna Clagett recorded deed 17 April 1805 from Benjamin Holland Jr. for $696 assigns part of *The Joseph,* containing, exclusive of one acre held by Daniel McCarthy, joining the second line, 116 acres. Alice wife of Benjamin Holland Jr. released dower rights.

M:181-182. William Steel recorded bill of sale 10 April 1805 from Rebecca Steel, for £20, one mare about 7 years old and all my household goods. Signed by mark.

M:182. Basil M. Beall recorded certificate 17 April 1805, as Deputy Sheriff before John Fleming.

M:182-184. Joseph Cahill recorded deed 22 April 1805 from William Cahill and Orson Cahill of Frederick County for part of *Leakin's Lot*, devised to them by their grandfather, William Cahill around 11 November 1782.

M:184-185. Henry B. Harrell recorded deed 22 April 1805 from Joseph Cahill of Frederick County, for $453 tract called *Leakin's Lot,* as conveyed above Elizabeth Cahill released dower rights.

M:185-186. Adam Robb recorded bill of sale 22 April 1805 from Thomas Waring of Montgomery County, for £53, livestock. Signed before Lewis Duvall.

M:186-187. John Aldridge recorded bill of sale 24 April 1805 from Singleton Ricketts for valuable consideration, assigns one Negro boy, Abraham about 12 years old, provided nonetheless if sum of £87 and etc. paid, then bill of sale is void.

M:187-188. Laurence O. Holt recorded deed 24 April 1805, from James Suter for $211.50 parcel called *Constant Friendship,* containing 11 3/4 acres. Ruth Suter released dower rights.

M:189-190. Michael Letton recorded deed 24 April 1805, from James Suter, for $37.12 sells part of tracts *Resurvey on Saint Marys,* and *Oatry,* containing 2 1/16 acres. Ruth, wife of James Suter released dower rights.

M:190-192. Clement Smith recorded deed 24 April 1805 from Charles C. Jones, to secure large note from the Bank of Columbia. Portion of tract called *Clean Drinking.*

M:192-194. Philip B. Key of Washington, D.C. and Joseph W. Clagett of Prince George's County, as trustees, recorded deed 27 April 1805 from William Digges of Montgomery County, for 5 shillings, all his slaves, Negroes, stock, etc. to pay debts due to Charles Carroll of Carrollton with interest and then for maintenance of said William and Catherine his wife. Catherine to have the following Negroes: Frank, Kitt, ... (illegible). And a further trust to convey one Negro boy, Bill, son of Harry to my grandson William D. Clagett; and to convey one Negro girl Hennry to my daughter Eleanor Clagett; and the residue to my two daughters Eleanor Clagett and Susannah Digges in equal proportion. Signed by William Digges, Philip B. Key and Joseph W. Clagett.

M:195. Edward Owen Jr. recorded release 29 April 1805 on *Resurvey on Friends Advice* for 400 acres by mistake, a quantity sold was left out of deed. Signed 15 April 1805 in Bath Co. Virginia by Elisha Williams. Wit: Frank Crutchfield, Samuel C. Fleming.

M:195. Benjamin Nicholls of Thomas recorded schedule, 30 April 1805. 2 pots, 1 Dutch oven, 1 looking glass, 1 shaving box & razors, debts: Hezekiah Veirs, Solomon Veirs, John Trott, Benjamin Tucker, Edward Harding. Witness: Lewis Duvall, John Fleming.

M:196-197. Edward J. Dorsey recorded deed 1 May 1805 from Jesse Hyatt for £157, two lots in Hyattstown, lots #16 & 70. Signed and acknowledged.

M:197-199. Charles Perry recorded deed 4 May 1805, from Richard Johns of Georgetown, Washington, D.C. for $1000 assigns parcel, the *Resurvey on Piney Grove,* beginning at tract *The Pines,* originally granted James Holmead and Joseph West, for 497 acres on 5th line of tract called *Hunting Hills,* Signed and acknowledged.

M:199-201. Charles Perry recorded deed 4 May 1805 from Joseph Rowles and Jeremiah Williams of the District of Columbia, a certain parcel transferred to them in trust, from Richard Johns, in consideration of above and $10 transfers same to Charles Perry.

M:201 Samuel Nicholls recorded 6 May 1805, list of slaves consisting of girl Annie, about 16 years old, who resided in Maryland until 2 years ago, when he sent her to Virginia, and is now bringing her back to Maryland.

M:201-202. Valentine P. Luckett recorded deed 8 May 1805 from Elizabeth Luckett of Frederick County, Maryland, for $3000. Two tracts of land *Georgia*, and *Conjurers Disappointment* containing 86 acres more or less.

M:202-203. Samuel Clapham of Loudoun County, Virginia recorded deed for sale from Val P. Luckett of Baltimore County, Maryland, for $2580 tracts *Georgia* and *Conjurers Disappointment*, opposite to *Fair Island* in the Potomac. Metes and bounds for 36 acres and 50 acre parcels given.

M:204. Otho H. W. Luckett of Loudoun County, Virginia, recorded deed of surrender, 8 May 1805 from Elizabeth Luckett of Frederick County, Maryland, for $300. *Resurvey on Discord* containing 171 acres.

M:205-206. Samuel Clapham recorded deed 8 May 1805, from Otho H. W. Luckett, description of tract, called *Resurvey on Discord,* between the two ferry landings, mentions Conrad's Upper Ferry, containing 171 acres

M:206-207. Val P. Luckett recorded deed 8 May 1805 from Elizabeth Luckett, two tracts containing 104 acres, called the *Gleanings*.

M:207-209. Samuel Clapham recorded deed 8 May 1805 from Elizabeth Luckett and Val P. Luckett, tract called *Rich Bottom*, adjacent to *Georgia*

M:209-211. Samuel Clapham of Loudoun County, Virginia, recorded deed 8 May 1805 from Val P. Luckett of the City of Baltimore, for £1851.. 5 two parcels known as *Gleanings.*

M:211. Rebecca Casey recorded bill of sale 9 May 1805 from Barton Harris for $1. Sells one Negro woman, by name of Vilet.

M:211. Barton Harris recorded bill of sale 9 May 1805 from Rebecca Casey for $1. Sells one Negro boy named Charles. Signed by mark before John Fleming.

M:212-213. William Magrath recorded deed 16 May 1805, from Elizabeth Magers for £37 tract called *Pyramid* adjacent to *Haymond's Addition.*

M:213-215. John Carroll and Robert Brent recorded mortgage 18 May 1805, from Henry Baggerly on part of *Joseph's Park,* beginning at Leonard H. John's part to south end of Thomas Cramphin's part to corner of Benjamin Becraft's. Schedule of payments recorded.

M:216-217. John Plummer recorded deed 18 May 1805, from Robert Dent, for £50, part of *Resurvey on Jeremiah's Park* on main road leading to Baltimore, it being the beginning of two acres formerly laid out for William Bennett. Mary Dent, wife of Robert released dower.

M:217. Henry Lodge recorded certificate 21 May 1805, as deputy sheriff

M:217-218. Thomas Linsted recorded bill of sale 24 May 1805 from Richard Turner for £108, one Negro boy, Joseph, about 18 years old, and one Negro girl called Darkey about 14 years old. If sum paid before 5 April next, bill of sale is void. Signed before Wm Holmes.

M:218-219. Thomas Hickman recorded bill of sale 24 May 1805 from John Walter for £35 one Negro man about 25 years old, is sum paid, bill of sale void. [name omitted].

M:219-220. Nathan Moore recorded deed 30 May 1805 from Mordecai Moore to his son, for $600 land purchased of Thomas, Samuel and John Snowden, 21 December 1768, part of *Snowden's Manor Enlarged,* adjacent to part conveyed to James Brooke, containing 100 acres. Signed before Jno Thomas 3d, Wm Culver.

M:220-221. Isaac Lancaster Lansdale recorded deed 3 June 1805, from Benjamin Berry of Baltimore County, but formerly of Montgomery County, for £500 part of *Resurvey on James and Mary,* conveyed by Samuel Hanson on 23 December 1793, and on which said Berry and Lansdale have erected a merchant mill. Elizabeth wife of Benjamin Berry released dower rights.

M:222. Samuel Clapham recorded one Negro man, named Kit, 24 years old, brought into the state from Virginia, where he was born, to work on his plantation in Montgomery County.

M:222. Philip Darrell and others [George Darrell and Augustus Darrell] recorded lease 6 June 1805 from Edward Willett of Fairfax County, for $150, lets to them *Trammell Island* in the Potomac, formerly the property of Sampson Trammell, deceased, containing 17 3/4 acres, for and during the natural life of Karan Willett (it being part of the dower of lands of said Karen)

M:222-223. Edward Willett of Fairfax County, Virginia, recorded deed 5 June 1805, made 20 December 1804, from Ninian Willett of Montgomery County, for £25, all his right or interest in *Trammell's Island* in the Potomac River. No dower release.

M:223-224. Lewis Duvall recorded schedule 5 June 1805 to Sheriff of Montgomery County. Viz: sundry accounts deposited in the hands of Henry Poole amounting to £172..10..0 and judgment in the hands of Joab Waters, 17..0..0. Witness Benjamin Gaither.

M:224-225. Frances and James McElvane recorded bill of sale 6 June 1805 from Archibald Orme for $400 sell one Negro woman named Let and her two children viz Westley and Amy.

M:225. Daniel Gue recorded list of Negroes brought into Maryland from Virginia. One Negro woman Nancy about 30 years old and one boy named Leonard about 19 years and one boy Rezin aged six years; one child Mahala. Signed by mark.

M:225-226. Van Swearingen recorded bill of sale, 12 June 1805 from Mary H. Swearingen for $5000; Negro woman Fillis, 55 years old; Negro Fider 40 years old and Rachel 35 years old; and boy Dick, age 5 years old; horses, hogs, lambs and household goods. Signed by mark 29 May 1805. Wit: John Adamson, John Fleming.

M:227. Creese Swearingen recorded bill of sale 12 June 1805, for Negro girl Anna 6 years old and Bett 4 years old. Signed by mark, Mary H. Swearingen, before same witnesses.

M:228. Van Swearingen, recorded bill of sale 12 June 1805 from Thomas Poplin, for livestock, corn, and oats growing in fields. Signed by mark. Wit: John Thomas 3rd.

M:228-230. Thomas Watkins recorded deed 5 June 1805 from Ephraim and Elizabeth Burgess of Allegheny County, Maryland, for $200. Sells an undivided part of three parcels of land devised by Joseph Magruder, *Addition to Hansley*, and finish of *Trouble Enough* and *Bedfordshire Carrier*.

M:230-231. John Lodge recorded certificate June 1805 for Negroes imported into Maryland from Virginia, viz: one Negro man Bill, about 28 years old; one Negro man Harry about 25 years old; one Negro named Bob about 15 years old; one Negro woman named Sucky, 24 years old; one Negro boy named James about one year old; one Negro woman named Ann about 20 years old; one Negro boy Ben, about 3 years old; one Negro boy Charles, about 2 years old.

M:231-232. Philip Duvall recorded deed 19 June 1805 from Thomas Orme for £9..7..6 tract called *Denmark,* adjacent to *Franklin,* containing 2 3/4 acres. Signed & acknowledged.

M:232-233. Joshua Stewart recorded deed 19 June 1805 from Charles H. Davis for £75, tract called *Fair Hill,* on road from the mouth of Monocacy to Baltimore, containing 10 acres. Signed, ack. Loriday, wife of Charles H. Davis released dower.

M:233-235. Richard L. Hall recorded deed 20 June 1805, from Alexander Whitaker for £8..2..6, tract called *Squabble,* on road commonly called Coxon's Road, containing 3 5/8 acres. Signed and acknowledged, and wife of Alexander Whitaker, examined apart (but not named) released dower.

M:235-236. James Allnutt recorded deed 20 June 1805, from Jesse Allnutt for $1800, assigns part of tract *Thomas's Discovery,* which was conveyed to James Allnutt the father of the said Jesse and James Allnut. Ann, wife of Jesse Allnutt released dower.

M:236-238. Christian Getzendanner recorded deed 20 June 1805 from Thomas Nicholls, tract called *Nicholls Discovery*, beginning at 12th line of tract called the *Pines* granted to Joseph and James Holmead, 20 May 1723, to 12th line of the *Younger Brother*, then with the 8th line of *Wickham's Park*, containing 10 ½ acres. Cassandra wife of Thomas Nicholls released dower right.

M:238-239. Ann Minor recorded list of Negroes, 22 June 1805, a resident of Montgomery County, but late a resident of the state of Virginia, on 28th of March last removes to Maryland, Negro man named Peter about 60 years, woman named Susannah about 26 years old, Negro woman Milly about 18 and Negro girl Kitty about 11; Negro girl Eliza about 4 years old; one Negro girl named Lucy about 3 years old. Ann Minor signed before Thos Offutt, Jr.

M:239. John M. Reed recorded bill of sale 25 June 1805, from William Orr, for £75, one Negro man named Van, about 30 years old. Signed before John Henderson.

M:239-240. John M. Read recorded lease 25 June 1805, from Jesse Browning, Meshack Browning and Nathan Browning and Zadock Browning, assigns yearly rent of £37..10 and agrees to keep house in good order and repair. Signed before Abraham Dawson, James Anchry, Nathan Browning of N.

M:241. Thomas C. Nicholls, with M. Browning, recorded bond to State of Maryland, regarding obligation of duties and trust reposed in him by act of Assembly, passed November session 1801, a supplement to act entitled an Act for regulating ___ of staying executions and repealing the acts of assembly therein mentioned ...

M:241-243. Thomas Lewis recorded deed 26 June 1805 from John Lewis, estate . Made by John Lewis of Ross Co., Ohio, son and heir of John Lewis late of Bedford County, whereas the said John Lewis, father to the said John, died intestate before 1st January 1788, and at the time of his death part of a tract of land called *Strathanover* originally in Frederick County, but now in Montgomery County, conveyed to John Lewis deceased by James Pearrie by deed 5 March 1771, and John Lewis as eldest son, for £150 conveys tract beginning at end of 65th line of *Resurvey on Happy Choice,*

M:243. Evan Belt recorded bond, 26 June 1805 with William Price Jr., references same act as Thomas Nicholl's bond above.

M:243-245. John Adlum Jr. of Frederick County, recorded deed 26 June 1805 from Charles Crabb for £150, sells part of tract *Chapple Forrest,* containing 10 3/8 acres. Susannah Crabb, wife of Charles Crabb released dower rights.

M:245. John Poole Jr. recorded bill of sale 27 June 1805 from John Campbell, for £8..10 bay mare.

M:246-250. John Poole Jr. and Priscilla his wife recorded deed 27 June 1805 from Daniel Jarrett and Margaret Jarrett his wife both of Jefferson County, Kentucky in consideration of 141 1/4 acres and also 5 shillings, grant part of *Happy Choice Fortifyed,* containing 182 acres, one undivided third part. Signed with power of attorney from Kentucky.

M:250-252 Benjamin Cecil recorded deed of gift 2 July 1805, from William Cecil Senior to his son, 2 July 1805 for natural love and affection and 50 cents, confirms parts of parcels of land called *Chance* and *Widows Purchase* and one part of *Resurvey on Wildcat Spring,*

M:252-253. Thomas Winsor recorded bill of sale 12 July 1805 from Joseph Brown for $200 sells and assigns personal property, six head of sheep, two feather beds and all household and kitchen furniture. Signed before Edward Burgess Jr.

M:253. Clement Jarboe recorded constables bond 16 July 1805.

M:253-255. John Cecill recorded deed 19 July 1805 from William Cecil Senior for 50 cents, part of tract called *Chance,*

M:255-257. Daniel Jarratt and Margaret Jaratt his wife both of Kentucky, recorded deed 25 July 1805 from John Poole Jr. and Priscilla his wife, part of *Happy Choice Fortyfied,*

M:257. Patrick Magruder and Lloyd Magruder recorded bond 26 July 1805 for £117 to State of Maryland, that they were appointed by Montgomery County Levy Court, to wit, William Offutt, William Offutt Magruder and Barton Duley for the building a bridge over the water course on the River Road, called Captain John Run, near Patrick Magruder's farm, for the sum of $156. And to maintain and keep in good repair the aforesaid road bridge for the term of seven years, from the 2nd April 1805, and whereas the said Patrick Magruder has completed the said bridge, now the obligation is that he shall maintain and keep it in good repair. Signed before Charles Young.

M:258. Thomas Austin Sr. recorded release 27 July 1805 from Robert Wallace, Thomas P. Willson and Jesse Leach For Negro boy Tom, 9 years old and John 7years old, wagon and desk and other items conveyed in bill of sale in July 1804.

M:258-259. James H. Rawlings recorded bill of sale 31 July 1805 from Aaron Henry for $192 quantity of tobacco, bay mare, silver watch.

M:259-261. Robert Peter recorded deed 1 August 1805, from Susannah Birdwhistle and Thomas Birdwhistle her son, for $60, two parts of tract, *Second Resurvey on Friend in Need,* beginning at 42nd line of *Resurvey on Friendship,* to tract *Nothing Venture Nothing Get,* 11 acres, and a one acre part next to a line of Zachariah Offutt's land.

M:261-262. Archibald Cecill of Montgomery County recorded deed 2 August 1805 from William Cecill of Frederick County, for £78..10 tract *Chance,* to 5th line of part laid off for John Cecill, containing 78 ½ acres. Signed and acknowledged.

M:262-263. Lloyd Beall recorded bond as constable 2 August 1805 with Samuel Beall.

M:263-264. Edward Howse recorded deed 5 August 1805, from Joshua Stewart for £75, part of *Fair Hill,* on east side of the road from Mouth of Monocacy to Baltimore, containing 10 acres. Signed by mark.

M:264. Edward Howse recorded constable's bond 5 August 1805 with Thomas Winsor.

M:264-265. John Sheckells from John Arvin for £10 recorded bill of sale for one bay horse, two feather beds, crops of corn, wheat and rye; all my household furniture and plantation utensils, sale void if sum paid by end of December.

M:265-266. Bennett Clements recorded constable's bond 5 August 1805, with William Darne and John Candler.

M:266-267. Ruthy Etchison recorded deed 5 August 1805 from John Simpson for $1. Part of *Pleasant Plains of Damascus* and part of *Bite the Biter* containing 54 acres. Elizabeth Simpson, wife to John Simpson released dower.

M:267. Richard Key Watts recorded deed 8 August 1805, from Thomas H. Wilcoxon for $858, parcel called Anthony Willcoxen's lot, #22 on the plat of *Bradford's Rest,* laid off into lots by Archibald Orme for George Plater, and sold to Anthony Willcoxen, father of the said Thomas H. Willcoxen, containing 191 3/4 acres.

M:268-269. John Sanders recorded bill of sale 12 August 1805, from Susannah Sanders; one Negro woman named Rachel; one Negro boy named Sam and one Negro girl named Jane. Signed by mark.

M:269-271. Jeremiah Watkins recorded bill of sale 13 August 1805, from Henry Lashore for £20 one feather bed and furniture, other household items itemized.

M:271. James H. Rawlings recorded bill of sale 15 August 1805 from Horatio Beall one Negro girl named Bett, about 18 months of age; one Negro woman, Lydd about 24 years of age and two horses.

M:272-273. Walter Brooke Beall recorded deed 15 August 1805 from Hezekiah Baggerley for $800 assigns tract *Beall and Edmonston's Discovery,* containing 138 ½ acres. Charlotte wife of Hezekiah Baggerly released dower.

M:273-274. John Lodge recorded deed 16 August 1805 from Richard Allison for $704.25 sells tract, *Resurvey on Martha's Delight,* containing 78 1/4 acres. Signed by mark. Sarah Allison released dower rights.

M:274-278. Henry Camden and Mary B. Camden his wife, recorded deed 20 August 1805 From Daniel Jarrett and Margaret his wife of Jefferson County, Kentucky, one undivided part of *Happy Choice Fortyfied,* metes and bounds given for 192 ½ acres..

M:278. John Orme recorded certificate 20 August 1805 that he is bringing in Negroes acquired by his marriage to Sarah McAllister of York County, Pennsylvania. Negro Peter 15 years old, Negro Jean 13 years old. They were willed by Sarah's brother, Richard McAllister of 24 June 1802.

M:278-279. Margaret Hopkins recorded bill of sale from Elisha Walker for 2000 pounds of tobacco, one black mare. Signed by mark.

M:279-280. Thomas Perry recorded bill of sale 24 August 1805, from Francis Perry for $336 sells Negroes: woman Henn about 25 years old; girl named Bett about 4 years old; boy named Scott about 2 years old.

M:280-281. Mary Maccubbin recorded deed 26 August 1805 from Benjamin Ray Jr., Sheriff. Whereas by writ of fi fa, for William A. Needham against Elizabeth Lanham and Walter Lanham, heirs of Aaron Lanham, plaintiffs, against Zachariah Maccubbin defendant; to lot called *Pritchett's Purchase,* bounded by tracts called *Huntington,* and *Contention,* the property of Robert Peter,

M:281-282. Benjamin Ray Jr. recorded bond 27 August 1805, as collector with Henry O'Neale and Joseph Slater.

M:282-284. Charles Gassaway recorded deed 28 August 1805, from Benjamin Cross and Ann F. Cross. Whereas William Hickman of Stephen, died possessed of a tract *Cider and Ginger* and *Three Springs,* descended to his children who were under age, and chancery court directed sale, tract divided into four lots, and Ann Fletchall Hickman, one of the children was entitled to one part, lot #2, and she married Benjamin Cross.

M:284-286. Edward Godman recorded deed 2 September 1805 from John Benson for £600 tract now called *Tom's Lott,* a part of *Edmonston's Range,* containing 53 acres. Ann Henrietta Benson his wife released dower.

M:286-288. James W. Perry, Thomas Edmonston and Peter Kemp recorded articles of agreement 2 September 1805, made 24 April 1802 between Absalom Beddoe, James Willson Perry, Thomas Edmonston, Zachariah Downs and Peter Kemp, who variously own parts of *Bear Garden Enlarged, Deer Park, First Mistake, Second Mistake,* and Peter Kemps survey of *James and Mary,* adjoining above, all are contiguous with each other, agree to survey together, and make permanent boundary, a fence that was put up between Absalom Beddoe and James W Perry.

M:288. Kinsey Talbott recorded bill of sale 6 September 1805 from John Sheats for £16..16 one bay horse, 4 years old.

M:289. Isaac Lansdale of Prince George's County, recorded bill of sale 7 September 1805 from John Hutton of Montgomery County, for 7 shillings, 7 pence sells one Negro woman Daphne, and one Negro girl, Celia her daughter, which Negroes were previously sold him from the said Isaac Lansdale

M:289-290. Philbert Greenwell of Frederick County, recorded deed 7 September 1805 from Raphael Melton of Montgomery County for £100 tract whereon Melton now lives, a part of *Beallmont,* containing ½ acre more or less. Signed.

M:290-291 John Hughes and James Hughes recorded mortgage from Brice Letton, Negroes, Jenny about 30 years old; Norwald about 15 years old; Ary 12 years old, Leath 10 years old; and Joseph 2 year old. Nevertheless, if Brice pays the full sum of £400 bill of sale is void.

M:291-292, John Cushman recorded bill of sale 17 September 1805 from Frederick Linthicum for £126, one Negro man Sam, about 23 years old.

M:292-293. Nehemiah Lowe recorded schedule 17 September 1805 as insolvent debtor. Bennett Smith's note for $14.22.

M:293-294. Zachariah Austin recorded deed 20 September 1805 from Hezekiah (and Elizabeth his wife) and John (and Cassandra his wife) Austin, David Clagett and Sarah Clagett his wife, Archibald Offutt and Jane Offutt his wife, Kesia Odle, Margaret Odle, all of Montgomery County, sell part of *Grubby Thickett* conveyed to Baruch Odle from Joshua Beall.

M:294. Leonard Watkins recorded certificate 20 September 1805, as Deputy Sheriff

M:294-295. Thomas Perry recorded deed 20 September 1805, from Basil Perry for £12..15 tract *Trouble Enough,* adjacent to *Addition on Ray's Adventure,* and part of *Hope Improved,* adjacent to part he conveyed to Samuel Phillips, for 135 acres; containing 4 1/4 acres. Signed by mark.

M:296-297. Thomas Perry recorded deed 20 September 1805, from Hannah Perry and Francis Perry assigns 80 acres of *Point Look Out*, and part of *Resurvey on Ray's Adventure,* adjacent to *Hutchcraft's Range.*

M:297-299. Thomas Perry recorded deed 21 September 1805, from Francis Perry for $300, Tracts adjacent to that conveyed by James Perry to William Gartrell for 105 acres, containing 45 ½ acres.

M:299. Joseph Soper recorded release 21 September 1805 from William Ray, tract of land called *Beall's Seat,* on east side of Paint Branch,

M:299-300. Francis C. Brown recorded schedule 21 September 1805, as insolvent debtor. List of items includes tools, 5 augers, drawing knife, 10 iron rings, hand saw.

M:300. Schedule of Peter Truax. Schedule included one feather bed, pots and pans, small crop of corn and potatoes, some cabbages, table, crockery.

M:300-301. Joseph Forrest from John Chambers of Henry, bill of sale for furniture, housewares.

M:301-302. Hezekiah Thomas recorded bill of sale 26 September 1805 from John George Sauders one black horse, cows, stock of poultry and hogs

M:302-303. James Willson Perry recorded deed 27 September 1805 from Tyson Beall for 5 shillings, tract called *Tyson's Third Lot,* Willa Jemima, wife of Tyson Beall released dower.

M:303-305. Jane Ober recorded deed 4 October 1805 from Kinsey Gittings for 5 shillings, part of *Drane's Luck,* containing 10 3/4 acres, as sold by John Hewitt as trustee, under the decree of chancery, in the case of Charles and Frances Lowndes and others against Richard Ober to Anthony Reintzel, and afterwards sold to the said Jane Ober, but was conveyed to me. Nelly Gittings wife of Kinsey Gittings released dower rights.

M:305-306. Benjamin Waters recorded deed 4 October 1805 from Rebecca Browning and Lucretia Mitchell for $721.50 sell two parcels, part of *Snowden's Manor Enlarged,* beginning at a tract formerly belonging to James Duncaster, 138 acres, and a tract called *Browning's Folly,* on the west side of the Paint Branch, from the lower end of *Snowden's Manor,* containing 14 acres. Both ladies signed by mark before Wm Culver, Wm Smith.

M:306-308. Washington Bowie recorded deed of trust from Joseph E. Rowles. Whereas heretofore Leonard Hollyday Johns and Richard Johns sold real estate in trust to Joseph E. Rowles, to secure and pay certain bank debts Washington Bowie to be endorser for Johns to Bank of Columbia for $5350 and also $1302, and to notes held by John Barnes for $250 and a note held by Burnett and Rigdon for $514.78 to secure Bowie in endorsements above, assigns tract devised to Leonard H. Johns by his father, one tract of 700 acres, being part of *Dan,* contiguous to the *Mill Seat,* being the tract on which Newport Mills stand. Acknowledged before R. Turner, Associate Justice.

M:308-310. Walter Smith recorded deed of trust from Joseph E. Rowles, et.al. [Leonard Hollyday Johns and Richard Johns]. Same premises as above, endorser for Richard Johns to be Jeremiah Williams of Georgetown, for papers held by the Bank of Columbia for $3850 and a note for $1302, also notes held by John Barnes and Burnett and Rigdon, the following three tracts of land devised to Richard Johns by his father, land lying on the Potomac containing 400 acres, another tract, an island in the Potomac containing 97 acres, and tract of land in the piney woods near Upton Beall, containing 300 acres, part of *Pine Grove.*

M:311. Samuel Pumphrey recorded list of slaves, 8 October 1805, from Virginia to Maryland, seized as a right of inheritance. James age 39, Mariah 1, Mill 16, Tom 13, Zachariah 13. Signed by mark before Zachariah Walker.

M:311. Zachariah Muncaster recorded list of slaves removed from Virginia to Maryland, 8 October 1805, viz: Negro man Jess 21, girl Amy 15, girl Ann 9 years and Betty 35 years old, boy Jack 1 year old. Signed by Zachariah Muncaster.

M:311-312. Richard Anderson recorded 17 October 1805, manumission for Negro woman, Margaret, aged 39 years and able to work. Signed before John Flemming.

M:312-313. Norris Hoskinson recorded 17 October 1805, schedule of goods and chattels, including 15 lbs. Of new iron and 15 lbs of old iron, proved account against Richard Dunn, now in the hands of Robert H. Whittaker, constable for collection, and accounts against Richard Taylor and Daniel Collins. Signed before John Adamson, Samuel Elgar.

M:313. William Carlin recorded schedule 18 October 1805. Signed by mark before John Fleming, Samuel Elgar.

M:313-315. Josias F. Beall and James A. Beall recorded deed 21 October 1805 from Ann Fendall Beall of Prince George's County, for $1332, two tracts, *Layhill,* and *Beall's Reserve.*

M:315. William Vinson recorded mortgage 23 Oct. 1805 from Robert D. Hooker for 3984 lbs. crop tobacco, sells slaves, one Negro boy named Peter and one girl named Barbary. Nevertheless if sum paid by 18 Oct. 1807, then sale is void. Signed Robert D. Hooker, Witness Thos F. W. Vinson. Taken before justice of the peace, 18 Oct. 1805, G. W. Harwood.

M:316-317. John Hampton recorded deed 24 Oct 1805, from Richard Thomas for $1. Part of *Addition to Charley Forrest,* adjacent to Bernard Gilpin's orchard, 110 acres. Signed before Wm Holmes, Wm Thomas of Richard. No dower release.

M:317-319. Bernard Gilpin recorded deed 24 October 1805, from Richard Thomas for $1, two parts of *Addition to Charley Forrest,* 255 acres, and second parcel on north side of Baltimore Road, 9 ½ acres. Signed before Wm Holmes, Wm Thomas of Richard. No dower release.

M:319-320. Archibald Orme recorded deed of trust 25 October 1805 from Samuel Williams, who applied for benefit of insolvency laws 23 December 1801 and Archibald Orme appointed trustee. Samuel Williams assigns all property (not specified.)

M:320-322. Daniel Jarret and Margaret his wife of Jefferson County, Kentucky, recorded deed 26 October 1805, from Henry Camden and Mary B. Camden his wife, in consideration of 133 acres in exchange and 5 shillings, sells part of *Happy Choice Fortified.*

M:322-324. John Poole Junr recorded mortgage 26 October 1805, from Christopher Miller. Whereas Christopher Miller is indebted in the sum of $45, to secure payment, assigns tract called *Hobson's Choice.*

M:324. Henry Bowen recorded schedule 28 October 1805, as insolvent debtor. One small corn field about 3 acres.

M:324-325. Hammutal Welsh recorded manumission 29 October 1805, for Jack, about 11 years old to serve until he attains age of 35 years. Wit: Richard Green, Amelia Green.

M:325. Hammutal Welsh recorded manumission 29 October 1805, for Mary, about 37 years old. Wit: Richard Green, Amelia Green.

M:326. Archibald Trail recorded receipt 31 October 1805. Received 19 Oct. 1805, a note of hand drawn on Samuel Lane for £13..5..7 and interest on said note of £1..7 3/4. Also $30 in cash. Signed from Zachariah Bogeley.

M:326-327. Christopher Miller recorded deed 26 October 1805, from Jacob Howard for £130..1, tract *Hobson's Choice,* adjacent to tract *Happy Choice,* containing 86 3/4 acres. Rachel Howard released dower.

M:327-332. George Beall recorded deed 26 October 1805 from Ellender Hopkins, wife of John Hopkins, deceased; John Hopkins and Barbara his wife; Alexander Hopkins and Rosanna his wife; Thomas Hopkins and James Hopkins all of Washington County, Pennsylvania . Case in Chancery Court, George Beall, complainant, October term 1805. For $500 sale of *I Was Not Thinking of it,* 170 ½ acres, beginning at *Boylstone's Discovery,* Also tract *Hopson's Choice,* beginning at *Evans Chance,* 63 acres, and tract called *Evan's Lookout,* containing 20 acres.

M:333-334. Benjamin Ricketts recorded deed 1 November 1805 from Benjamin H. Jones, Sheriff. Judgment obtained by Ignatius Davis, administrator of Sarah Perry against John B. Magruder, 42 acre part of *Eden.*

M:334-336. Joshua Pearre recorded deed 2 November 1805 from William Trail for $29, assigns tract called *Fruitful Plains,* on 12th line of *Happy Choice Fortified,* containing 3 5/8 acres. Signed and acknowledged - no dower released.

M:336-338. Joshua Peare recorded deed 2 November 1805, from Henry Camden and Mary his wife for part of *Happy Choice Fortified.*

M:338-342. Walter Hodges and Peter Hawkins recorded deed 2 December 1805, from Peter Arnold and David Arnold of the State of Kentucky for $2000 sell their undivided moiety in tract called *Mount Vernon* at 6th line of *Self Defense,* to 5th line of *Happy Choice,* to part conveyed by Thomas Morton to John Bennett, to end of 5th line of *Final Conclusion,* containing 389 ½ acres, about 2 miles from Sugarloaf Mountain. James Pearre given power of attorney to make deed. Nancy Arnold wife of Peter, and Eleanor Arnold wife of David, released dower rights.

M:342 John Rigges recorded manumission 2 November 1805, for Nell, a mulatto girl about 20 years old and 6 months, to be free from this date. Wit. Richard Green.

M:342-343. Commission to William Holmes and Richard Wootton, as Associate Justices recorded 4 November 1805.

M:343-344. William Waters recorded bill of sale 4 November 1805 from Christian Leaman for $414, three horses, wagon, wheat and corn, other livestock, housewares and farming tools, a parcel of cabbages and Irish Potatoes.

M:344-345. Thomas Green recorded bill of sale 4 November 1805 from Susannah Douglas widow of Samuel Douglas for and in consideration of his being security for John Douglas in the sum of 2500 pounds crop tobacco; one Negro boy named Noble about 10 years old, to be free at the age of 31 years; also one bed and furniture, and a chest; if bond is secured, bill of sale is void.

M:345-346. Patrick Orme recorded deed 4 November 1805, from James Willson Perry for £26..8..9, for *Tyson's Third Lot,* on 8th line of *Addition to Easy Purchase,* for 11 3/4 acres. Margaret Perry his wife released dower rights.

M:346-347. Patrick Orme recorded deed 4 November 1805, from Thomas Trundel for £105..18, tract *The Addition to Easy Purchase,* to 10th line of Isaac Lansdale's part of tract, containing 35 3/10 acres. Leah Trundle released dower rights.

M:348-349. Thomas Fletchall recorded deed 4 November 1805, from Solomon Davis surviving executor of Col. Solomon Simpson who appointed his wife Dorcas, and his nephew Solomon Davis his executors to sell certain real estate at auction. For $1868.11 ½ he sells tract *Flint Grove*, containing 152 3/8 acres.

M:349-356. Christian Hempstone recorded deed of partition 4 November 1805, between William Hempstone, Zephaniah Plummer and Charity his wife for the third part; Elias Spalling [signed Spalding] and Eleanor Spalling his wife for the 4th part; and John Mullican and Mary Mullican his wife for the fifth part. Whereas Mathias Hempstone late of Montgomery County, died seized in fee of tract *Resurvey on Trouble for Nothing,* divided into 5 parts each containing 26 acres for his five children: Christian, William, Charity, Eleanor and Mary. Adjoining tracts *Round Knowl and Woodstock* mentioned. Signed by all parties.

M:356-363. James Day recorded deed 5 November 1805 from Hannah Perry and Francis Perry for £40, all that tract called *Resurvey on Point Look Out,* [pg. 357-362 are missing from microfilm. However, this appears to be a numbering problem, because the edges of page 356 visible on page 363 appear to be the same deed, and on page 363 is the signatures and release of deed to James Day from Hannah Perry and Francis Perry.]

M:363-365. William Willson of John recorded deed 5 November 1805, from James Day for £322..10 tract *Point Look Out,* likewise a part of 244 acres of said tract laid off by Hezekiah Veatch for the dower of Hannah Perry and Francis Perry, and by them conveyed to James Day in two separate parts, 1st part 74 ½ acres, and second for 6 7/8 acres, the whole containing 81 3/8 acres. Sarah Day released dower rights

M:365-367 Zachariah Knott recorded deed 5 November 1805, from Francis Deakins of Georgetown, for $165, sells part of *Fruitful Plains,* adjacent to *Resurvey on Wolf's Cow,* to the 17th line of *Conclusion,* adjacent to part conveyed to Thomas Knott, containing 33 acres.

M:367-369. Zachariah Knott recorded deed 5 November 1805, from Leonard M. Deakins and John Hoye of Georgetown, executors of Francis Deakins, who in his lifetime, made deed 8 March 1804, for $165 selling to Zachariah Knott, part of *Fruitful Plains,* containing 33 acres, and left instructions in his will to make good deed.

M:369-372. Thomas Knott recorded deed 5 November 1805, from Francis Deakins for £86, parts of three tracts, 25 acres of *Fruitful Plains,* which was resurveyed for William Deakins Jr., 15 June 1784; second an undivided moiety or half part of 87 acres of *Conclusion,* lots #12 & #13, conveyed by William Deakins to Francis Deakins and Andrew Leitch, 7 Oct 1771, but actually containing 84 ½ acres clear of elder surveys, and third containing 4 ½ acres, *The Slipe,* which was willed to Francis Deakins; and whereas a certain Zachariah Knott, brother to the aforesaid Thomas Knott, has contracted with the heirs of Andrew Leitch for their undivided part of the aforesaid 84 ½ acres, it is understood, and intended that they divide the 84 ½ acres and 4 ½ acre tracts equally.

M:372-376. Thomas Knott recorded deed from Leonard M. Deakins and John Hoye of Georgetown, executors and devisees of Francis Deakins deceased, who in his lifetime, made deed 8 March 1804, for £86 selling to Thomas Knott, his rights in above, and instructing executors to make good deeds.

M:376. Benjamin Becraft recorded certificate of slaves 6 November 1805, imported into Maryland within three months, for his own use, Alice, a female slave about 20 and her son, Sam about 18 months.

M:376-377. Richard Wootton recorded deed 7 November 1805, from Solomon Davis for £131..5, tract *Retreat,* being part of several tracts beginning at 8th line of *Friendship,* to the Old Georgetown Road, containing 6 acres. Signed and acknowledged before Wm Clagett.

M:378-379. Walter Prather recorded deed 7 November 1805, from Henry Culver of Prince Georges County for $300 part of *Resurvey on the Farm,* containing 50 acres. Signed before Gab'l P. VanHorne, Geo Page. Mary Culver released dower rights.

M:379-381. Henry Culver recorded deed 7 November 1805, from Richard Jones of Joseph for $303, *Addition to Culver's Chance,* and also part of *Two Farms.* Signed and acknowledged before Wm Smith, and Wm Culver. Susanna Jones released dower

M:381-383. Robert D. Dawson recorded deed 7 November 1805 from John Linthicum two lots in Clarksburgh, upon which Charles Rogers had entered into possession, but taken from sheriff by writ of fi fa, for which John Linthicum was the highest bidder. Priscilla Linthicum released dower rights.

M:383-385. Richard Jones of Joseph recorded deed 7 November 1805, from Evan Thomas for $15. part of *Two Farms* tract, at 4th line of *Addition to Culver's Choice,* containing 3/4 acres. Signed by Evan Thomas. Rachel Thomas released dower

M:385 Asa Dent recorded manumission 8 November 1805, for Amy, about 10 years old, she has been sold to William Bennet for term of 18 years to expire 10 October 1823, and then she is to be free. Wit: Joshua Pearie, Vachel Hall.

M:385-387 Arnold Lashley recorded deed 8 November 1805, from Henry Baggerly for $1505.25, for part of *Beall's and Edmonston's Discovery,* conveyed to Henry from Hezekiah Baggerly and Charles Phillips, containing 150 acres. Mary Baggerly released dower

M:387-388. Solomon Davis recorded deed 8 November 1805, from John Hewett of the City of Washington, trustee for the sale of the real estate of Gerrard T. Conn, in case of Benjamin Stoddert and Uriah Forrest, complainants, sold tract called *Elizabeth.* Solomon Simpson, was the highest bidder, and is since deceased, and Dorcas Simpson is also now deceased, leaving Solomon Davis as his surviving executor. Deed made for negotiated sum.

M:388-390. William H. Dorsey and John Mountz recorded mortgage 9 November 1805, from James Redman, justly indebted for $600 money loaned to Henry Fox, of Georgetown, in order to secure payment, mortgages tract called *Pleasant Fields,* containing 422 3/4 acres.

M:390-391. Ephraim Etchiston recorded bill of sale 11 November 1805 from Elisha Walker, livestock and furniture. Signed by mark.

M:391-392. Mary Costigan recorded deed 11 November 1805, from Michael Costigan of Baltimore County for £100 assigns tracts *Charles and John's Choice,* and *Fellowship,* recently resurveyed as *Fair Rosamon's Bower,* willed to him by his father Dennis Costigan. Mary Costigan, wife of Michael Costigan released dower rights.

M:392-393. Lewis Beall recorded bill of sale 14 November 1805. I Benjamin Norris for valuable consideration assign the woodwork of one new wagon made for John Lodge of said county and now in possession of Hewes and Riley, blacksmiths. However, if Benjamin Norris pay Lewis Beall £8..5..4 with interest this sale is null and void. Signed 24 October 1805 by Benjamin Norris, Wit: Samuel Elgar.

M:393-395. Leonard Hays recorded deed 12 Nov 1805, between Henry Camden and Mary his wife for £166..10, sells part of *Happy Choice Fortified,* containing 55 ½ acres.

395-396. Barton Harris recorded deed 20 November 1805, from Robert P. Magruder. Whereas John B. Allison, did by deed of 25 February 1797, grants an alley way over part of lot he then held in Town of Williamsburgh, now called Rockville, but since sold to Barton Harris, now grants forever right of passage, 4 feet in width over lot of ground, adjacent to the garden fence of Honore Martin, in Rockville, parallel to Commerce Avenue

M:396-398. John Willson and Richard Wootton recorded deed 26 November 1805 from Thomas Nicholls of Simon for a valuable consideration sold unto James Perry, now deceased, the land hereafter mentioned, and which James Perry by his will bequeath unto the aforesaid John Willson and Richard Wootton the whole of his real estate. Metes and bounds on the main road from Montgomery Court House to the Mouth of Monocacy. Signed before John Fleming, Samuel Elgar.

M:398-400. Leonard Howard recorded deed 26 November 1805, from Charles Howard for $2370.25 assigns tracts *Addition to Peter's Favor,* adjacent to *William and Ann*, containing 11 7/8 acres, and tract *Hopewell,* adjacent to *Resurvey on Gum Spring,* and *Resurvey on Wolf's Cow,* containing 237 5/8 acres; also his interest in 11 1/4 acre part of *Wolf's Cow,* being within the plantation, which for many years has been held in peaceable possession by the said Charles Howard and his father, Jacob Howard, but never conveyed by original patentee, but intended to have been conveyed. Signed before Wm Smith and Greenbury Howard. Anna wife of Charles Howard released dower rights.

M:400-402. Verlinda Beatty, widow of Col. Charles M. Beatty, recorded deed 26 November 1805, from Elizabeth Clements, widow of Francis Clements deceased, and Jacob Clements, son of the said Francis Clements. Whereas Francis Clements by his will devised part of *Brother's Industry,* to his sons Joseph and Jacob, and part of his widow Elizabeth, and Joseph and Jacob previously conveyed their part to Col. Charles M. Beatty, who paid for purchase in his lifetime, but deed not made. Deed is now recorded and made.

M:402-403. William Willson recorded bill of sale 26 November 1805, from Edward Burgess Sr. for £100 one Negro man called James, provided nevertheless that if sum paid in one year, bill of sale is of no effect.

M:403-404. John Magruder recorded bill of sale 26 November 1805 from Eleanor Magruder for $400 assigns one Negro man Jack about 32 years old; now in the employ of Charles Miles until 1st January next.

M:404-405. William Lodge recorded bill of sale 30 November 1805 from Frederick Sparrow for £9 mortgage on livestock and furniture.

M:M:405-406. George Cross of Anne Arundel County, recorded bill of sale 3 December 1805 from Leonard Aldridge of Montgomery County for $200 sells furniture and housewares

M:406-407. George Deakins Church recorded bill of sale 3 December 1805, from Joseph Church for £100 furniture and housewares.

M:407-409. Edward Crow Sr., late of Montgomery County, but now of the western country, recorded deed 4 December 1805, from John Hilleary of Frederick County for 5 shillings, tract in conveyance of 1782 by Hezekiah Veatch, called *Peace and Plenty,* with part of *Younger Brother,* to 10th line of *Peckerton,* to 1st line of *Rose's Delight,* containing 91 1/4 acres; 2nd part of *Peace and Plenty,* beginning at part conveyed to Nathan Trail, containing 173 1/4 acres. Anne Hilleary released dower.

M:409-411. Samuel Magruder recorded deed 4 December 1805 from John Dent for £12..3..8, assigns part of *Hannah's Inheritance,* for 125 ½ acres. Signed before Ozias Offutt, Richard West. Verlinda, wife of John Dent, released dower.

M:411-413. William Smith recorded deed of trust 4 December 1805, from Thomas Orme. Whereas Thomas Orme is indebted to many persons he assigns all real estate and personal property to sell to pay creditors, including *Discovery,* 89 acres; *Portland,* 13 ½ acres; *Red Oak Bottom,* 11 acres; *Mount Vernon,* 125 acres; *Cumberland,* 46 acres; *Saplin Ridge,* 21 acres; *Hispanolio,* 12 1/4 acres, *Addition to Story's Grove,* 63 acres, *Yorkshire,* 26 ½ acres; *Addition to Fancy,* 5 ½ acres; *Addition to Saturday's Work,* 8 1/4 acres; *Addition to Saplin Ridge,* 5 ½ acres; *Addition to Very Good,* 12 ½ acres; *Neglect,* 6 acres; *Mount Etna,* 35 acres; *Sporting Ground,* 96 acres; *Second Addition to Saplin Ridge,* 1 3/4 acres; any other lands omitted here, receipt for *Halifax,* sold Thomas A French, but not conveyed, and all personal property in annexed inventory. Inventory on inserted sheets: Thomas Nicholls of John, note for £10..6..8, Jesse Hyatt on bond on William Magrath's judgment, £8..17..6; book of accounts with sundry small balances; desk, bookcase and parcel of books, three trunks and chest, 1 horse. Dated November 6, 1805. Signed by Thomas Orme.

M:413-414. Lewis Duvall recorded deed 6 December 1805, from Samuel Welsh Sr. For £300, tracts in deed to Welch of Anne Arundel County, from Isaac Webster of Harford County, tracts on Seneca Creek, *Richardson's Range,* 383 acres, *Bristol,* 50 acres and *Rogues Harbor,* 50 acres.

M:414-416. Thomas Benson recorded deed 9 December 1805, from John Harding for $1800, tract called *Forrest,* as resurveyed for Elias Harding, containing 150 acres. Signed by mark.

M:416-418. Thomas Reid recorded deed 9 December 1805, from George Reid for £1200 tracts *Ray's Adventure,* and *Resurvey on Buckfield,* part of *Good Cheer,* and part of *Mount Carmel,* on the north side of Little Monocacy adjacent to Thomas Talbott, containing 96 3/4 acres. Rosannah Reid, wife of George Reid released dower rights.

M:418-419. William H. Pleasant recorded bill of sale 9 December 1805 from Jacob Brown for $40. Sells one black walnut desk and bookcase.

M:419-422. William Trail recorded deed 10 December 1805, from Daniel Jarret of Jefferson County, Kentucky, and Margaret his wife, daughter and heir of Frederick Sprigg. Appointed John

Poole to have power of attorney to make deed to William Trail, for £600 for *Happy Choice Fortified,* containing 207 1/4 acres.

M:422-426. Thomas Sprigg recorded deed 10 December 1805 from Daniel Jarrett and Margaret, his wife, daughter and heir of Frederick Sprigg, of Jefferson County, Kentucky, for £568..6..3, part of *Happy Choice Fortified,* containing 216 ½ acres.

M:426-427. Thomas Peter recorded bill of sale, 11 December 1805, from Benjamin Higdon, for £12 and 167 pounds of tobacco, due to Robert Peter; sells livestock including 2 mares, 4 cows, 4 yearlings, 10 head of sheep, 3 sows, 12 shoats.

M:427-428. Daniel Browning recorded deed 12 December 1805, from Archibald Browning for $1. Grants parcel of land called *Resurvey on Long looked For,* containing 44 acres; Signed before G. Howard, M. Browning.

M:428-429. Benedict Clark recorded bill of sale 13 December 1805, from William Steel, wagon, horses and farm equipment.

M:429-432. Ruth Trundle recorded deed 16 December 1805, from Leonard M. Deakens of Prince George's County, and John Hoy, of Washington, D.C., executors of Francis M. Deakins, a 9 acre part of *Mount Carmel* which James White had passed bond on 25 July 1801 for £3500, and then conveyed part to Ruth Trundle for 58 acres for £302..10 adjacent to *Meredith's Hunting Quarters,* the executors are making good on bonds by deed to Ruth Trundle.

M:432-433. Thomas Burgee recorded deed 18 December 1805, from Charles Busey Jr. Of Frederick County, sells lots #21 & 75 in Hyattstown, to pay annual rents of 5 shillings to Jesse Hyatt.

M:433-434. Richard Ricketts recorded mortgage 18 December 1805 from Archibald Trail for $115. Part of tract *Rockhead, Pleasant Fields,* supposed to contain 16 1/4 acres; and part of *Younger Brother,* for 27 3/4 acres. Nevertheless if sum paid, sale is void.

M:434-435. George Reed Jr. Bill of sale 19 December 1805 From Alexander Reed for £196 one Negro girl about 7 or 8 years named Sarah; and four head of horses.

M:435-436. Elisha Lanham recorded certificate of importation of slaves 20 December 1805 from Virginia for one Negro woman named Pat about 32 years old; one Negro boy named Samuel Henson about 3 years old and a girl child (unnamed) about 11 months.

M:436-437. Singleton Owen [and Rosanna Owen and John Candler Owen] recorded deed December 1805 from Benjamin Pelly for £80 one undivided seventh part of a tract called *Wickhams Chance.* Ann wife of Benjamin Pelly released dower rights.

M:437-438 Robert Doynes Dawson recorded bill of sale 30 December 1805 from Basil Mockbee for $50. Sells one mare and two feather beds.

M:438-439. Samuel Elgar and Westley Pigman recorded bill of sale 30 December 1805 from Thomas Pitt Hays and Elizabeth Hays his wife for £400 sells one Negro man named Moses, a blacksmith, now in the possession of Samuel Thomas Junr., one other Negro man called Sam, now in possession of John Thomas, 3rd; one Negro woman named Kate now in our possession

M:439-440. Samuel Elgar and Westley Pigman recorded mortgage 30 December 1805 from Thomas Pitt Hays and Elizabeth Hays his wife, who was one of the heirs of Jeremiah Ducker, deceased. For £300 assign right to his lands.

M:440. Walter S. Alexander, trustee for Catharine Dade of the State of Virginia, a list of slaves was recorded 30 December 1805, Frank 40 years old; Dick 28 years old; Benjamin 30 years old and Dick 17 years old; James 8, Rippen 6 years; Edmund 5, Danny 3 and Dick 2; female slave Prece 30 and Easter 30; Judy 1 year and Prece 24 years; Maria 7 and Henny 1 year; Patience 40 and Sucky 10; Patty 5, Milly 30, Betty 5; and Peggy 6 years old.

M:440-441. Benjamin Ray Jr. 31 December 1805, Recorded sheriff's bond with Henry O'Neall, Nathaniel Beall and Benjamin G. Orr.

M:441-442. Eleanor Ayton recorded bill of sale 31 December 1805 from Beal Ayton for £150 Negro man called Joshua.

M:442-443. John Aldridge recorded bill of sale 1 January 1806, from Joshua Brashears for valuable consideration, one Negro woman named Priss about 40 years old; but if he pays by 1 January next $162.50 bill of sale is void.

M:443. Samuel Nally recorded schedule 2 January 1806, to sheriff as an insolvent debtor: some fodder, some corn, some hoes and two axes.

M:443-444. Henry Clements, insolvent debtor recorded schedule 2 January 1806; a parcel of corn, a parcel of fodder, 1 plough, 4 hoes, 2 axes, a parcel of crockery, some old knives and forks.

M:444-445. Samuel B. Magruder recorded bill of sale 2 January 1806 from William Collins for $60 one gray mare, my crop of tobacco, etc. Signed by mark.

M:445-446. John Sheets recorded bill of sale 2 January 1806 from Richard Sheets for £100 sells livestock including pigs, pork and barrels of corn, fodder other housewares.

M:446 Vachel Hall recorded 3 January 1806, manumission for George to be free from 25 December 1825.

M:446-447. Benjamin Ricketts recorded release 3 January 1806 from Solomon Holland for bill of sale made 5 January 1791 for mulatto Bill, Negroes Jerry and Rose and boy Charlie and also one mulatto boy Erasmus and furniture and kitchen ware from bill of sale in 25 October 1797.

M:447-450. Robert Waters recorded deed 4 January 1806 from John Bowie for £2295 part of *Wickinger and Pottingers Discovery* and part of *Piney Thickett*.

M:450-452. George Davis recorded deed 6 January 1806 from Charles Busey Junr. of Charles lots #3 & 4 in Hyattstown,

M:452-454. Henry Gaither recorded deed 6 January 1806 from George Upton for $225 part of *The Resurvey on the Farm,* adjacent to *Greenwood,* containing 36 ½ acres. Elizabeth wife of George released dower rights.

M:454-455. Hugh Anderson recorded deed 6 January 1806 from Henry Gaither for $18.12 ½ part of *Resurvey on John and Sarah,* beginning at Philemon Plummer Jr's lot, containing 36 1/4 square perches. Signed and acknowledged.

M:455-457. Philemon Plummer Jr., recorded deed 6 January 1806 from Henry Gaither for $47.62 ½ part of *Resurvey on John and Sarah,* containing 95 + acres.

M:457. Thomas Hilleary recorded bill of sale 7 January 1806 from Richard Farmer for 1250 pounds of neat crop tobacco, sells one horse and one feather bed. Signed by mark before Clement Wheeler, Wm Darne Jr.

M:457-458. Thomas Hilleary recorded bill of sale 7 January 1806 from Zedekiah Willson for 1500 pounds of neat crop tobacco, one bay horse about 6 years old.

M:458-459. John Baden of Robert, recorded schedule 11 January 1806, as insolvent debtor. Lists Basil Talbott for bill for geers, 4 old chairs, 1 pot, 1 small table, ½ dozen knives and forks, 1 pewter dish, 2 pewter plates, 3 earthen plates, 1 earthen dish, 3 tubs, 1 wedge, bed, bedstead and furniture, 1 old bedstead & furniture, 1 old table, 1 broad ax. Signed by mark befoer John Fleming, Samuel Elgar.

M:459. Rebecca Moran, aged 9 years recorded manumission 12 January 1806, to be free on 1 September 1820, and her offspring to be free at 21 if males and 16 if females. Signed by Edward Lancaster.

M:460-463. John Bealmar recorded deed 18 January 1806 from Lawrence O'Neale, William Vears and John Vears of Daniel. Whereas John Bealmar did heretofore convey several tracts of land, and all his Negro slaves, to wit: Jacob, Eve, Biney, Nace and also livestock and household goods; they are now reconveying those two tracts which remain unsold, and have paid debts, excepting parts sold to Matthew Reid

M:463-465. Robert Jones of Prince George's County, recorded deed 14 January 1806, from Richard Jones of John, of Montgomery County, for $1130 part of *Beall Christie* and *Bealls Manor* containing 113 acres.   Susanna Jones released dower rights.

M:465-466. Robert Jones of Prince Georges County recorded deed 14 January 1806, from James Willson Perry for £66..12 tract called *Rural Felicity,* on 16th line of *Easy Purchase.* Margaret wife of James released dower rights.

M:466-467. Robert Jones of Prince George's County, recorded deed 14 January 1806, from Thomas Trundell for £148..4 part of tract called *Addition to Easy Purchase,* containing 49 4/10 acres. Signed before Wm Smith, Thos Simpson. Leah Trundle released dower.

M:467-469. James Wilson Perry recorded deed 14 January 1806, from Thomas Trundel for £114..18 assigns part of tract *Addition to Easy Purchase,* containing 38 3/10 acres . Leah Trundle released dower.

M:469-470. Charles Gassaway recorded bill of sale 17 January 1806, from Eleazor Standage, for 2000 pounds neat crop tobacco, mulatto girl Leathe, about 13 years old. If sum paid, bill of sale is void.

M:470. Commission for Justices of the Peace 17 January 1806 to William Smith, Laurence O'Neale, Richard Green of Hds Run, Henry Brookes, Greenbury Howard, Edward Burgess, Junior, Benjamin Gaither, James Lackland, Ozias Offutt, John Thomas, John Burgess, William Culver, Thomas Simpson, Richard West, John Adams, Camden Riley, Warren Magruder, Richard Beall, John Fleming, Samuel Elgar, Meshech Browning, John Belt, Gassaway Harwood, Walter Brooke Beall, William Garrett and William Darne, all of Montgomery County.

M:470-474. Nicholas Rhoades recorded deed 20 January 1806, from David Arnold and Peter Arnold of the State of Kentucky for $1000. Part of *Resurvey on Williams Chance,* adjacent to *Plummer's Hunting Lot,* for 34 acres. Also part of *Labyrinth,* laid out for 60 acres. Nancy Arnold wife of Peter, and Eleanor Arnold wife of David released rights.

M:474-475. Samuel Bealmar recorded bill of sale 23 January 1806, from John Bealmar for £59..2 sells two young Negroes, one Biney 8 years old and Nace 6 years old.

M:475. Robert Peter recorded bill of sale 23 January 1806 from Patrick Lyddane for livestock and furniture.

M:475-476. Thomas Garrett recorded release 25 January 1806 from Solomon Holland for £50 one Negro girl Harriett about 8 years old conveyed to me in a bill of sale 28 April 1804.

M:476. James Carey recorded bill of sale 25 January 1806 from Thomas Garrett, for £50, one Negro girl Harriett about 8 years old.

M:477-479. Jesse Hyatt recorded deed 25 January 1806, from Thomas Orme for £901..10, the following tracts, *Resurvey on Long Looked For,* part of *Rising Sun,* part of *Trouble Enough,* part of *Solomon's Roguery,* and part of *Pleasant Plains,* contiguous to each other, metes and bounds given, adjacent to part of *Solomon's Roguerey* conveyed to said Orme by Boyer and Day for 29 ½ acres; reversed with given line, and continuing to contain 466 ½ acres in all. Signed and acknowledged before Wm Smith, Lewis Duvall.

M:479-481 Jesse Hyatt recorded deed 25 January 1806, from John Tolly Worthington and Mary (Polly) Worthington his wife of Baltimore County for £702..6..4, for 390 acres, land that was devised to said Polly by her father Brice Thomas Beall Worthington, late of Anne Arundel County, deceased, and any right to her sister Henrietta's heirs coming to inherit land in Ann Arundel County near Severn River, Signed by both.

M:481-482. Gerard Brooke recorded deed 27 January 1806, from Caleb Pancoast and Mary Pancoast his wife for £193..15 all those lots in town of Brookeville, #10, 11, 12, and 13, adjoining each other, Signed and acknowledged by both..

M:482-483. Elizabeth Thomas recorded 27 January 1806, manumission for Syrus/Cyrus, from date hereof; for Sarah 10 years on 15 December next to be free at age 18. Wit: John Thomas 3rd.

M:483-485. James Peter Soper of Anne Arundel County, recorded deed 28 January 1806, from John C. Herbert and Mary his wife, formerly Mary Snowden, of Prince George's County, for $703 tract called *Moore's Rest,* now called *New Birmingham,* on the 11th line of *White Marsh,* containing 93 3/4 acres. Signed and acknowledged.

M:485. Ignatius Clarkson and William Hempstone recorded bill of sale 29 January 1806 from Zadock Brashears one Negro boy named Ben, one wagon and other plantation and kitchen furniture.

M:486-488. William Marbury recorded deed 4 February 1806, from Benjamin Stoddert, for $8535 part of *Friendship*, land bought of Joseph Belt adjacent to Wm Digges part of *Chevy Chase*, containing 271 acres. Also one other parcel he bought of Joseph S. Belt, adjoining the aforesaid, being a part of *Chevy Chase*, beginning on 12th line of *Friendship*, and also of *Oatland*, to Wm Digges part of *Chevy Chase*, containing 13 1/4 acres. Signed by Ben Stoddert before Benjamin Stoddert Jr. And Elizabeth Stoddert as witnesses. Acknowledged before John Fleming, Samuel Elgar.

M:488-489. Van Swearingen recorded bill of sale 5 February 1806 from Henry Lanham dark bay horse and other livestock. Signed by mark, Henry Lanham.

M:489. Thomas Garrett recorded release 6 February 1806 from Solomon Holland for $275 for one Negro woman, Jenny about 18 years old on bill of sale dated 24 April 1804.

M:489-491 Christian Getzendanner recorded deed 10 February 1806, from Alexander Contee Hanson, Chancellor of State of Maryland, whereas William Marbury, agent became the purchaser of two tracts, *The Pines*, containing 200 acres and *Bampton*, containing 50 acres, as may appear in deed from Solomon Holland to the said William Marbury, on 12 May 1796, and he contracted to sell same to Thomas Nicholls of Simon, contracted for tracts, and by assigned in 1805 to Christian Getzendanner all his right to same, and that *The Pines* contains only 171 acres and the tract *Bampston* contains only 30 1/4 acres; metes and bounds follow for tracts, signed by A.C. Hanson.

M:491-493. Nathan Talbott recorded deed 11 February 1806, from William Brewer for $1206 tract of land called *Fortune*, on a small branch that falls into Beaver Run, on south side of a tract taken up for Mr. Daniel Carroll, containing 100 ½ acres. Mary Brewer released dower rights.

M:493. Hannah Offutt recorded release 13 February 1806 from Mordecai Burgess Offutt and Jane Offutt all their right and claim to the personal estate of Zadock Offutt, deceased.

M:493-495. Elijah Viers, recorded deed 14 February 1806 from Lawrence O'Neale. Witnesseth that a certain John Bealmear did heretofore on 12 August 1799 convey a tract called *String About*, purchased of John Goshen for 55 acres, to the above named Laurence O'Neale, William Viers and John Veirs of Daniel, did sell the aforesaid tract to several persons, and one part thereof to Elijah Veirs for a valuable consideration, in consequence thereof the aforesaid William and John Veirs of Daniel did afterwards, about 18 April 1801 by deed of bargain convey to the aforesaid Elijah Veirs part of said tract, but as Laurence O'Neal was not part of deed of conveyance he was advised his title may be defective, this indenture therefore in consideration of the premises and the further consideration of $5 makes good deed. Signed by Laurence O'Neale before Richard Beall, G. W. Harwood.

M:496-497. William H. Willson recorded deed 13 February 1806, from Ben Ray, Jr., sheriff. Whereas Jonathan Rawlings, administrator dbn of Francis Rawlings, did recover a judgment against Lewis Duvall for £3333..6..8 with interest from 19 May 1797, by writ of fieri facias, takes six lots in Hyattstown, #22, 76, 23, 77, 24, 78 and all improvements thereto belonging sold at public sale to high bidder for $490.

M:497-498. Mareen Howard Duvall recorded deed 15 February 1806, from William H. Willson of Prince George's County, for $490 six lots #22, 23, 24, 76, 77, 78 in Hyattstown. Signed before John Fleming, Samuel Elgar.

M:499. Charles O. Jones and Daniel Robinson recorded bill of sale 17 February 1806, from Richard Steward , two feather beds for the purpose of their being security on a note unto William Offutt of James, Administrator of Zadok Offutt deceased.

M:499-500. Benjamin T. Busey recorded bill of sale 17 February 1806 from Henry Busey for $300 sells one bay horse, one bay colt, one cow and yearling, one iron pot, one Dutch oven, one frying pay, 8 shoats, sow and 7 pigs, 12 geese, two feather beds and furniture, two bed steads, 2 tables, trunk and cupboard, one little wheel and three chairs, corn, two plows, 7 hoes, 18 dung hill fowls, 16 pewter spoons, 30 pieces earthenware, 600 weight bacon, about 500 lbs tobacco, a quantity of corn fodder. Signed by mark.

M:500-501. Benjamin Poole recorded deed 19 February 1806, from Joseph Poole Senr. For £7..10 sells parcel number 3, part of tract called *Poole's Hazard,* beginning at stone on 3rd line of lot #2, then straight line to 1st beginning, containing 15840 sq. ft., or one fourth of an acre, signed before G.W. Harwood, Laurence O'Neale.

M:501-502. Walter Poole recorded deed 19 February 1806, from Joseph Poole Senr for $50 sells parcel part of tract called *Poole's Hazard,* on 13th line of *Aix La Chapelle,* to 7th line of *Eleanor's Purchase,* containing 4 ½ acres. signed before G.W. Harwood, Laurence O'Neale.

M:503-504. William Poole recorded deed 19 February 1806, from Joseph Poole Senr. for £7..10 sells parcel number 6, part of tract called *Poole's Hazard,* containing 15840 sq. ft., or one fourth of an acre, signed before G.W. Harwood, Laurence O'Neale.

M:504-505. Walter Poole recorded deed 19 February 1806, from Joseph Poole Senr. for £7..10 sells parcel number 4, beginning at 3rd line of lot #3, part of tract called *Poole's Hazard,* containing 15840 sq. ft., or one fourth of an acre, signed before G.W. Harwood, Laurence O'Neale.

M:505-507. Joseph Poole Jr. recorded deed 19 February 1806, from Joseph Poole Senr. for £7..10 sells parcel number 2, part of tract called *Poole's Hazard,* beginning on north side of main road, commonly called Coxon's Road, about 2 perches southwest of the well now in possession of Jacob Howard, it beginning the first beginning of lot number 1, containing 15840 sq. ft., or one fourth of an acre, signed before G.W. Harwood, Laurence O'Neale.

M:507-508. Samuel Poole recorded deed 19 February 1806, from Joseph Poole Senr. for £7..10 sells parcel number 5, part of tract called *Poole's Hazard,* containing 15840 sq. ft., or one fourth of an acre, signed before G.W. Harwood, Laurence O'Neale.

M:508-509. William Collins recorded schedule as insolvent debtor, 22 February 1806, consisting of three old chairs and one shovel plough. Signed by mark, witnessed by John Fleming, Samuel Elgar

M:509. Zachariah Duly recorded schedule as insolvent debtor, 22 February 1806, consisting of 1 ax and one shoe bench. Signed before John Fleming, Samuel Elgar.

M:509-510. Commission from State to Jeremiah Townley Chase of Anne Arundel County appointed Chief Judge of third district 3 March 1806.

M:510. Commission to Henry Ridgley of Anne Arundel County as Associate Judge 3 March 1806.

M:510-511. Jeremiah Townley Chase recorded certificate of qualification, 3 March 1806, and his belief in Christian religion.

M:511-512. Henry Ridgley recorded certificate of qualification, 3 March 1806, declaring his belief in Christian religion.

M:512-513. Richard H. Harwood recorded certificate of qualification as Associate Judge of Third Judicial District 3 March 1806.

M:514. Lewis Beall recorded bond, 3 March 1806, with Zachariah Dowden and Henry Lansdale bound to Benjamin Holland Jr. In sum of $50. Whereas Benjamin Holland Jr. Has applied to three county justices of the peace for relief as insolvent debtor, and whereas Lewis Beall, and Zachariah Dowden, two of the creditors alleged that Benjamin Holland Jr. hath lessened or otherwise disposed of his property, objecting against his discharge, on the above recited allegations, they shall be overruled, then the within obligation or bond will be of no effect; otherwise in full force.

M:514-515. Schedule of Benjamin Holland Jr recorded 3 March 1806. Basil Perry per account £27. Signed before John Fleming, Samuel Elgar.

M:515-517. Thomas Fletchall recorded deed 3 March 1806, from Elizabeth Hickman, one of the daughters of William Hickman of Stephen, for tract *Cider and Ginger* and also all her right to leased land, part of *Preston March*. Elizabeth is now 21, received $160 for one moiety of land containing 80 odd acres. William Hickman left a widow and the following children, all under age, to wit: Thomas, Ann Fletchall, Elizabeth, William and Mary

M:517-518. Joseph Poole Senr recorded deed 3 March 1806, from John Poole Senr. for £13..15 part of tract known as *Poole's Right,* beginning at tract *Pooles Hazard,* containing 2 3/4 acres.

M:518-521. Samuel Clapham recorded deed 3 March 1806 from Joseph Newton Chiswell and Thomas Fletchall, executors of Stephen N. Chiswell, late of Montgomery County, deceased, for conveyance of tract called *Accord,* and agreement between Chiswell and Eneas Noland and Otho H. W. Luckett to altar the bounds lines and corner of a part of the aforesaid tract. Now for sums of money paid to them they convey to Samuel Clapham (assignee to Eneas Noland) tract *Accord,* and also part of *Resurvey on Discord,* beginning on 12th line of tract *Concord,* established in a boundary line agreement in August 1788, between Isaac Hite, William Hough, Leonard Deakins and Simon Nicholls, containing 202 acres.

M:522-523. William Willson of John recorded deed 4 March 1806, from Nacy Waters. Whereas Richard Waters by his will in 1794 gave to my three granddaughters, daughters of my deceased son Azel Waters, viz. Amelia, Anna and Katy Waters, tract called *Timber Creek* on Ten Mile Creek, two years after my decease; and whereas two of the girls have since married, viz Amelia to John

Flanagan and Katy to Moses Hedges, all of Frederick County, he now sells tract with express purpose to divide proceeds among the three granddaughters of Richard Waters. Deed signed by Amelia Flanagan, John Flanagan, Anna Waters, Caty Hedges, Moses Hedges, before Middleton Smith and Lewis Browning of Frederick County.

M:523-525. William Willson of John recorded deed 4 March 1806 from Nacy Waters for 60 acre tract called *Timber Creek,* bequeath to Amelia, Anna and Katy Waters, sold for $5 per acre. Signed before Greenbury Howard, Edward Burgess Jr.

M:525-527. Robert Fisher recorded deed 4 March 1806, from George Hussey and John Fisher of Baltimore County. Whereas Christopher Hussey to secure debt mortgaged part of tract *Charley Forrest,* now called by the name of *Pigman's Inheritance,* containing 50 acres. If land sold, out of the surplus intent to pay and satisfy Curtis Grubb, on sum of money due from the said Christopher Hussey, for $200 recorded in Liber L:98 . Signed 20 December 1805.

M:527-528. Charles Gassaway recorded bond 5 March 1806, to serve as Coroner with Hezekiah Thomas and Joseph Burnsides.

M:528-530. Beal Gaither recorded deed 6 March 1806, from Philemon and Joshua Griffith, executors of estate of Henry Griffith, part of tract called *Snowden's Purchase,* containing about 4 acres of land for $24. Signed by Philemon Griffith and Joshua Griffith before John Belt, Edward Burgess Jr.

M:530-531. William Benson recorded deed 7 March 1806, from Nicholas Pegno. Whereas Nicholas Pegno has applied to the judges of Montgomery County for benefit under laws for relief of insolvent debtors, and above William Benson was appointed trustee to sell property, he assigns all goods and furniture, effects and chattels belonging to and due to him.

M:531-532. Caleb Pancoast recorded deed 6 March 1806, from Gerard Brooke for $150 lots #14 & #15 in town of Brookeville. Signed before Richard Green, Jno Thomas 3d.

M:532-534. William Brewer Jr recorded deed 8 March 1806, from Jesse Hyatt for £6 lots #31 & #32 in town of Hyattstown.

M:534-536. Philip B. Key recorded deed 8 March 1806, from Thomas Plater and John Rowsby Plater, all residing in the Territory of Columbia, for $2500 sells all their interest in a tract called *Bradford's Rest,* devised to Thomas by his father George Plater, except fore two leases, distinguished by the numbers two and 10 which were heretofore assigned to William Bayley, and also two lease by number 20 and 21, which were heretofore sold to a certain William P. Williams, and they do hereby appoint Richard Key Watts and Lewis Beall of the Court House in Montgomery County, their attorneys.

M:536-541. Soloman Glissan recorded deed 8 March 1806, from Ann Mc Kay, Ann Shaw, Mary Boyd and Margery Reed (Margery Gun at time of will), the devisees of the will of William Mc Kay, of Montgomery County; also Andrew Boyd husband of Mary Boyd of Frederick County; and John Reed, husband of Margery Reed of the City of Washington. Assigns tract of land called *Mackey's Chance,* to part of tract called *Wilson's Discovery,* as now laid out for Walter Simpson for 80 acres; to first line of *William's Chance,* containing 50 acres more or less.

M:541-547.   Samuel Simmons recorded deed 8 March 1806, from Ann Shaw, of the City of Washington; Witnessed that by an instrument of Writing, by Ann McKay, Mary Boyd, and Marjery Read, on 25th August 1803, on division line of a tract called *Mackey's Chance,* between the heirs of William Mackey and William Knight, containing 50 acres more or less, they confirm deed, and all that part of a tract called *Wilson's Discovery,* and part of *Mackey's Chance,* as devisees of William McKay, the said Ann McKay, Margery Read, then Margery Gun, Mary Boyd and Ann Shaw.

M:547-549. Joseph Clagett recorded deed 8 March 1806, from Ninian Benson. Whereas Ninian Benson, together with his brother William Benson and Sarah who intermarried with Allen Simpson, were entitled in fee simple to two tracts of land, *The Retrospect,* containing 10 acres more or less, and *Critical Review,* containing 5 3/4 acres; which Nicholas Pegno, guardian made a bond to sell to Joseph Clagett, and thereafter on 10 December 1803, William Benson and Sarah and her husband, conveyed their interest; recorded in Liber L:208-209; and Ninian Benson having now attained to full age, in consideration of above and 5 shillings, grants his interest.

M:549-551. George Bowman recorded deed 8 March 1806 from Mary Edmonston, Robert Edmonston, Eden Edmonston and Dorothy Edmonston of Montgomery County and Thomas Edmonston and Edward Edmonston of Prince George's County, and Andrew Scholfield and Betsy Scholfield of the City of Alexandria, in Virginia for $1033.50 sell part of tract called *Delay,* and resurvey thereon, beginning at tract called *Stoney Range,* to tract *Hutchcraft's Range,* to part of tract called *Pleasant Plains of Damascus,* and *Very Good,* containing 172 ½ acres. Signed by parties above, and   Mary Edmonston wife of Robert Edmonston, Ruth Edmonston wife of Thomas Edmonston, Peggy Edmonston wife of Edward Edmonston and Betsy Scholfield wife of Andrew examined apart released dower rights.

M:552. George Bowman recorded instrument of writing 8 March 1806, from Thomas Edmonston, with survey in metes and bounds for tract *Delay,* per Jos Elgar Surveyor.

M:552-554. Basil Offutt recorded deed 10 March 1806, from Andrew Offutt for £20..16, part of a tract of land called *Resurvey on William and Ann,* containing 5 3/10 acres. Eliza Offutt, wife of Andrew, released dower rights.

M:554-557. Basil Offutt recorded deed 10 March 1806 from Zachariah Offutt for $5. Part of tract called *Petersburgh* adjacent to 18th line of *Resurvey on Black Rock,* to the beginning os Offutt's part of *William and John,* to first line of tract, *Mother's Good Will,*   to main road leading to the Mouth of Monocacy, containing 382 and 45/100 acres . Eleanor Offutt wife of Zachariah Offutt released dower rights.

M:557. Rebecca Self recorded list of Negroes 10 March 1806, late a resident of Louden County, Virginia, brought with her a Negro girl, Esther, about 12 years old, which I purchased of Mrs. Elizabeth Hickman. Signed before Nathan T. Veatch.

M:557-558. Negro Betsy Tar, aged 38 years old, and able to gain a sufficient livelihood, to be free after 1st January 1810, received manumission from Thomas Batson, recorded 11 March 1806 for diverse good reasons

M:558-560. Hugh Conn of Fairfax County, Virginia recorded deed 11 March 1806, from Nathaniel Crawford of Prince George's County, for $1100 *Resurvey on Bishop's Island,* about a mile above the spout of the Great Falls of Potomac. Sarah B. Crawford, wife of Nathaniel released dower.

M:560-561. Lewis Beall recorded bill of sale 12 March 1806 from Brice Letton for £300 sells one black gelding 5 years old, one sorrel gelding, other horses, and household furniture and items.

M:561-562. Zadock Holland recorded deed 15 March 1806,, from Benjamin Holland Jr. of Fleming County, Kentucky for £75 parcel of land called *Gipson's Choice,* 22 acres more or less.

M:562-563. Ann Roberts recorded on 17 March 1806, manumissions for Lucy Bowman, and her three children: David Boman, Bob Boman and Henny Prather; also for the children of said Henne, to wit: Harry, Pegg, Middleton and Delilah, when they arrive at age. Harry now 8 to be free at 21; Pegg now 6 free at 16; Middleton now 4, free at 21; Delilah to be free 16 years from the date hereof; and any other children free at age 21 (males) and 16 (females). Other children of Lucy Bowman: Bedford, Adam and Sarah to be free at 21 years of age, or at my death, whichever is later. Wit: Hezekiah Ward, Jesse Hyatt.

M:563-565. Henry Roberts recorded deed 19 March 1806 from Benjamin Ray, Sheriff land recovered from Thomas Orme, known as *Mount Vernon,* lying on the Potomac, near Great Falls,

M:565-567. Barton Harris of the town of Rockville, recorded deed 21 March 1806, From John Burch Allison of Bourbon Co., Kentucky; part of two lots #40 & #41, in Rockville. Deed by William Garrett, attorney for John Burch Allison. Elizabeth Allison relinquished dower rights.

M:567-569. Basil M. Perry recorded deed 22 March 1807 (?) from Celia Beall daughter of James Beall deceased, deed made 2 March 1806. Tract devised to her by James Beall of Jas called *Greenland,* and adjacent to part sold to Tyson Beall, containing 50 acres. Signed before John Fleming, Samuel Elgar.

M:569-571. Samuel Willson recorded deed 24 March 1806, from George W. Haymond for $1954.62 sells land devised to him in will of William Fee dated 26 December 1790, part of *William's Meadows,* and *Rocky Point,* except for 4 acres leased to Will Carroll, together containing 102 acres. Mary Haymond released dower rights.

M:572-573. William Hilton recorded deed 25 March 1806 from Christian Hempstone for £42..3..9 part of *Hempstone's Discovery,* containing 11 1/4 acres. Signed before Richard Beall, Gass W. Harwood. Dorcas Hempstone released dower rights.

M:573-574. Mary Hungerford recorded certificate and list of slaves 25 January 1806, imported from Loudon Co., Virginia by Mary, wife of Charles Hungerford, late deceased. Woman Hannah age 14; Peggy age 14; Gabriel 9 years and Jenny 25 years; Phillis a 6 year old girl; Mary 9 months and Sarah 30 years old.

M:574. John Simpson recorded manumission 26 March 1806 of Negro man Anthony. Wit: Edw Burgess, Ephraim Etchison.

M:574-576. John Fleming recorded deed of trust 27 March 1806, from Talbott Allnutt, an insolvent debtor, all property, real, personal or mixed, to sell to satisfy creditors.

M:576. Hanza Lanham, an insolvent debtor, recorded schedule of personal property 27 March 1806, lists right to bill of sale to Van Swearingen, and 2 spinning wheels.

M:576-577. Eleanor Ayton from Beal Ayton, recorded 28 March 1806, bill of sale for Negro man, Charles, age 25 years. If $270 paid by 1 March next, bill of sale void. Wit: John Adamson.

M:577-579. James Beall recorded power of attorney 29 March 1806, from Alexander E. Beall of Columbia County, Georgia, to sell and settle real estate from his father, James Beall of James for him, on Paint Creek, in Montgomery County, containing 200 acres.

M:579. Elizah Collins recorded schedule 31 March 1806, of estate debts and credits list includes 1 wire riddle, iron pot, woolen wheel, 2 old axes, 4 knives and forks, 5 old chairs, 3 old barrels, washing tub.

M:579-580. Edward Owen recorded manumission 31 March 1806 for Negro Priss 35 years old after the date hereof, 29 March 1806. Wit: Jono. Thomas 3d, John Fleming..

M:580-582. John Adamson recorded 31 March 1806, deed made 29 March from Edward Owen and Washington Owen for $2935 tract *Mount Arratt, Owens Lott, Addition to Owens Lot, Little Profit, Contentment, What you Please;* at forks of Rock Creek. Metes and bounds given for 293 ½ acres. Receipt, acknowledgment. Dower releases from Rachel Owen, wife of Edward and Ruth Owen wife of Washington Owen.

M:583-584. Nathan Suter recorded deed 31 March 1806, from James Suter for £21..3..4 part of *St. Mary's* and *Resurvey on St. Mary's,* beginning at 5th line of deed from Robert Peter to Michael Letton, containing 2 acres. Ruth Suter released dower rights.

M:584. Zadock Holland recorded bill of sale 1 April 1806. Nathan Pelly for $500 sells Negro boy George age 14 and woman "Finder" 50 years old. Witness B. Gaither.

M:585-586. John Nicholls son of John H. Nicholls, late of Prince George's County, recorded deed 1 April 1806, from Mary and Robert Edmonston, executrix and executor of the late Thomas Edmonston, deceased, tract called *Edmonston's Enclosure,* partly in Prince George's and partly in Montgomery Counties, at 32nd line of *Deer Park and Bear Garden Enlarged,* to 4th line of *Edmonston's Range,* to 4th line of *Addition to Deer Park* containing 211 3/4 acres. Signed before Gabriel VanHorn, and Geo Page.

M:586-588. Edward Owen recorded 2 April 1806, from John Adamson, for $497 ½, part of *Mt. Arrarat, Contentment, Little Profit,* 49 3/4 acres. Signed John Thomas 3d, John Flemming, Sarah Adamson released dower.

M:588-589. Thomas Pollard Jr. Recorded list of slaves 2 April 1806 imported into Maryland to wit: Moll 50, Nero 30, Beck 20 and Sarah 12.

M:589-590. William Holmes recorded bill of sale 2 April 1806 from Thomas Lazear Junr., for 1000 lbs of tobacco, sells two horses, one a flea-bitten grey about 14 years old, and one 3 year and one dark bay colt, 3 years old this spring, and four hogs.

M:590-591. Nathaniel Edwards Magruder recorded deed 4 April 1806, from Elizabeth Lowe, for $100, sells any right to tract called *Lowes Purchase*.

M:591-592. Robert Briggs recorded deed 4 April 1806, from Archibald Orme for £264, tract called *Paris*, containing 44 acres. Elizabeth wife of Archibald Orme released dower rights.

M:592-595. Joel Brown recorded deed 5 April 1807 from Adam King of Washington, D.C. part of *Owen's Resurvey*, adjacent to part conveyed by Samuel Crow to William Bernard, and part conveyed to John Owens. Containing 2 3/10 acres. Also part of a tract called *Philemon and Sarah*, adjacent to *Brooke Park*, and land to William Redman from William Bernard and *Merryman*, for 15 ½ acres, all rights belonging to the said Adam King assigned to the said Joel Brown. Receipt for $1500. Acknowledgment. Grace, wife of Adam King released dower.

M:595-597. Thomas Fletchall recorded deed 8 April 1806, from Joseph N. Chiswell for $300. Part of *Resurvey on Wolf's Cow* beginning at *Resurvey on Hanover*, containing 172 acres. Eleanor wife of Joseph N. Chiswell released dower

M:597-600. Thomas Fletchall and Joseph N. Chiswell, executors of Stephen N. Chiswell, recorded deed 8 April 1806, from Samuel Clapham of Loudon County, Virginia, to secure debt of £700 assigns tract called *Accord*, together with part of *Resurvey on Discord*, references boundary agreement in August 1788, between Isaac Hite, William Heugh, Leonard M. Deakins and Simon Nicholls.

M:601-602. Thomas Fletchall recorded deed 8 April 1806 from William Brewer for $480 for part of *Resurvey on Wolf's Cow*, to part formerly conveyed to James Hawkins for 50 acres; containing 60 acres. Mary Brewer released dower rights.

M:602-604. Lloyd Dorsey recorded deed 8 April 1806, from Obed Leeke, for $173. part of *Gittings Hah Hah*, *Leeks Venture*, and *Leek's Lot*, on road from Green's Bridge. Page 604 missing from microfilm, however it is on digital version. Elizabeth Leeke wife of Obed released dower. Witnesses John Thomas 3d, Richard Green.

M:604-606. George Hussey and John Fisher recorded deed 10 April 1806 from Robert Fisher for $900, *Pigman's Inheritance*, on NNE line of *Charley Forest*, 50 acres. Same land conveyed to Robert Fisher from George Hussey and John Fisher. Witness Owen Dorsey. Acknowledgment from Baltimore County of deed from Robert Fisher to George Hussey and John Fisher. Hannah Fisher acknowledged releasing right of dower.

M:606-607. Hezekiah Ward recorded deed 13 April 1806 from Jesse Hyatt for £7..10, sells two lots in Hyattstown, lot #46 and 47.

M:608-609. Basil Waters recorded deed 18 April 1806 John Adamson for $632 sells part of tract, *Clean Shaving*, containing 158 acres. Sarah Adamson released dower

M:609-611. Benjamin Craycraft recorded deed 19 April 1806 from John Adamson for $1607.50, tracts *Owen's Lot*, and part of *Addition to Owen's Lot*, to the 8th line of *Beckwith's Range*, bounding Rock Creek, containing 160 3/4 acres. Sarah Adamson released dower rights.

M:611-613. John Willson Jr. Recorded deed 23 April 1806, from Nicholas Rhodes for £105 sells part of *Resurvey on William's Chance*, on a line of *Plummer's Hunting Lot*, containing 34 acres, also part of *Labyrinth*, for 60 acres. signed before Greenberry Howard, M. Browning.

M:613-615. Thomas Cramphin recorded deed 24 April 1806 from Zachariah Offutt for £96 sells part of *Petersburgh*, beginning at end of 1st line of *Mother's Good Will*, to tract *Last Choice*, containing 13 3/4 acres exclusive of the main road running through. Eleanor Offutt released dower rights.

M:615-616. Lewis Tabler recorded deed 24 April 1806, from Jesse Hyatt, for £7..10, lot #107, in Hyattstown to pay annual rent of 5 shillings in January each year to Hyatt or heirs.

M:616-618. Lewis Tabler recorded deed 24 April 1806, from William Willson for $204, five lots in Hyattstown conveyed to him by Adam Ramsower, lots #51, 52, 53, 105 & 106. Sarah Willson released dower rights.

M:618-619. Charles Busey Jr., recorded deed 28 April 1806 from Jesse Hyatt for $16, sells two lots #36 and #90 in Hyattstown.

M:619-621. James M. Lingan recorded deed 30 April 1806 from Ozburn Trail, relating to legacies of his father James Trail to himself and to his brother Archibald Trail on tract *Trail's Addition*. Whereas Archibald Trail who inherited 23 acres of tract, surveyed for 50 acres, conveyed the same on 12 April 1800, and Ozburn Trail received the remainder, he now conveys all his right to tract, for $254.58.

M:621-622. Hezekiah Thomas recorded bill of sale 1 May 1806 from Daniel Smith for £51..16, a Negro boy, Basil about 14 years old.

M:622. William Alba recorded schedule 1 May 1806 as insolvent debtor lists one scythe and one cradle.

M:622-623. Commission to Justices of the Levy Court dated 5 May 1806, to Henry Brookes, Edward Burgess Jr., Richard West, Ozias Offutt, George Riley, Warren Magruder and Thomas West.

M:623-624. Isaac Lansdale recorded bill of sale 7 May 1806 from Zachariah Willson for $50, gelding, but if sum paid, mortgage is void.

M:624-627. Charles Henry Waring Wharton recorded deed 7 May 1806 from Edward Crow of Mercer County, Pennsylvania, for £587..15, part of tracts *Peckerton, Quince Orchard*, *Peace and Plenty* and part of *Resurvey on Younger Brother*, beginning at *Resurvey on Younger Brother*, at part conveyed by Joseph West to David Trail, to the 4th line of *Rose's Delight*, to part conveyed by Basil and Margaret Trail to Henry Brookes, to 1st line of *Peckerton*, surveyed by Thomas Pecker, to part of *Quince Orchard*, formerly conveyed to David Low by John Fleming, containing in all 226 acres.

M:627-628. Andrew Scholfield of Alexandria, recorded bill of sale 8 May 1806, from George Gue, Rezin Bowman, Allen Bowman and George Bowman. For £200; one black stud, one bay horse, one sorrel mare, one stud colt, eleven sheep, seven lambs, three cows, two heifers and other livestock and crops growing by grantees.

M:629-631. Henry Clarke Sr. Recorded deed 10 May 1806 From Thomas Rhodes for $291.25 part of tract called *Hard Struggle,* at the 6th line of Thomas Hewett's part. Containing 29 1/8 acres. Signed before Walter B. Beall, Thos Simpson. Polly Rhodes wife of Thomas released dower.

M:631-633. Henry Clark recorded deed 10 May 1806 from John Laird of Georgetown, for $200 all his interest in *Hills and Dales,* granted Jonathan Nixon Jr., 19 July 1787, beginning at *Fenwick,* to tract *Elizabeth's Delight,* containing 70 1/4 acres, as deeded from Jonathan Nixon to Thomas Dick, late of Bladensburgh, deceased, whose will was recorded in Prince George's County, and devised real estate to John Laird. Thomas Perry Willson of Montgomery County, served as attorney for conveyance.

M:633-635. Godshall Douglass recorded deed 12 May 1806 from Ozburn Trail for £1..17..3, for part of *Father's Good Will,* containing 94 acres. Frances, wife of Osborn Trail released dower.

M:635-637. Enoch George recorded deed of trust 12 May 1806 from Archibald Orme. Administrator of James Orme. Whereas James Orme, deceased of Washington, District of Columbia, died intestate in March 1802 leaving a considerable estate, and whereas Mrs. Octavia Smith, wife of William Smith, and sister of Archibald and James, is entitled to a distributive share of the estate; and whereas Henry Woodward of Ann Arundel County, by reason of his marriage with Mary White, and Thomas Hodges of Prince George's County, by reason of his marriage with Elizabeth White, daughters and co-heirs of Elizabeth a sister of James Orme; conveys tract *Paris,* adjacent to *Resurvey on Boylestone's Discovery,* containing 179 ½ acres. , with the agreement of the co-heirs, for the use and benefit of said Archibald Orme and his wife, during their life, and afterwards, to be sold, and from the proceeds £300 with interest to be paid to Mrs. Octavia Smith or her heirs; and £250 plus interest each, to Mary Woodward and Elizabeth Hodges or their heirs.

M:637-639. James B. Higgins recorded deed 13 May 1806, from Elemelech Swearingen and Richard Watts. Whereas Richard Allison, on 15 June 1796, sold 2 ½ acres of *Resurvey on St. Mary's* to Elemelech Swearingen, and the balance of *St. Mary's* was sold to Richard Watts, as 110 acres, this deed sells part of tract to James B. Higgins.

M:639-643. Honore Martin recorded deed 13 May 1806, from John Suter and Sarah Suter of Georgetown, District of Columbia, administrators of the estate of John Suter Sr., deceased, sells part of tract *Earn Hill,* at *Wickham's Good Will,* and granted to James Plummer for 270 acres, metes and bounds for 22 ½ acres.

M:643-644. Benjamin Ray Jr., bill of sale 15 May 1806 from Thos Pitt Hays and Elizabeth Hays his wife for £100 sells Negro man, Moses, a blacksmith by trade aged about 37 years; Sam, about 40 years; one woman, Lott, aged 27 years; and her two children, about 18 months, and 2 years old.

M:644-647. Andrew Offutt recorded deed 16 May 1806 from Zachariah Offutt, for $5., part of a tract, called *Petersburgh,* beginning at 34th line of part conveyed to Basil Offutt, where tract intersects the main road leading from the Mouth of Monocacy, to 12th line of *Resurvey of William and Ann,* containing 371 45/100 acres. Eleanor Offutt released dower rights.

M:647-648. John Garrett recorded deed 19 May 1806, from Gerard Brooke for £80 sells lot #18 in Brookeville. Signed and acknowledged.

M:648-649. Basil Offutt recorded bill of sale 29 May 1806 from Dorothea Hawkins, for 5 shillings, the three following Negroes: Sal 26, Mariah 8, and Frank about 3 years old.

M:649-650. Richard Berry recorded deed 30 May 1806 from Samuel Brooke, trustee for sale of real estate of Peter Casanave, deceased, for $62, *Berry's Neglect,* beginning at *The Charles and Benjamin,* to *Shepherd's Hard Fortune,* containing 10 acres. Signed before Richard Green, John Burgess.

M:650-651. Michael Letton recorded deed 31 May 1806, from Nathan Suter for $16.00 part of tract called *The Resurvey on Saint Mary's,* beginning at end of 5th line of part sold by Robert Peter to Michael Letton, and part of *Oatry,* containing 1 acre and 107 sq. perches. Signed and acknowledged.

M:651-653. Kinsey Gittings recorded deed 2 June 1806, from Jane Ober for $950. Two tracts of land. *Drane's Final Conclusion,* beginning at 2nd line of *Outlet,* for 6 acres, also *Drane's Luck,* conveyed by Anthony Reintzel to Jane Ober for 10 acres more or less.

M:653-654. Thomas Linstead recorded bill of sale 2 June 1806 from Christopher Cool for $50. Housewares and furniture, one milch cow and 3 hogs.

M:654-655. William Warren King recorded deed 2 June 1806, from Arnold Warfield for $450 parcel in Clarksburg, part of lot #9 and #10. Containing 6357 sq.ft. Margaret, wife of Arnold Warfield released dower.

M:656. James Rawlings and Richard Rawlings executors of James Rawlings deceased, recorded Bill of sale 3 June 1806, from Charles Soper for $129. 50 owed to them assigns gelding, other horses and livestock. Sale void if sum paid with interest.

M:656-659. James Maccubbin Lingan recorded deed 3 June 1806 from Ninian Benson, Allen Simpson and Sarah Simpson his wife, and William Benson. Whereas William Benson, deceased father of Ninian, Sarah and William made bond to Philip Hocker for conveyance of *Gray's Discovery*, 60 ½ acres, and 40 acre part of *New Holland,* adjacent to *Addition to Trail's Choice,* sells tract. Signed by all parties. Sarah wife of William Benson, and Sarah Simpson released dower rights.

M:659-660. Nathan Soper of Zadock recorded bill of sale 3 June 1806 from Basil Soper of John, Negro man called Wall about 35 years old; Negro man Tom, 25 or 26 years; Negro woman Kitty, 23 years old; Negro boy Hanson about 18 months, son of Kitty; and Negro girl Nelly about 15 years old; wagon, several horses and other livestock, provided nonetheless that if sum owing is paid, bill of sale is void.

M:661-662. Richard Key Watts recorded deed 4 June 1806 from Philip B. Key for $5 conveys right to part of *Bradford's Rest,* lot #22 called Anthony Willcoxon's lot, sold by his heir and son Thomas H. Wilcoxon to Richard K. Watts for 71 3/4 acres.

M:662-663. Richard K. Watts recorded deed 4 June 1806 from Richard Allison for $1320, part of *Resurvey on Saint Mary's,* beginning at tract called the mill land. Sarah Allison released dower rights.

M:664-665. Jesse Willcoxon recorded deed from 4 June 1806 Benjamin Pelly and Ann Pelly his wife of Montgomery County, for $250, piece of land formerly conveyed by William Diggs to Samuel Green, to 4th line of part conveyed by Joseph Wheat to Thomas Birdwhistle, to north side of road to Zachariah Maccubin's mill, devised by Thomas Birdwhistle to Ann Pelly and her heirs; *Resurvey on Friend in Need*, adjacent to tract called *Italy* containing 50 acres,

M:665-667. William Hickman of Arthur recorded deed 10 June 1806 from Elizabeth Hickman for $1000. Land division of William Hickman of Stephen. Lot #3 of part of *Cider and Ginger*, 50 acres.

M:667-669. Archibald Mason recorded deed 11 June 1806, from Charles Rogers, John Warfield and Ann his wife, Deal Dorsey and Mary his wife; Mordecai Ijams and Catherine his wife, for £30, tract *John and Joan's Choice,* adjacent to tract sold from John Rogers to Richard Estep, containing 80 acres.

M:669. Charlotte Frazier recorded bill of sale recorded 16 June 1806 from Thomas Pitt Hays for 5 shillings, for the benefit of her mother, Elizabeth Hays, one mare, one brown cow, other items listed.

M:670-672. Elizabeth Hays recorded deed 16 June 1806 from John Snowden of Ann Arundel County. Whereas John Snowden or about 23 June 1764 did sell to Jeremiah Ducker, a part of a parcel then in Frederick County, a part of *Snowden's Manor* containing 1000 acres, and whereas said Jeremiah Ducker died intestate without paying the full amount of said deed, and the court directed the division of the said land among Jeremiah Ducker's four children, Jeremiah Ducker, Henry Ducker, Elizabeth Hays and Ann Ducker; and Elizabeth Hays was appointed executor de bonis nom of Jeremiah Ducker, but cannot divide land because of lack of clear deed of title, she paid $200 to John Snowden the balance due on deed, and receives title.

M:672-673. Verlinda Beatty, widow of Col. Charles Beatty late of Georgetown, deceased, recorded deed 16 June 1806, from Joseph Clements of the State of Virginia. Whereas Francis Clements late of Montgomery County devised to his sons Joseph Clements and Jacob Clements and his widow Elizabeth, part of tract *Brother's Industry,* which he sold for $1200 to Charles Beatty, before his death. Heirs of Charles Beatty, have already made deed to Verlinda Beatty for their interest in property. Deed made.

M:674. David Clagett recorded deed of gift 18 June 1806, from Ann Clagett for and in consideration of natural love and affection for her son, and for his better maintenance and support assigns one Negro girl called Tabitha about 11 years old.

M:674. John Orme recorded list of Negroes, 21 June 1806, imported into the State of Maryland. Negro Hector 23, Sarah 22, Stephney 12. Acquired by marriage with Sarah McAllister of York County, Pennsylvania, which descended to her from the death of her brother Richard McAllister, late of the state of Georgia.

M:675-677. Richard Ricketts recorded deed 21 June 1806, from Edward Crow of Mercer County, Pennsylvania. For £553..4, sells part of *Peace and Plenty,* and part of *Peckerton,* surveyed for

Thomas Pecker, beginning at *Rose's Delight,* metes and bounds for 134 2/10 acres, also part of *Peckerton,* containing 1 4/10 acres.

M:677-680. Richard Montgomery Boyer recorded deed 21 June 1806 from Adam King of Washington, D.C. for $3000 sells parcels, part of the *Land of Goshen,* and part of *Pigman's Purchase,* beginning at a tract called *Very Good* surveyed for Mathias Pigman, 1750; and part of *Pigman's Purchase,* and part of other tracts as conveyed to Williams Fipps for 66 1/4 acres; to tne of 52ⁿᵈ line of the mill seat as laid out for Edward Crow for 150 acres; then with the line of said mill seat reversed, the 23 following courses, containing 513 3/4 acres. Signed and acknowledged. Grace King released dower.

M:680. Beal Ayton recorded bond to State of Maryland as constable on 21 June 1806 with Robert Swailes and Nathaniel Beall.

M:681-682. John Willson Junr. recorded deed 24 June 1806, from Leaven Wilson for $700 part of *Labyrinth,* and *Resurvey on None Left,* beginning at a line of tract *Happy Choice,* to *Wilson's Discovery,* to *Mackey's Chance,* to 151 acres laid off for Hugh Jones, of which this is a part containing 101 acres. Signed before Laurence O'Neale, G. W. Harwood.

M:682-683. Thomas Beall of George recorded deed 24 June 1806, from Benjamin Ray Jr., Sheriff, for property acquired by writ of fi fa issued against Archibald Orme, a part of tract called *Paris,* on which said Orme now lives, containing 96 acres, for high bid of £248..15..9.

M:684-685. James Desellum recorded deed from William Fulks, Thomas Rawlins, Elizabeth Rawlings, Jacob Swamley, Eleanor Swamley and Mary Fulks, for sum (left blank in recording) current money, sell all their interest in two lots in Clarksburg, parts of lots #9 and #10, as devised by Gerard Briscoe of Virginia to Baltis Fouts, 18 March 1789, being part of *Robert's Delight,* containing one acre.

M:685-686. Zachariah Walker and Benjamin F. Mackall recorded certificate of qualification as Deputy Clerks, 30 June 1806.

M:686. John Bonifant recorded constable's bond 1 July 1806 with Edward Berry, Robert Lazenby and James Lazenby.

M:686. Evan Belt recorded constable's bond 2 July 1806 with Henry Cooley.

M:687. Thomas McBee recorded schedule as insolvent debtor 7 July 1806, listing crops of wheat and corn growing, and debts: Thomas C. Nicholls, $4. Signed by mark.

M:687. Zachariah Halsey recorded bill of sale 7 July 1806 from Mary Downs, in consideration of the love and affection that she has for her three grandchildren, she grants to them Zachariah, Mary and Stacy, six Negro slaves: to grandson Zachariah Halsey, to have Charles and Mahala, and also Theresa for term of 5 years, then she is to be free; to grand daughter Mary, to have Melinda, and after my death to have Kitty; to granddaughter Stacy, shw is to have Matilda and Maria. Whereas Theresa has always behaved well and is the mother of the other slaves, she is to have her freedom in five years from this date. Signed by mark before Wm Culver, Lancelot Griffin.

M:688-689. These two pages on the digital site from the Maryland State Archives, seems to start in the middle of a deed [see pg 327]. No page numbers are discernable, and edges are ragged and not complete. They are missing from microfilm copy of deed book. Pages begin with mention of tracts to be sold, *Evans Chance,* 171 acres, also *Hopson's Choice,* [? 75 acres] and *Evan's Lookout,* 20 acres. from Ellener Hopkins, wife of John Hopkins, deceased, John Hopkins and Barbara His wife, Alexander Hopkins and Rosanna his wife, Thomas Hopkins and James Hopkings, to the said George Beall, appoint James S. Morsell and John M. Gantt of Georgetown, Montgomery County, Maryland, their attorney, to make deed. Signed and dower releases made in Washington County, Pennsylvania.

M:688-690. According to index, deed begins on page 688: Charles Welsh recorded deed from George Ellicott and wife. Pg. 690: George Ellicott and Elizabeth Elicott signed deed before Andrew Ellicott and John Ellicott.

M:691. Rachel Cooke, administrator of Nathan Cooke, recorded bill of sale 22 July 1806, from Zadok Ricketts, for £81..3..2, one Negro slave named Jack, about 20 years old; that in case he pay sum by 20 July 1809 then bill of sale is void.

M:691-694. John Figg recorded deed 23 July 1806 from Benjamin Ray, Jr., sheriff. Whereas in a case of Richard P. Richardson for the use of Richard Richardson, against Joshua Dorsey, late of Montgomery County, a writ of fieri facias was issued against his property, including two lots in Hyattstown, which were sold at public sale and John Figg was high bidder.

M:694-695. Thomas Moore recorded deed 24 July 1806 from Caleb Bentley for $23.75 sells part of *Addition to Brooke Grove,* a moiety of lot beginning at south corner of David Newlin's mill lot, containing 2 acres and 19 perches.

M:695-696. Barton Soper recorded bill of sale from 25 July 1806 Charles Soper, for $60, sells 3 sows, 20 shoats, two feather beds and furniture, and other kitchenware and furniture enumerated.

M:696-697. Thomas Green recorded deed 26 July 1806, from Solomon Davis for $894, part of tract *Elizabeth,* containing 111 3/4 acres. Mary Davis released dower rights.

M:698-699. William Layman recorded deed 26 July 1806, from Richard Thomas and Deborah Thomas for $40, lots #53 and #54 in town of Brookeville.

M:699-700. Abijah Taylor recorded deed 26 July 1806, from Caleb Pancoast for $50, lot #16 in Brookeville. Mary Pancoast released dower.

END OF LIBER M

Montgomery County Liber N, Land Record

N:1.   Bond for $200, of Charles C. Jones with Edward Burgess, 28 July 1806, bond for keeping in good repair the bridge whereon said Jones contracted with the commissioners Zadock Willson and Daniel Lee for building for £90 on Rock Creek near said Jones' mill.

N:1.   Constables Bond of Benjamin Hoves recorded 29 July 1806 with Nathan Musgrove and Henry Counselman.

N:1-2.   For natural love and affection, which I have for my son Daniel Allnutt, assigns all eight Negroes: Ruth, Harry, Tom, Jude, John, Tilman, Eve and Luce, seven cows, 4 calves, 13 sheep, two horses. August 1806. Signed Jean Alnutt by mark. Wit: Laurence O'Neal, Wm. Darne, Jr.

N:2-5. Peter Gardner recorded deed 2 August 1806, made 21 June from Gerard T. Hopkins of Baltimore County, merchant, and Dorothy his wife, for $3000, part of several tracts, *Addition to Brooke Grove, Fair Hill, Resurvey on Brooke Park,* and *Sure Bind, Sure Find,* metes and bounds given for 255 acres, the same tract conveyed to Dorothy Brooke as her share of the estate of her uncle Thomas Brooke's land, as recorded in Liber F:66-68.

N:5-6. Adam Robb recorded bill of sale 11 August 1806 from Thomas Waring for sorrel horse, grey mare, furniture. Wit: John Fleming, John Bowers.

N:6-8. Levi Hayes and Eleanor, his wife and daughter of Joseph Harris, recorded deed 12 August 1806 from Jesse Harris, administrator of his father Joseph Harris, who had on 24 August 1786 surveyed *Mount Zion,* for 1217 acres which was unpatented. This deed is to correct an earlier deed to provide her share of estate, metes and bounds adjacent to 10th line of *Beall's Good Will,* to waters of the mill dam formerly the property of Thomas Morton, containing 75 3/8 acres.

N:8-9. Nathaniel Clagett recorded deed 13 August 1806 from Jacob Bowman for £250 tract *Hygham* 103 acres and also tract taken up by James Brooke, the elder, beginning at *Joseph and Margaret's Rest,* on line of Thomas Pleasant's mill seat, 59 ½ acres. Signed before John Burgess, John Belt.

N:9-10. William Hempstone recorded 11 August 1806, bill of sale. I Sango Rice for $100 sells one bay horse, crop of corn, 18 bushels of wheat, 10 hogs, 2 iron pots, other personal property.

N:10-13. Dorothy Hopkins recorded mortgage 14 August 1806 from Peter Gardner for $2000 same tracts in deed above, metes and bounds included mention of James Thompson's spring, 255 acres. Payments scheduled through 1816 $200 on 1st of January with interest. Signed by mark.

N:13-14. Aeneas Campbell, the high bidder, recorded deed 15 August 1806, from Solomon Davis executor of Solomon Simpson. Tracts *Elizabeth,* 111 3/8 acres, and second tract of 57 acres.

N:15-16. Solomon Davis recorded deed 15 August 1806 from Aeneas Campbell for $976. Two tracts sold in preceding deed. Henrietta Campbell released dower rights.

N:16-17. Henry Culver, recorded bill of sale 18 August 1806 from Edward Browning (signed by mark), for feather beds and furniture.

N:17. James Willson recorded 19 August 1806, list of Negroes imported to Maryland. Willson was formerly a resident of Jefferson County, Kentucky. Negroes Barbara 48, Luce 12, Phillis 12 and Sam 9 years old. Girl Phillis was a gift from my father to my son Wadsworth, now a minor; other two born of my property.

N:17-18. Road plat recorded 19 August 1806. Change in road moved to east side of Captain John's meeting house. New road 153 perches, old road 150 perches.

N:18. Robert Swailes recorded bill of sale 19 August 1806 from James W. Ward for $70.50 amount Swailes is bound to pay James H. & Richard Rawlings for Wards use, for property purchased 26 November 1804: one grey gelding 12 years old, one pied cow 9 years; one other cow and bull calf. Wit. John Adamson, Beal Ayton.

N:18-20. Benjamin Davis recorded 30 August 1806 from John Hobbs and Charlotte his wife and Elizabeth Hobbs mother of the said Charlotte for £843..15, part of *Wolf Den,* and *Snowdens Manor Enlarged,* deed by the Snowden's to Benjamin Joseph Perry for 70 acres, adjacent to Samuel Bonnifant's part of *Wolf Den,* to the given line of *Beall's Reserve,* now laid out for 375 acres..

N:20-21. Aquila Gatton recorded deed 1 September 1806 from George Riley for £100 all his right to *Wickham's Chance,* formerly the property of Colbert Pelly, 21 2/3 acres, which he purchased of Richard Thompson and Elizabeth Thompson his wife. Sarah Riley, wife of George released dower rights.

N:21-22. John Trigg recorded deed 3 September 1806 from Joshua Inman of Frederick County for $21 lots #14 and #68 in Hyattstown.

N:22-24. Richard Wooton recorded deed 8 September 1806 from John Baptist Medley for £43 part of *Resurvey on Disappointment,* 4 5/8 acres.

N:24. Bond for Benjamin Ray Junior, made 11 September 1806, with Henry O'Neale, Nathaniel Beall and William Benson, that he will pay to the levy court several sums which he shall receive.

N:24-25. William Candler recorded deed 12 September 1806 from Benjamin Ray sheriff, by judgment obtained for writ of fieri facias for Adam Robb against Thomas Orme, sells tract *Saplin Ridge.* 21 ½ acres to high bidder. Signed before John Flemming, Samuel Elgar.

N:26-27. William Candler recorded 12 September 1806 from Thomas Magruder Claggett for £422..14, sells *Owen's Conclusion,* adjacent to *Pleasant Plains of Damascus,* containing 167 acres. Martha Clagett released dower.

N:27-28 Ignatius West recorded bill of sale 13 September 1806. Whereas a bill of sale made 1 Feb.1805 for £75..14..3 from Thomas Linsted and Solomon Holland, for Negro man Frank, 28 years old, has been redeemed, this releases bill of sale as paid in full. Wit. Samuel Elgar.

N:28-30. William Kelly recorded deed 20 September 1806, from Richard Berry for $630, tract, *Shepherd's Hard Fortune,* a resurvey for Edward Owen in 1745, containing 31 ½ acres. Sarah Berry released dower rights.

N:30-31. Richard Beall recorded 26 September 1806 from John Gartrell and Lucretia Gartrell his wife for $65, assigns 13 5/8 acres, part of *Snowden's Mill Land,* which descended from Lawson Beall to his daughter, Lucretia. Witnesses Richard Green, Allen Green.

N:31-32. John Fleming recorded bill of sale 6 Oct. 1806, for £750 Negro man Joe 21 years, boy Harry 15 years; Patrick 12, Vachel 11, Will 7, woman Henny 30 and her child; women Lydia 40 and her child; Nann 55 years and Jenny 57 years old. Signed Edward Burgess Sr., before Edward Burgess Jr.

N:32-33. John Fleming recorded deed 6 October 1806 from Basil Musgrove Beall for $840, part of tract called *Prevention,* otherwise called *Welshman's Purchase,* sold by James Perry and William Williams, son of Thomas, to Jacob Barnes, for 84 acres.

N:33-35. Thomas Morton of Ann Arundel County recorded 7 October 1806 from Christian Hempstone for £56..5 tract *Resurvey on Trouble,* 25 acres. Dorcas wife of Christian Hempstone, released dower.

N:35-36. Thomas Morton recorded 7 October 1806 from Zephaniah Plummer and Charity Plummer his wife for £59..5 part of tract called *Resurvey on Trouble for Nothing,* containing 26 acres. Acknowledged before Greenberry Howard, Edward Burgess, Jr.

N:36-38. Henry Griffith Junr. recorded deed 8 October 1806 from Basil Brooke for $1141.33 land devised to him by his father, part of several tracts, *Addition to Brooke Grove, Resurvey on Brooke Park, Fair Hill,* and *Crow's Content,* for 107 acres. Mary, wife of Basil Brooke released dower.

N:38. Richard Lyles recorded bill of sale 8 October 1806 from Joseph Hall, for $25 one red cow, two feather beds and furniture, 4 iron pots, 2 fish barrels, some old pewter dishes, etc.

N:38-40. William Joy of Loudoun Co., Virginia, recorded 8 October 1806, from William Norris of George, for $1425. *Hopewell* and part of a tract of land called *Father's Gift,* and part of a tract called *That's It Resurveyed,* metes and bounds, courses given for 178 acres. Signed before Richard Beall, G.W. Howard. Receipt. Acknowledgment. Mary Norris, wife of said William released dower rights.

N:41. Edward Willett, recorded certificate as deputy sheriff 14 Oct 1806, at request of Benjamin Ray Junior.

N:41-43. Rebecka Magruder et.al., representatives of Ninian Magruder recorded 10 October 1806, from Ariana French, executrix of George French, deceased, late of Georgetown, District of Columbia. To Elizabeth Perry, Rebecca Perry, Rachel Magruder and Mary Ann Magruder of Montgomery County, who are the heirs and representatives of Ninian Magruder. The said Magruder not having fully paid the conveyance price, and in consequence thereof Eleanor Magruder relict and executrix of the said Ninian Magruder deceased has since fully paid the said Ariana French the balance due, now the said Ariana French, in consideration of the sum of $1450, sells tracts in common as joint tenants, part of *Friendship Resurveyed,* for Zachariah Magruder, containing 145 and 6/10 acres. Signed by Ariana French before Joel Brown, Robert P. Magruder. Receipt. Acknowledgment. Ariana French appoints Upton Beall as her attorney to make full acknowledgment according to the laws of Maryland.

N:43-44. Manumissions recorded 18 Oct. 1806 from John Thomas 3rd: Joseph Briscoe[2], aged 38 years and able to work, and for David age 11 years old to be free 1 January 1820. Wit: Philip B. Key, William Culver.

N:44-45. Joshua Johnson recorded 18 October 1806 from Thomas Morton, lately of Montgomery County, but now of Ann Arundel County, to perfect agreement lately made for £2000, sells one undivided moiety in grist and saw mills lately occupied by Thomas Morton and Ignatius Davis, now in possession of Joshua Johnson. Also land conveyed by Lenox Martin and by Barton Harris. 11 April 1801. Wit: Lawrence Owen, G. W. Harwood.

N:45-47. William Clagett recorded deed 20 October 1806 from Benjamin Ray Jr., sheriff, writ of fi fa of Adam Robb recovered against Thomas Orme, for tract *Neglect,* 6 ½ acres. Clagett was high bidder at $9.60.

N:47-50. Henry Brooke of Prince George's County, recorded 20 October 1806, from Thomas Howard, tract called *Transylvania,* and also part of *The Pleasant Plains of Damascus,* and part of *Resurvey on Green Spring,* Eleanor Howard released dower.

N:50. John L. Trundle recorded 24 Oct. 1806 on 15 August 1806 I removed into the state of Maryland from the State of Kentucky and at that time I brought with me the following slaves, Sarah aged about 36 years, Coleman aged about 24 years and Harry aged 21, Eve aged 9 years and Jane 8 years, Margaret 6 years and John aged 3 years, which were my slaves in the former state of Kentucky.

N:50-51. Daniel Schley recorded schedule as insolvent debtor 6 October 1806. Debts from John Brown, Thomas Garrett, John Gray, Aquilla Pearce, James Welsh, Mr. Layton, Jonas Pasley, Francis Johnson, Basil D. Beall, William Garrett, Elizabeth Crabb, Daniel Renner. Signed before John Fleming, Samuel Elgar.

N:51-53. Lawson Clarke recorded 6 October 1806 from Zebedee Beall of Montgomery County, as attorney for Patrick Carten and Dorothy Brook his wife, Joshua Broten and Betsy Eddy his wife and Notley Brooke Beall of the State of Georgia, in reference to deed in Liber M:104-105. Part of *White Oak Valley,* adjacent to Thomas Simpson's part of said tract containing 93 5/8 acres.

N:53. Manumission from William Norris recorded 31 October 1806, for Bob age 28 years, and Rachel age 22 years old. Signed 22 October 1806, before M. Browning, Charles G. Linthicum.

---

[2]Joseph Briscoe and Charlotte Briscoe, no ages given are found on the 1832 Free Negro Census for Maryland.

N:53-54. Samuel Robertson 3rd, recorded receipt for £500..14..6 in full of a mortgage dated 16 November 1799 to John Clark, dec'd, from Edward Crow. Wit: Samuel Waters, Wm Willson executor of John Clark, deceased.

N:54. William T. Mason recorded commission 3 November 1806 as constable.

N:54-58. William Norris of George recorded mortgage 3 November 1806 from William Joy of Loudoun County, Virginia, for sum of $1424. To pay with legal interest. Same as tract above.

N:58. Manumission for Nace from Philemon Plummer recorded 4 November 1806, released from bondage my Negro man named Ignatius aged about 35 years to be free at the expiration of six years from the date hereof. Signed 22 October 1806 in the presence of Richard Green, Amelia Green.

N:58-59. Samuel Thomas recorded Bill of sale from Samuel Moore, for $162. Negro girl named Nell to be free at the age of 18 years; livestock and household furnishings. Signed before Jno Thomas 3rd, Israel Leeke.

N:59-60. Bennet Clements recorded constables bond 3 November 1806 with Thomas Brown and William Candler

N:60-61. John Walker of Francis recorded bill of sale 5 November 1806, Elisha Walker for $80 crop of corn and tobacco. Signed by mark.

N:61-62. Edward Ward recorded deed, 5 November 1806 from William Cecill, for £24..15..10, part of tract, *Wild Cat Spring* containing 31 3/4 acres.. Signed by mark.

N:63-64. Edward Ward recorded deed 5 November 1806 from William Cecill, for $318. deed, land called *Chance,* adjacent to *Ward's Inheritance.* Signed by William Cecill by mark.

N:64-66. John Duvall recorded deed 7 November 1806, from Thomas Perry for $369..7.., part of several tracts, *Hope Improved, Resurvey on Rays Adventure, Trouble Enough,* adjacent to *Resurvey on Point Lookout,* conveyed by Hannah and Francis Perry to Zachariah Thompson for 8 acres, and to deed formerly conveyed by James Perry to William Gartrell for 125 acres, to the 1st line of *Hope Improved,* then to lines of *Bristol,* containing 129 1/4 acres. Signed by mark.

N:66-67. Thomas Peter of Washington County, District of Columbia, recorded 8 May 1806, from John Ward for $391.66 sells lands, part of *Bealls Design and Wards Chance,* No dower release.

N:67-69 Thomas Peter from Ann Ward, for $391.66 bargains and releases her undivided fourth part of *Bells Design and Wards Chance.* Signed by mark before Wm Darne, Jr., Wm Smith.

N:69-71. Thomas Peter recorded 7 November 1806, from Thomas Beall of George, tract *Seneca Ford,* containing 33 24/100 acres. Nancy, wife of Thomas Beall, released dower.

N:71-72. Hannah Chanai recorded bill of sale 8 November 1806, from John Riley, for $100. 110 tanned hides.

N:72-73. Francis Jamison recorded deposition 11 November 1806. To William Owens deposeth that in the month of November 1803 he was employed by Thomas O'Drane to go with him to Lancaster Jaol to bring home a Negro man named Charles which he had purchased of said Jamison.

He appeared in good health when he took him of Lancaster, and brought him home. He was in the habit of seeing Mr. Drane often, and had no complaint of Charles lack of health until Charles was taken ill which was in the month of June following. Contention regarding value of slave. Sworn to Richard Beall.

N:73-74. Leven Warfield recorded deed 11 November 1806, from Daniel Ballinger of Frederick County, for $600 tract called *Resolution,* containing 107 acres. . Signed before Joab Waters and Henry McElfresh, Justices of the Peace for Frederick county, attested to before Wm Ritchie Clerk of Frederick County Court.

N:74-75. James Simpson recorded power of attorney 12 November 1806. James Simpson Sr. Of Gallatin County, Kentucky appoints his son, his lawful attorney Allen Simpson witnessed.

N:75-78. William Baker recorded deed 12 November 1806 from Richard Jones (of Joseph). Lot of land, a part of *Beall Christie* and a part of *New Purchase*, the very same lot on which Adam B. Freeman and his wife Mary have lived since 1801 until the current year, beginning at a stone on the old road, a drive of Robert Jones' land. Richard Jones appoints as attorneys Henry Culver and Josiah Jones of Prince George's County. Signed by Richard Jones and Susannah Jones before John Sheckell, James B. Mower. Attestation from the State of New York, Ontario County.

N:78-79. Richard Wootton recorded deed 12 November 1806 from Solomon Davis for £5, part of *Resurvey on Disappointment*. Signed before John Fleming, G. W. Howard

N:79-80. Solomon Davis recorded deed 12 November 1806 from Richard Wootton for £5..6, part of *Resurvey on Disappointment,* containing 1 1/4 acres. Signed and acknowledged.

N:80-81. Bond recorded 14 November 1806 for John Fleming as Sheriff of Montgomery County presented by Benjamin Ray Jr., Henry O'Neel, Nathaniel Beall, William Benson, James Magruder, Van Swearingen, Benjamin Grayson Orr and Robert A. Whitaker.

N:81-84. Lewis Beall recorded lease 17 November 1806 between William O'Neale and Sarah O'Neale his wife. Benjamin Adams by his will recorded in Frederick County in 1764, devised to his wife Sarah Adams, now Sarah O'Neale land lying on north side of road commonly known as Falls Road, for term of her natural life, land a part of *Exchange and New Exchange*, for rents herein lease to Lewis Beall for the life of said Sarah, to pay £55 per year and not destroy property. Signed by all parties.

N:85-87. William O'Neale Jr. Recorded deed from William O'Neale for part of *Exchange and New Exchange,* adjacent to tracts called *Pig Pen* and *Partnership*, containing 98 acres, including part of a tract called *Sandusky*. Signed before William Smith, Richard West. Sarah, wife of William O'Neale released dower rights.

N:87-89. Armistead Long recorded deed 19 November 1806 from Isaac Hite of Frederick County, Virginia. Part of *Black Walnut Tree Island*. Signed before G. W. Harwood, Richard Beall. Receipt for $3300. Acknowledged.

N:89-91. Joshua Shelton recorded deed 19 November 1806, from Isaac Hite of Frederick County, Virginia for $6800. Tract called *Concord*, on bank of Potomac River, adjacent to *Resurvey on*

Discord, as laid out and to be conveyed to Leonard A. Deakins. Signed before same witnesses. Receipt. Acknowledgment.

N:92. Jacob and Richard Bowman recorded bill of sale 20 November 1806 from George Bowman for $3000. Livestock described, furniture, crop of tobacco in the house and all household and plantation utensils. Signed by mark before Ed Burgess Junr.

N:92-93. Edward Willett recorded certificate of qualification as Deputy Sheriff, 24 Nov. 1806.

N:93. Henry Lodge recorded certificate of qualification as Deputy Sheriff, 24 November 1806.

N:93-96. Jacob Bowman recorded deed 20 November 1806 from Gerard T. Hopkins, of Baltimore County, and Dorothy his wife, for $5040, daughter and heir of Roger Brooke, deceased, late of Montgomery County, her part of four separate tracts of lands, *Addition to Brooke Grove, Resurvey on Brooke Park, Fair Hill and Long Chance,* laid off for Roger Brooke by the division of his father's lands (for 931 acres). Metes and bounds given to division line of Margaret Brooke's part of tracts, containing 420 acres. Signed, acknowledged and dower released.

N:96-99. John B. Dyson recorded deed 26 November 1806 from Edward Brashear and Ann his wife of Bullett County, Kentucky, for £58..10 all their right, title or interest in tracts *Resurvey on Non Eaten,* supposed to contain 21 acres, and *Thomas's Discovery,* as descended from Samuel Dyson, late of Montgomery County deceased. Signed by marks.

N:99-102. John B. Dyson recorded deed 26 November 1806 from Samuel Bird and Sarah Bird, both of Bullett County, Kentucky for £58..10 all their right, title or interest in tracts *Resurvey on Non Eaten,* and *Thomas's Discovery,* as descended from Samuel Dyson, late of Montgomery County deceased. Both signed by mark and clerk recorded as Samuel Beard and Sara Beard.

N:102-103. John B. Dyson recorded deposition November 1806. Whereas George Dyson late of Charles County deceased bequeath to his two sons Samuel and Basil Dyson, a tract called *Resurvey on Non Eaton,* 150 acres. Division not found, so depositions taken of Edward Veirs and Hezekiah Veirs, agreeing on the division line.

N:103. James Trail recorded list of Negroes, removed from the state of Kentucky into Maryland, Kitt, a black woman 36 or 37 years; Lyd a black woman 25 years and Ben a black man, aged 21 years. November 26, 1806.

N:104. Henry Lansdale recorded certificate of qualification as Deputy Sheriff 27 November 1806..

N:104. Philip Cornell recorded certificate of qualification as Deputy Sheriff 28 November 1806.

N:104-105. Archibald and Richard Orme recorded bill of sale 28 November 1806 from John Orme for large bay horse and dark brown horse, white horse and black horse, seven horn cattle, 10 head of hogs, one elegant clock, mahogany clock case, mahogany desk and two dining tables, 7 leather bottomed walnut chairs.

N:105. Stephen Adams recorded certificate 5 December 1806, as Deputy Sheriff.

N:105. Basil M. Beall and Benjamin Ray Junior recorded certificate 5 December 1806, for both as deputy sheriffs.

N:105-107. Joshua Johnson recorded deed 11 December 1806 from Ignatius Davis of Frederick County for £1000 sells one undivided moiety of the grist and saw mill in Montgomery County lately occupied by the said Ignatius Davis and Thomas Morton and now in the occupation of the said Joshua Johnson. Signed and acknowledged.

N:107-108. Nathan Thompson recorded 11 December 1806, from John Belt for £254..12..9 sells parcel, a part of *Three Brothers,* beginning at *Pleasant Plains,* containing 96 5/8 acres. Signed before G. Howard, M. Browning.

N:108-109. Margaret Anderson recorded 15 December 1806 from Richard Thomas Jr. And Deborah Thomas of Montgomery County for $2080, lot #52 in town of Brookeville. Signed, acknowledged before Richard Green, Jno Thomas 3d.

N:110. Van Swearingen and William Prather, recorded bill of sale 18 December 1806, from Walter W. Summers for household furniture, one saddle, two bridles, one gun, powder horn, shot bag, 2 brass candlesticks, for $400 if paid then this is void. Signed in presence of Samuel Elgar.

N:111-112. Washington Bowie and Benjamin Hersey recorded deed 16 December 1806, from Thomas Beall of George, assign the *Millford Mills* near the mouth of Great Seneca, and all the lands and houses belonging to said mills, bounded by the lands of Richard Thomas Esq., John Threlkeld and Thomas Peter Esq., reference to a deed from William Deakins Jr. And Bernard O'Neale, 27 January 1796. Nancy wife of said Beall released dower rights.

N:112-116. Thomas Howard recorded deed 18 December 1806 from Henry Brooke of Prince George's County, for $2209.32 part of *Pleasant Plains of Damascus*, also part of *Johnson's Discovery*, together with part of *Resurvey on Gumspring*, all contiguous to each other, beginning at a tract of land called *Transylvania*, and adjacent to tract *Indian Fields* containing 274 ½ acres. Signed and acknowledged by Henry Brooke before M. Browning, G. Howard..

N:116-118. Kinsey Gittings of Benjamin recorded deed 22 December 1806 from Nicholas Brewer, trustee, for certain real estate mortgaged by Patrick Durham, 7 July 1799 to John Pleasants, Israel Pleasants and Samuel Pleasants,. Whereas by advise of the high court of Chancery, where John, Samuel and Israel Pleasants were complainants and John Kelly and Patrick Durham were defendants, the said Nicholas Brewer of Anne Arundel County, was appointed trustee for the sole purpose in the above recited mortgage, and on 13 March 1803 sold and conveyed tracts *Riley's Chance, Appernine Hills,* and a part of *Harrison's Delight,* the *Addition to Higgs*, and *Let no man deceive you,* to the said Kinsey Gittings for $1400. Payment having been made, deed is recorded.

N:118. Thomas Jones recorded schedule of debts &credits, 23 December 1806, an insolvent debtor. Debts James Winset, Rezin Harding, Thomas Conner, Thomas D. Mahay Jr., Josiah Beans Jr.

N:118. Gassaway Cross recorded certificate 22 December 1806, as deputy sheriff.

N:118-119. Samuel B. Brooke recorded bill of sale 27 December 1806 from Isaac Miller for $94.79 1/4 cents sells one bay horse, 10 years old; one gray gelding, other livestock.119-120. William Kelly recorded schedule 31 December 1806 of goods and credits. Debtor. Schedule: a barshear, one shovel plow, 2 wooden hoes.

N:120. Nicholas Haney listed the following schedule 31 December 1806, debts and credits: one sorrel colt in possession of Samuel Golding Junr., 3 gelts on Zachariah Offutt's plantation, 2 year old heiffer and one bay mare at Samuel Goldings Junr. One chair in the jail to John Thompson . Per act. 2/4; Basil Ricketts and John Easton, to an account agt. Solomon Holland for 6 1/4$. Signed before B. Gaither, Samuel Elgar.

N:120-123. Mordecai B. Offutt recorded 31 December 1806, from Ann Clagett guardian of Hezekiah, Ann, William, Elizabeth, Samuel, Mary Ann and Thomas Clagett, heirs of Samuel Clagett deceased who was heir at law to Henry Clagett of the one part and Mordecai Burgess Offutt of the other part. Witness that whereas in the High Court of Chancery for Maryland, November 1805, decreed in the bill of complaint filed against the heirs of Samuel Clagett deceased, the sale of a certain piece of land was ordered, called *Friendship.*

N:123-124. William Vinson recorded 1 January 1807 from Richard Thomas. Richard Thomas being legally possessed of tract, *Thomas Discovery Fortified,* for £529 sells tract beginning at *Father's Gift,* to 11th line of *Conclusion,* containing 157 acres. Signed and acknowledged.

N:124. Schedule of Christian Leaman recorded 2 January 1807. Names Robert Moore's note of hand, 1 scythe & cradle, to the benefit of an agreement with Walter Fryer.

N:124-125. Commission of appointment to Justices of the Levy Court, 8 January 1807 to Henry Brookes, Edward Burgess Jr., Richard West, Ozias Offutt, George Riley, Warren Magruder and Normand West.

N:125-126. Philip B. Key recorded deed 8 January 1807, from John Rowsby Plater of Saint Mary's County for $300 assigns lot, a part of *Bradford's Rest,* adjacent to Mr. Williams' lot, containing 199 ½ acres. Elizabeth Plater released dower rights. Acknowledged before Edmund Key, an Associate Judge of Maryland.

N:126-128. Basil M. Beall recorded deed 12 January 1807 from Benjamin Ray Jr. Sheriff, Selling land recovered in suit against Thomas Orme by Samuel Hammett. Tract *Cumberland,* 43 acres by patent, sold at auction.

N:128-129. Evan Jones recorded deed 12 January 1807 from William O'Neale for $1. Sells lot in Town of Rockville, part of lot #71, 72 & 73,

N:129-131. Dorcas Clapham of Frederick County, Maryland recorded deed 13 January 1807 from Samuel Clapham of Loudon County, Virginia. Whereas Samuel is indebted to Dorcas on two bonds, with interest, assigns *Fair Island* in the Potomac.

N:131-133. Leonard Hays recorded deed 14 January 1807, from Vachel Hall and Margaret Hall, for $1300 part of *Resurvey on Jeremiah's Park,* beginning on north side of town of Barnesville, on 2nd line of lot laid out for William Bennett, containing 108 acres.

N:133. Elizabeth Hobbs recorded list of slave 15 January 1807 that I removed from the State of Virginia with intention to reside in said County, the following Negroes have been my property from their birth: one woman, Ellenora, 25 years; one boy, son to Eleanor 5 years old called Joe and one girl, Kitty her daughter one year old; one boy called Ned five years old last June. Signed before Horatio Hobbs.

N:133-134. Jesse Phillips recorded deed 15 January 1807 from Samuel Allison of Brooke County, Virginia for £8..6 sells tract called *Hard to Get,* 8 ½ acres.

N:134-135. Commission recorded 15 January 1807 appointment of Justices of the Peace to William Smith, Lawrence O'Neale, Richard Green, Henry Brooke, Greenbury Howard, Edward Burgess Junr., Benjamin Gaither, James Lackland, Ozias Offutt, John Thomas, John Burgess, William Culver, Thomas Simpson, Richard West, John Adamson, Camden Riley, Warren Magruder, Richard Beall, Samuel Elgar, Meshack Browning, John Belt, Gassaway Harwood, Walter Brooke Beall, William Garrett, William Darne, Jesse Leach, Nathan Holland and Edward Tillard of Montgomery County. Honorable William Kilty, Esquire, Chancellor.

N:135-136. Mary Sands recorded deed 16 January 1807 from Frederick Duvall for $128, lot #46 in the town of Brookeville. Emsey Duvall wife of Frederick released dower rights.

N:137-139. James Simmons recorded deed 22 January 1807, from Susanna, Thomas and James Birdwhistle, part of *Friend in Need,* and *Second Resurvey on Friend in Need,* beginning at tract called *Father's Good Will,* conveyed by Benjamin Pelly and Ann Pelly to Jesse Wilcoxen, to tract formerly conveyed by Robert Peter to Thomas Birdwhistle for 45 acres; containing 246 ½ acres. Susanna Birdwhistle signed by mark, Thomas Birdwhistle and James Birdwhistle signed before G. Howard, M. Browning. Elizabeth, wife of Thomas Birdwhistle released dower.

N:139-142. Elizabeth Johnson recorded deed 23 January 1807 from Richard Thomas and William Thomas, sons of Richard Thomas late of the County, deceased, and Elizabeth Johnson, daughter of the said Richard Thomas for $5. Tracts, *Thomas's Discovery Fortified,* devised to them by deceased father's will. Deborah, wife of Richard Thomas and Martha, wife of William Thomas released dower rights.

N:142-144. Thomas Robertson, and Sarah Robertson, two of the grandchildren of Richard Thomas, deceased, recorded deed 23 January 1807, from Richard Thomas and William Thomas, sons of Richard Thomas, late of Montgomery County, and two of the grandchildren of the said Richard Thomas deceased of the other part, for $5. part of *Thomas's Discovery Fortified,* adjacent to part conveyed to Elizabeth Johnson. Deborah, wife of Richard Thomas and Martha, wife of William Thomas released dower rights.

N:144-145. Thomas Gittings and Nathaniel Willson recorded bill of sale 24 January 1807 from Henry Willson for $200. Assigns four wagon horses, one wagon and gare, one sorrel mare, two feather beds and furniture.

145. Lewis Beall recorded 26 January 1807, from John and Patrick Lyddane, bill of sale, livestock.

N:146-147. Thomas Frederick Brooke of Prince George's County, recorded deed 20 January 1807 from Samuel Craigh and Joanna his wife of the town of Alexandria in the District of Columbia, assigns part of tract known as *Dann*, sold by Clement Brooke unto Richard Forrest, containing 66 acres. Acknowledged before John Fleming, Samuel Elgar.

N:147-148. Stephen Anderson recorded deed 26 January 1807, from George Bowman for $955.55 sells part of tract called *Delay* granted in 1785 to Thomas Edmonston for 197 acres adjacent to *Pleasant Plains of Damascus* to second line of *Addition to Stony Range,* metes and bounds for 147 acres. George Bowman signed by mark, Elizabeth Bowman his wife relinquished dower.

N:149-150. John Gittings, recorded bill of sale 26 January 1807 from John McDonald for $14. One red cow and one brown yearling.

N:150. Benjamin White, recorded 26 January 1807 bill of sale from Anne Hoskinson, livestock.

N:150-151. Thomas Jones, recorded bill of sale from James Gatton for £70 assigns two feather beds, two iron pots.

N:151. Joseph Clarke, recorded bill of sale 2 February 1807, from Joseph Astlin for $200. One Negro male slave named John Carroll about the age of 15 years . Signed 19 January 1807. Wit Thomas Simpson.

N:152. Sabrina Beall records manumission 2 February 1807, for diverse good causes, declares free Negroes Nan, aged 39 years; Cesar aged 37 years, signed by mark before Joseph Joy, Nathan Holland Junr.

N:152. Evan Belt records certificate 3 February 1807, as Deputy Sheriff.

N:152. Samuel Nicholls records list of slaves 2 February 1807 brought into Maryland from Virginia. Flora about 38 years. Wit. Hezekiah Walker.

N:152-154. Joseph Poole and Benjamin Poole recorded deed 5 February 1807, from John Poole Junior for £11..5 part of tract called *Poole's Right,* which was conveyed to me by my father John Poole, Senior, on north side of main road called Coxon's Road, containing 3/8 of an acre. Prissa W. Poole released dower.

N:154. William Magrath recorded bill of sale 9 February 1807, from William Darne, being indebted to William Magrath for £25, sells one cart, one dark bay mare, one bay horse, one brindle cow, one red cow and one pied cow. If sum paid before 1 Nov. 1808, sale is void.

N:154-156. John H. Simmons of Frederick County, recorded deed 10 February 1807 from Leonard Hays and Eleanor Hays for $300 part of *Resurvey on Jeremiah's Park,* to part formerly conveyed to James Barnes for 2 acres. Signed by Leonard Hayes, Eleanor Hays by mark.

N:156. Henry Culver of Prince George''s County, recorded bill of sale 10 February 1807 from William Wheeler Sr., horses, sheep, milch cows, wagon and gears, furniture and farm equipment.

N:156-157. Nathan Jones recorded bill of sale 11 February 1807 from Archibald Trail for $50. one Negro girl named Nance aged about 13 years old and one Negro boy named Jack about 11 years old. Signed before Samuel Elgar.

N:157-160. Samuel H. Wheeler recorded deed 12 February 1807 from Isaac Hite of Frederick County, Virginia, for $5565. grants and bargains tract called *Concord,* beginning at fork in River Road and the road leading to Joshua Hickmans, containing 16 acres, and also part of tract called

Forrest, containing 50 ½ acres; and one other tract, *Resurvey on Discord,* containing 104 7/8 acres. Signed before G. W. Harwood, Richard Beall.

N:160-161. John Lyons recorded 13 February 1807 from Benjamin Norris, bill of sale for £27..1 ½. Sells two feather beds, bedsteads and furniture, six windsor chairs, 3 splinter bottom chairs, one cherry tree breakfast table, one woollen wheel, one women's saddle and poplar corner cupboard, other personal items, and wheel wrights tools. Signed before Nathan Holland Jr. Receipt recorded.

N:161. Negro Nancy recorded manumission from Eleanor Tippett 16 February 1807. Whereas Eleanor Tippett the elder, deceased by her will devised to her daughter Eleanor Tippett for the term of 12 years; she gives Nancy her liberty at an earlier period of time, Nancy to be free at the expiration of two years. Signed by mark before Nathan Holland Jr. and Upton Beall.

N:161-163. Upton Beall recorded deed 23 February 1807, from James Higgins and Luraner his wife, for 4 shillings, sells part of tract called *Joseph's Park,* of which the late Benjamin Becraft died seized, to contain 405 acres, their undivided half.

N:163-163. James Higgins recorded deed 23 February 1807, from Upton Beall for 5 shillings, sells one equal and undivided half of *Joseph's Park,* which the late Benjamin Becraft, died seized, to contain in the whole 405 acres.

N:163-167. Peter Becraft and James Higgins recorded deed of partition 23 February 1807. Whereas they are seized in fee simple and hold as tenants in common, dan equal share in certain parcel of land, called *Joseph's Park,* conveyed by Joseph Belt to Benjamin Becraft by deed dated 24 July 1759 for 321 acres, and the said Peter Becraft and James Higgins have made partition and all that piece as conveyed by Josias Talburt to Benjamin Becraft; adjacent to corner of land formerly belonging to Thomas Miles, on the east side of the road leading from Rock Creek to Bladensburg, also part of tract as conveyed by Doctor John Carroll and Robert Brent to Benjamin Becraft, containing in the whole 452 3/4 acres. Mary Becraft, wife of Peter released dower; and at the same time Luraner Higgins, wife of James Higgins, released dower rights.

N:167. Christopher Cole recorded schedule 23 February 1807, of debts and credits. Listed accounts due Jaret Kirkman, Charles Cooper, judgment, Basil Beall.

N:167-170. Alexander Whittaker recorded deed 24 February 1807 from Marian Soper of Prince George's County, executrix of James Soper late of Prince Georges County for £193..10 tract called *Difficulty,* containing 86 acres, also part of tract containing 14 ½ acres which George Wilson of Frederick County sold to James Soper. Signed by mark.

N:170-171. Pursuant to an Act of Assembly, the following bond was recorded 25 February 1807 by Richard Anderson, Solomon Holland, Honore Martin, Upton Beall and Lewis Beall, bound in the sum of $5000. They are jointly bound, by an act authorizing a lottery to raise a sum of money to purchase a fire engine and to purchase ground and build a school house in Rockville in Montgomery County, authorized to raise a sum of money not exceeding $2500, and to sell tickets thereof provided that they proceed in the sale, shall give good bond to State of Maryland in the penalty of $5000. And truly apply the moneys arising therefrom within 90 days to the payment of the prizes drawn therein to the adventurers to whom they shall be due; and after deducting the necessary expenses incurred in the management thereof shall apply the residue within 20 months to the purchasing ground in the said town, and building a school house thereon, and to purchase of a fire wagon.

N:171. Benjamin Bonifant recorded certificate of qualification 26 February 1807, as Justice of the Peace

N:171-173. Thomas Cramphin recorded deed 27 February 1807 from Benjamin Ray Jr. Late sheriff, selling property in case of Robert Christie plaintiff against Edward Veirs defendant and that of Samuel Sprigg for use of John Clarke, against Edward Veirs, defendant. Part of *Resurvey on Non Eaten* and part of tract called *Mary,* adjacent to Samuel and Basil Dyson's part of said tract, to Jonathan Swan's part to John Belmear's part. Containing ½ acre and 4 3/4 acres of land.

N:173-176. Thomas Cramphin recorded deed 27 February 1807 from William Harding, eldest son of Charles Harding, late of Frederick County, deceased. By authority of the will of his deceased father, for $766.50 sells part of three tracts, called *Hermitage* and *Chance,* as in deed of partition between Charles Harding and Elias Harding in January1787. Adjacent to Jeremiah Stimpson's land, to land laid out for Benjamin Perry,

N:176-178. Richard Gatton recorded deed 27 February 1807 from William O'Neale Sr., for £580..10 part of *Weavers Den*, and part of *Eleanor's Green*. Adjacent to each other, and adjoining *Piney Grove*. Sarah O'Neale released dower rights.

N:178-180. Dorcas Harris, widow of John Harris late of Montgomery County, deceased, recorded deed 2 March 1807 from Jesse Harris of Montgomery County, for part of *Mount Zion.*

N:180-183. Armistead Long recorded deed in trust 2nd Feburary1807 from Samuel H. Wheeler and Ann his wife; Samuel H. Wheeler is justly indebted to Major Isaac Hite of Frederick County, Virginia for $4,575.

N:183-185. Hezekiah Veatch recorded deed of trust 2 March 1807 from Armistead Long of Loudoun County, Virginia; whereas Armistead Long is justly indebted to Isaac Hite of Frederick County, Virginia, for £3000 lawful money of Virginia, and is desirous to provide for payment, for this and $1, he assigns tract in Montgomery County called *Black Walnut Tree Island,* that Hezekiah Veatch will sell for him.

N:186-188. Leonard Holliday Johns of Washington, District of Columbia, recorded deed 3 March 1807 from Kinsey Gittings of Benjamin for £754, part of tract called *Dann,* at 7th line of William Dent's part containing 25 acres; also part of tract called *Club's Delight,* on west side of Rock Creek, a little above Watry Branch, containing 88 ½ acres, Mary Gittings, released dower right.

N:188-190. Allen Green recorded deed 3 March 1807 from Caleb Gartrell for $2000 sells parcel of land sold by Ephraim Davis to my father, Aaron Gartrell, and will to me, part of *Benjamin's Lott,* containing 160 acres more or less. Signed before Richard Green, John Burgess. Rebecca wife of Caleb Gartrell released dower.

N:190-191. Robert Brown of the City of Washington, D.C., recorded deed 5 March 1807 from Samuel Davidson of Georgetown, Washington, D.C. for $2300 sells tract called the *Hermitage*, 129 1/4 acres, part heretofore conveyed to Davidson by Benjamin Ray, Sheriff 5 April 1796.

N:191-192. Edward Iglehart recorded bill of sale 2nd March 1807 from Jacob Hitechew of Montgomery County for $100, three black cattle, one sow and 8 shoats, all my crop of tobacco now hanging in the house, other crops now growing in the fields. Signed in German Script before Edward Burgess.

N:192-193. John Aldridge recorded bill of sale 3 March 1807, from Robert A. Whittaker for a valuable consideration, one Negro man Toney 37 years; woman Priss 35 years Negro boy Stephen about 5 years girl Sook about 3 years and their future increase. If full sum of $600 paid by 1st January next, bill of sale is void.

N:193-194. Charles Gassaway recorded bond 4 March 1807, as Coroner in Montgomery County with Hezekiah Thomas and John Candler.

N:194. James W. Perry and Peter Kemp recorded assignment 7 March 1807. I Thomas Reynolds of Prince George's County, for a valuable consideration, assign all my interest in and to a certain mill formerly owned by Walter Beall, and known by the name of Burnt Mill, and part of a tract of land known by the name of *Bealls Industry.* Signed February 1807. Wit. Wm Culver.

N:194-198. Leonard Boswell recorded deed 7 March 1807, from Greenberry Gaither of Nelson County, Kentucky, for £481 sells tracts, part of *Mitchell's Range,* and part of *Gaither's Range,* and part of *Gaither's Bastian,* beginning at *Resurvey on the Wolf Pit,* and *Pig Pen,* containing 121 ½ acres. Ann Gaither, wife of Greenbury Gaither released dower rights before Ninian Edwards. James Anderson served with power of attorney before Jesse Leach, Nathan Holland Jr.

N:198-199. Baruch Hall of Frederick County, Maryland, recorded deed 9 March 1807, from Charles Busey Junior of Jefferson County, Ohio, for $160 lots #36 and #90 in Hyattstown. Signed before Samuel Elgar, Benjamin Gaither.

N:199-203. John Linthicum recorded deed 11 March 1807 from Thomas Linthicum of Nelson County, Kentucky, for £600 part of tract called *Second Resurvey on Friend in Need,* conveyed to Ninian Beall by Thomas Birdwhistle, for 116 acres on 7th line of *Partnership.* Metes and bounds for part containing 26 2/3 acres. Another part adjacent to Jacob Water's part of the said tract, containing 26 acres, and part of *Partnership,* conveyed to Zachariah Linthicum by Benjamin Edwards, on 5th line of *Second Resurvey on William and John,* containing 146 acres. Signed by Thomas Linthicum, Ann Linthicum, wife of Thomas released dower.

N:203-204. William Bennett recorded deed 13 March 1807 from Henry Camden for $300 for part of tract called *Happy Choice,* for 99 1/4 acres. Mary B. Camden released dower.

N:204-206. Samuel Ridout recorded deed 17 March 1807 from William Stewart of Georgetown, trustee appointed by court of chancery of David Ross, Horatio Ross, and Archibald Ross, residuary legatees of Dr. David Ross late of Prince George's County. David Ross sold to said Ridout tract called *White Marsh,* and died before deed made.

N:206-207. Thomas Peter recorded deed 17 March 1807 from Richard Thomas and William Thomas, part of *Thomas's Discovery Fortified,* Deborah wife of Richard Thomas and Martha wife of William released dower.

N:207-208. Van Swearingen recorded bill of sale 19 March 1807 from Aaron Coaplin, for $56 for sorrell mare. Signed by mark.

N:208-210. James E. Wilcoxon recorded deed 21 March 1807 from William Willcoxon of Jesse for $24 assigns part of *Mount Zion,* on 26th line of *Resurvey on Jeremiah's Park,* containing ½ acre. Ruth Wilcoxon released dower rights.

N:210-211 Thomas Jenkins recorded deed 23 March 1807, from Solomon Holland, late sheriff of Montgomery County, whereas a judgment was obtained by Elizabeth Carroll against a certain Philip Jenkins, a writ of fi fa was issued, against two lots in town of Williamsburgh, now Rockville, lots #44 and #45, Thomas Jenkins was high bidder. Deed made for $1.

N:211-212 Thomas Jenkins recorded deed 23 March 1807, from Solomon Holland, late sheriff of Montgomery County. Whereas a judgment was obtained by John Janney against Philip Jenkins, a writ of fi fa was issued against property, for lot #24 in Rockville, for $600, sold to high bidder.

N:213-214. Leonard Edelin of Charles County, recorded deed 27 March 1807, from William Price Jr. For $20 part of tract called *Fat Bacon,* also part of tract *Conclusion,* on road leading from Mouth of Monocacy to Baltimore, containing ½ acre. Sarah Price, wife of William released dower.

N:214-215. Commission recorded 28 March 1807 to Henry Brookes, Edward Burgess Jr., Richard West, George Riley, Warren Magruder, Normand West and Henry Jones, to serve as Justices of the Levy Court.

N:215. Gustavas Easton recorded schedule 31 March 1807, includes 1 tea kettle, some earthen ware, table, six chairs, some pewter, 2 candle sticks, some knives and forks, a cradle, and case of razors.

N:215-216. Joseph Church recorded schedule 31 March 1807, one straw bed, one blanket, one quilt, ½ doz. Tea cups and saucers, two flower barrells, one ax, one grubbing how, one shovel plough, one small jug. Signed by mark.

N:216-217. Walter B. Beall recorded bill of sale 4 April 1807, from Zachariah Willson for $53. One bay mare, which I bought at the sale of Joseph Jackson.

N:217. George Jennings recorded schedule 4 April 1807, as insolvent debtor to sheriff of Montgomery County. Signed by mark.

N:217-218. Thomas West recorded bond, April 1807. We Thomas West and Samuel Middleton are bound for $600. Whereas by a judgment of Montgomery County Court at March Term, a Negro man named Hercules, the slave of a certain Thomas West was condemned to work on the public roads in Baltimore County for 18 months, and after that time to be sold for the use of the state of Maryland, and whereas the petition of the said West, the owner of the aforesaid slave, has directed the punishment of aforesaid, sell and transport the said Negro Hercules for his own benefit on his giving bond, the county court has approved. Signed Thos West, Sam'l Middleton. Wit. John Fleming.

N:218-220. Daniel Lee recorded deed 7 April 1807 from Joseph Simm, of Prince George's County for $1300 part of *Joseph's Park*. Beginning at lot #2, to a side of Benjamin Becraft's land, to 5th line of Leonard H. John's part of *Joseph's Park,* containing 210 ½ acres.

N:220-221. Charles A. And John Beatty recorded release April 1807, from James Offutt of Wm, administrator of Doctor Ozias Offutt . Whereas Col. Charles Beatty deceased, father of the said John and Charles, did 4 December 1804 as indemnity to a certain Zadock Offutt and the said Doctor Ozias Offutt, grant the lands herein mentioned, *New Harbour,* a resurvey on *That's It Resurveyed,* and whereas those engagements have since the death of the said Charles Beatty, been fully complied with by John M. Beatty, this release signed 30 March 1807, by James Offutt of Wm, administrator of Doctr. Ozias Offutt.

N:221-223 Joseph Elgar recorded deed 10th April 1807 from Alexander Allen. Whereas Allen many years ago passed his bond for the conveyance of 77 acres of land to Henry Townsend, which he afterwards conveyed and assigned to Mr. Barlow of Philadelphia, on whose death his executors entrusted Philip B. Key to sell said land, to any person who would purchase the same, and the said Key did lately sell lands at public sale and aforesaid Elgar became highest bidder; for $60 paid by him, Philip B. Key granted 77 acres, part of tract called *Outlett,* now in possession of William Wade, tenant, which came to him the said Alexander Allen as heir to his mother. Signed Alexander Allen before John Fleming, Samuel Elgar. Winfred, wife of Alexander released dower.

N:223-226. Henry Hawkins Young recorded deed 13 April 1807 from Francis McElewain, for £1152 tracts called *Aix La Chappelle* and *Utrecht*; Metes and bounds given. Signed before G. Howard, Benjamin Gaither.

N:226-227. Basil Musgrove Beall recorded deed 14 April 1807 from John Fleming for $840, part of tract called *Prevention,* otherwise called *Watchman's Purchase,* which land was sold by James Perry and William Williams (son of Thomas) to Jacob Barnes for 84 acres of land, see deed of conveyance.

N:227-228. Solomon Holland recorded bill of sale from Thomas Garrett, for £125..17 sells one mulatto woman named Beck about 45 years; one mulatto man named Owen 22 years old; one mulatto woman named Polly 17 years one mulatto boy named Bobb 11 years old and one dark bay mare 12 years old; one black mare 7 years old; one dark bay mare 7 years old; other livestock and furniture. If debt paid, sale is of no effect. Signed before Nathan Holland Jr.

N:228-229. At request of Benjamin Norris, an insolvent debtor, recorded schedule the 13 April 1807 of credits and goods given to Sheriff of Montgomery County. Debts: Elizabeth Crabb £1..13..9; Henry Dunlap, £7..0//6; Lewis Beall unsettled Montgomery County 0..15..0; John Eadler 0..15..0; Joseph Dove £3..14..0; Lance Willson £5..16..7 ½; John H. Barney .. 9..4 ½; Singleton White ..3..9; Thomas Most £1..4..9; John Burrass ..1..5 ½; Aquila Hall .. 2..6. Witness: Jesse Leach, Nathan Holland Jr.

N:229. At request of Jacob Hitechew, in insolvent debtor, recorded schedule 13 April 1807. Debt due from Thomas Sedgwick, acct. £2..12..6. Signed before Jesse Leach, Nathan Holland Jr.

N:229-230. Aquilla Cawood recorded schedule as insolvent debtor. Debts owed to Jesse Harbert, Stephen Tuttle. Signed before Nathan Holland Jr.

N:230-231. John Cunningham of Harford County recorded deed 20 April 1807 from Joseph Jackson of Montgomery County, for two tracts of land called *Saint Winexberg* and *Poplar Forest*. Guliana Maria, wife of Joseph Jackson released dower.

N:232. Isaac Miller recorded schedule 25 April 1807, as insolvent debtor. Debts James Anderson unsettled account, Zachariah Musgrove, ditto.

N:232. John Bealmar recorded release and receipt 27 April 1807. Samuel Bealmar received one Negro boy named Nace and one Negro girl named Berry, which were under bill of sale to me. Witnessed by William Bealmar.

N:232-233. David Clagett recorded bill of sale 27 April 1807. I Thomas M. King, for $150 sell livestock creatures, four cow kind, 19 hogs. Provided any balance should remain it is to be divided among my eight children with an equal distribution. Signed by mark before Martin Fisher, Thomas Fisher.

N:233-234. Thomas Buxton recorded deed 27 April 1807, from Kinsey Gittings of Benjamin. Whereas by a decree of the Chancery Court, the following lands, tracts *Riley's Chance, Appernine Hills,* and a part of *Harrison's Delight,* the *Addition to Higgs,* and *Let no man deceive you,* were deeded to the said Kinsey Gittings by Nicholas Brewer, and Gittings agreed to convey same as appointed trustee to Buxton, now indenture witnesses that for $1400 deed made for 194 ½ acres.

N:234-235. Levi Phillips recorded bill of sale 29 April 1807 from Jacob Droneberger for £25 sells blacksmith tools, belles, anvill and vice, a parcel of hammers and all the tools thereto belonging. If sum paid, bill of sale to have no effect.

N:235. John Baker recorded list of slaves, May 1807, late of the commonwealth of Virginia, brings in Martha, 26 years; Milly, about 5 years and Edy, age 3 years. Wit. Zachariah Walker.

N:235-237. Nicholas Pegno recorded deed 15 May 1807 from Philemon Griffith and Joshua Griffith, executors of the will of Henry Griffith of Frederick County for $80 assigns tract, containing 7 ½ acres.

N:237-240. Henry Howard of John recorded deed 15 May 1807 from Philemon Griffith and Joshua Griffith, executors of the will of Henry Griffith of Frederick County. Whereas the above Henry Griffith in his life time purchased of John Beal Bordley of the City of Philadelphia, for £1700 sterling, purchased *Tusculum, Elk Ridge, Resurvey on Griffith's Chance, Inman's Plains,* and *That's All,* and Henry departed this life before the purchase money was paid, which the executors paid, and in June 1797, John Beal Bordley deeded to the said Philemon and Joshua Griffith, a legal title, now for $10/acre or sum of $5400 current money, they convey *Tusculum, Resurvey on New Years Gift, Jones Chance,* and part of *Ward's Pleasure,* by whatever names, running reversed of given line of Samuel Griffith's land devised him by his father Henry Griffith, then adjacent to

Henry Gaither's lands, to intersect John Burgess' lands, to a line leading from the pear tree standing in the old field, containing 550 acres.

N:240-241. Evan Thomas recorded release 18 May 1807 from Thomas Brown. Whereas Evan Thomas did by indenture of lease on 11 April 1803, part of *Two Farms* and *Addition to Culver's Chance,* and *Berry's Meadow,* for the term of 99 years; subject to yearly rent of £72 for $1 he now assigns remainder of term of lease.

N:241-243. John Henderson recorded deed 21 May 1807 from James Maccubbin Lingan for $5 assigns *Zoar,* on north side of Long Draft Branch, containing 395 acres, by reference to deed of Robert and Gerard Briscoe to James Maccubin Lingan, in 1797, recorded in liber G, and also another part of tract, containing 23 acres. Signed and acknowledged and Janet Lingan released dower rights.

N:243-244. James M. Dawson recorded deed 25 May 1807 from John Belmair, for $1390 deed for part of *Resurvey on Friends Advise,* containing 105 acres. Mary Belmair, wife of John released dower.

N:245-246. Samuel Brooke recorded deed 25 May 1807 from Caleb Panacoast for $1000 confirms lots #14 and #15 lying in town of Brookeville.

N:246-247. Alexander Adams recorded deed 26 May 1807 from Archibald Orme for £56 ..5 shillings, grants tract called *Piney Grove,* containing 25 ½ acres. Signed and acknowledged.

N:247-249. William Trail and Anne Belt, the following marriage contract was recorded 26 May 1807. Articles of agreement. Anne Belt is seized of three tracts, from her deceased husband Carlton Belt, and personal property consisting of 18 Negroes: Stephen, Os, Bill, Moses, Joe, Tom, Jack (little), Moses, Sandy, Lucy, Eve, Candis, Charity, Hanner, Ann, Liley (little), Lucy and Sall; 35 head of cattle, 14 head of horses, 48 head of hogs, 35 head of sheep, together with household and kitchen furniture, plantation utensils and a set of blacksmith tools; he agrees with Daniel Trundle and the aforementioned Anne Belt, that should marriage take place, she will manage them during her natural life, and may dispose of them as she sees fit, as if she had remained sole by will or otherwise in her life. Signed by William Trail before Tilghman Belt, Amos Belt.

N:249-250. Benjamin Willett Sr. Recorded bill of sale 27 May 1807 from Ignatius West for £75 all goods on schedule herein. Furniture listed.

N:250-251. Benjamin Stoddert recorded deed 28 May 1807 from Isaac Pollock late of Montgomery County, presently residing in Washington, D.C., for $6300 all his right to parcel called *Magruder's Purchase* and *Addition to Resurvey on Magruder's Purchase,* but latterly known as *Fruit Hills,* containing by estimation 295 ½ acres; being the farm whereon he lately resided.

N:251. Manumission recorded 29 May 1807, from John Thomas Senior for diverse good causes and considerations, manumit Priscilla aged 35 years, and Anthony age 31 years; Poll about 14; John about 11, Thomas about 9 years, Maria about 6 years; Anne about 4, William about 2 years and Rachel about 2 months, the children of the Priscilla above named. Recorded 29 May 1807. .Signed in the presence of Abram Jones, William West.

N:251-252. George Washington Haymond recorded deed 4 June 1807, from Will Carroll for 7 shillings, part of tract called *Williams Meadows,* lately conveyed by the above named George Washinton Haymond to Samuel Wilson, containing 4 acres more or less. Signed by mark before Nathan Williams Jr., Jesse Leach.

N:252-253. Commission recorded 5 June 1807 for Justices of the Levy Court to Edward Burgess Jr., Richard West, George Riley, Warren Magruder, Normand West, Henry Jones and Samuel Lane of Montgomery County.

N:253-254. Elizabeth Thomas, daughter of Samuel Thomas 3d, deceased, recorded deed 8 June 1807 from Richard Thomas and William Thomas, sons of Richard Thomas, deceased, late of Montgomery County, for $5 they assign part of *Snowden's Manor Enlarged,* devised to them by their father, by will dated 8 November 1806, beginning at second line that Richard Thomas deceased had conveyed to John Thomas 3d for 33 1/8 acres, and running thence to tract called *Charles and Benjamin,* to 8th line of *Snowden's Manor Enlarged,* formerly conveyed by Richard Snowden to Richard Thomas for 650 acres, then to the north side of the main road, to the beginning containing 221 ½ acres. Deborah, wife of Richard, and Martha wife of William Thomas released dower.

N:255-257. Peter Kemp recorded 8 June 1807 deed made 13 May 1807 between Mary, widow of Thomas Edmonston and Andrew Scholfield and Elizabeth his wife of Fairfax Co., District of Columbia, Robert Edmonston and Eden Edmonston of M.C., whereas Thomas Edmonston deceased, the father of Elizabeth Scholfield, and Robert and Eden Edmonston, by his last will, dated in 1801, among other things devised to his daughter, Dolly Edmonston, all that part of a tract called *Bear Garden,* conveyed to him by James Beall, containing 8 acres, Dolly Edmonston previously sold tract, but had only received a life estate from her father, this deeds property. Signed by all parties.

N:257-259. Baley E. Clarke of Prince George's County recorded deed 9 June 1807 from Thomas Rhoads for $4116. Sells part of *Rhodes Good Luck,* beginning at a line of *William and Elizabeth,* on 14th line of tract *Deakin's Hall.* To Bayley Erles Clark.

N:259-260. Ann Newton Chiswell recorded deed of gift 9 June 1807, from Joseph N. Chiswell for natural love and affection for his daughter, grants to her one Negro boy about 9 years old by the name of Tilman.

N:260. Manumission from James Spencer[3] recorded 9 June 1807, in consideration of £50 paid, release from slavery my Negro woman Lydia about 30 years and able to work and gain a sufficient livelihood, and her three children: Phillip, Mary and Caroline. Wit. Richard Beall, John Benson.

N:260-262. John Eliason recorded deed 11 June 1807, from Joseph Browning of Washington County, District of Columbia, for $300, sells part of the *Resurvey on Red Oak Slipe,* 100 acres; and a tract called *Fancy,* containing 30 acres more or less, and one called *No Name,* on north west side of Bennets Creek, containing 10 acres, which were devised to the said Joseph Browning, through Jeremiah Browning Senr. and Edward Browning the 3d, son and grandson of Edward Browning the first, and is intended to be all the land so as aforesaid devised to him under him, to hold the two undivided fifth parts of land. Signed and acknowledged by Joseph Browning.

N:262-263. William Prather recorded deed 13 June 1807 from Sykes Beckwith, for $150 sells part of *Adamsons and Beckwiths Discovery* adjacent to *Resurvey on the John and Rose.* 14 3/4 acres. Metes & bounds given.

N:263-264. Greenbury Murphey recorded deed 13 June 1807 from Caleb Pancoast for $45 lot #17 in town of Brookeville. Mary Pancoast released dower.

N:264-265. Artaxerexes Fisher recorded bill of sale 16 June 1807 from William Carroll (a free mulatto) of Montgomery County for $25. One sorrell mare and one brown mare. If sum paid with interest before 1st September next, then this bill of sale is void.

N:265-267. Lloyd Beall recorded deed 17 June 1807 from Samuel Beall for $10. Part of *Batchellor's Forest,* containing 33 perches. Elizabeth Beall, wife of Samuel released dower.

N:267. Nathan Prather Swailes recorded bill of sale 17 June 1807 from Robert Swails for natural love and affection for my four children: Nathan Prather Swailes, Ann Willcoxon Swails, Robert Goldsborough Swailes and Margaret Goldsborough Swailes, I grant and confirm to them in equal proportion the following property: one Negro man called Neal, one Negro woman called Beck; one woman called Dark; one boy called Bob; one boy called Dick; three feather beds, bedding and furniture, one cradle bed and furniture; one mare and her colt; one gray horse, one bay horse, one roan horse, 27 head of sheep, 24 head of hogs and 17 head of cattle. Signed before Jno Thomas 3rd, Thos C. Wilcoxon.

---

[3]James Spencer appears on the 1810 Census with a family of 7 in the "other free persons" column. He died intestate in Montgomery County, before June 1818, when Solomon Davis filed an administration bond and an estate inventory. Estate sales, showed most purchases made by the widow, Lydia Spencer. An administration account shows a balance of $3.80 from an estate worth $245.35. A deed was recorded to James Spencer, former servant of Thomas Morton, on 2 May 1814, from Joseph Morton, devisee of Thomas Morton of Anne Arundel County, for a 50 acre tract "*Trouble for Nothing.*" The 1820 Tax lists show that the heirs of James Spencer still held this property. Jerry Hynson, *Free African Americans of Maryland, 1832,* shows in Montgomery County: Lydia Spencer, 56, Philip Spencer 26, Mary Spencer 28, William Spencer 24, Rachel Spencer 22, and four other young children: George-4, Jim-3, Thomas-3 and Mary-1.

N:267-268. Nathan Prather recorded bill of sale 17 June 1807, I Robert Swailes for $500. Sell one Negro man called Jerry; 3000 pounds of tobacco in the house, all my crops of every time I have now growing; two desks; one cupboard, 2 tables, 8 chairs, a parcel of books and all household & kitchen furniture except what I have this day conveyed to my children. Signed before John Thomas 3rd, Thos C. Wilcoxon.

N:268-270. Richard Beall recorded deed 18 June 1807, from William Hilton for $250 part of tract, *It May be Good in Time,* in two parts one part containing 3 3/8 acres, adjacent to 12th line of *Hempstone's Discovery,* the second part containing 21 1/4 acres. Elizabeth Hilton released dower.

N:270-272. Richard Beall recorded deed 18 June 1807, from Thomas Reid for $680, part of tract called *Round Knowl,* and also *Mount Carmel,* containing 85 acres. Sarah Reid released dower.

N:272-273. William Hilton recorded deed 18 June 1807, from Richard Beall for $5 tract called *Resurvey on Trouble for Nothing,* containing 3/4 acre.

N:273. Elizabeth Johnson, recorded schedule as an insolvent debtor, 18 June 1807, which includes lots with furniture in the houses in the City of Philadelphia.

N:273-274. Jacob Swamley, recorded bond 19 June 1807, for office of constable.

N:274-275. Zachariah Dowden recorded deed 20 June 1807, from John Shook for $1 grants tract called *Brandy Hall,* on the third line of *Hunting Hill,* on the south side of the main road leading from George Town to the Mouth of Monocacy, containing 7/8 acre. Dorcas Shook, wife of John, released dower rights.

N:275-276. James M. Lingan recorded deed 20 June 1807 from Archibald Trail for $56. Tract on Seneca, called the *Resurvey on Mill* tracts, and tract of said Lingan heretofore purchased and his brother Ozburn Trail. Monica Trail wife of Archibald released dower.

N:276-277. Carlton Belt and Elizabeth his wife recorded release of dower 23 June 1807 from Sarah Jones, relict of Edward Jones late of Montgomery County, for $100 releases all her right to tract of land called *the Eleven Brothers,* containing 86 1/4 acres..

N:278-279. Charles Willson recorded deed 23 June 1807, from Carlton Belt, for £575, part of land called the *Whole Included,* near Sugarland Road on 24th line of tract *Wilson's Delay.* Elizabeth Belt released her dower rights.

N:279-281. Gerard Brooke recorded deed 23 June 1807 from Richard Thomas and William Thomas, sons of Richard Thomas late of Montgomery County, deceased for $5 part of *Thomas's Hog Pasture* containing 630 acres. Deborah wife of Richard Thomas and Martha wife of William Thomas released dower rights.

N:281-283. Jacob Marshburger recorded deed 27 June 1807, from Ephraim Warfield of Anne Arundel County, for £300 assigns lands lying partly in Montgomery County and partly in Anne Arundel County. 59 1/4 acres called *Hillsborough.* Signed and acknowledged.

N:283-284. George Culp recorded mortgage 27 June 1807 from Jacob Marshberger, for $4073 tract called *Advise,* lying partly in Montgomery County and partly in Anne Arundel County containing 59 1/4 acres; and a tract called *Hillsborough* containing 45 acres more or less. Signed by mark.

N:284-285. Christian Getzendanner recorded deed 27 June 1807, from Richard Wootton for £750 part of tract called *Younger Brother,* containing 203 1/3 acre. Martha Wootton wife of Richard released dower.

N:285-287. Thomas Clagett recorded deed 2 July 1807 from Zachariah Offutt for £100, deed for part of *Blackoak Thickett.* 205 acres. Eleanor Offutt released dower right before Benjamin Gaither and Wm Darne Jr.

N:288-289. Henry Griffith Jun recorded deed 3 July 1807 from Philemon Griffith of Frederick County, Maryland and Joshua Griffith of the state of Kentucky, executors of Henry Griffith Senr. Of Montgomery County. Henry Griffith had purchased from John Beal Bordley of Philadelphia, and departed this life before the purchase money for said lands was paid; tract known as *Borcham's Spring,* on branch of Hawlings River. Signed and acknowledgments in Frederick County.

N:290-293. Thomas O. Williams of Prince Georges County, recorded deed 3 July 3 July 1807 from Harriet Williams, Leonard H. Johns and John K. Smith of Georgetown, executors of the will of Elisha O. Williams late of Georgetown, part of *Exchange and New Exchange Enlarged.* Adjacent to part sold Philip Jenkins, and adjacent to the first line of the town of Williamsburg containing 67 ½ acres. The other part of 148 acres in the deed, is south ward of the main road from Rockville to the Mouth of Monocacy.

N:293-294. Samuel Griffith recorded deed 3 July 1807 between Philemon Griffith and Joshua Griffith executors of Henry Griffith Senr. Deceased. Whereas Henry Griffith by his will, gave to his son Samuel certain lands purchased from John Beal Bordley, for which a deed was not made, before he departed this life, now this confirms deeds.

N:294-295. Zachariah Warfield and William H. Pleasants of Goochland County, Virginia, recorded agreement 4 July 1807. Whereas a dispute exists regarding lines and boundaries of certain lands lying near Snells Bridge on Patuxent or Snowden's River held by said Warfield in his own right and the said Pleasants as executor of Thomas Pleasants deceased, the agree on Henry Griffith, Thomas Davis and John Chew Thomas as arbitrators. Description of lines between tracts given.

N:296-297. William Henry recorded deed 4 July 1807 from Jesse Hyatt for £75 lots #219, 20, 73 & 74 in Hyattstown.

N:297-298. Charles A. Beatty recorded power of attorney from his brother, J. M. Beatty, 5 July 1807, to Hezekiah Harris and others, to give efficacy and effect to deeds to Leonard Hays, William N. Silver, Otho Holland, Williams Luckett.

N:298-299. Peter Becraft recorded bill of sale 7 July 1807 from Mordecai Mobley for $450 sells Negro woman named Rebeckah, one iron grey horse, one brown horse, one brown & one red cow, other livestock, rye, corn and tobacco in the ground, and furniture. Signed before Nathan Holland.

N:299-301. James Wallace recorded deed 7 July 1807 from Daniel Lee of Montgomery County for $10, part of tract called *Joseph's Park.* Priscilla Lee wife of Daniel Lee released dower.

N:301-302. Robert Waters recorded deed 10 July 1807 from William Lodge for $101.25 sells parts of *Small Profit,* 2 ½ acres, *Hickory Grove,* beginning at 3d line of *Piney Level,* 5 acres and part of *Rich Meadow,* 1 3/4 acres, in all 9 1/4 acres. Signed and acknowledged.

N:303-304. William Willson recorded deed 14 July 1807 from Warren Magruder for $370, part of *Lick Hill,* beginning at *Allison's Park.* Harriot Magruder released dower rights.

N:304-305. Charles Courts Jones recorded deed 17 July 1807 from William Needham of Montgomery County, for $131. Part of *Labyrinth* to Andrew Hugh's part of *Labyrinth,* to 2nd line of *Clean Drinking,* containing 9 acres. Signed, acknowledged..

N:305-306. John Templeman recorded deed and decree 20 July 1807 from Samuel Brooke Beall and Thomas Brooke Beall, deed made 29 January 1795, for £150 land in Potomac called *Turkey Island.* Acknowledgment was recorded. "Samuel W. Brooke Beall, Roger Perry trustee of Samuel Brooke Beall; Harriet Beall and widow of Thomas Brooke Beall, Sarah Beall, Isaac Brooke Beall, Thomas Heugh Beall, Gustavus Beall, Mary Heugh Beall and Thomas Tilghman Beall, heirs at law of Thomas Brooke Beall in chancery, February term 1807, the said cause standing ready for — and being submitted by the complainant, the bill exhibit and publication together with all other proceedings were by the Chancellor read and considered and the chancellor being satisfied that the omission to record the deed in the bill mentioned was without any fraudulent design or intention in the party claiming" ... decree by William Kilty that deed should be recorded.

N:306-307. Henny Ann Campbell Belt recorded deed of gift 21 July 1807 from Anne Trail, formerly wife of Carlton Belt, and since his decease, wife of Mr. William Trail, by and with the full consent of Mr. Trail, gives to my daughter Henny Campbell Belt, daughter of the said Carlton Belt, the following Negro slaves: one boy Jack 4 years old; Sall a girl about one year old, to be delivered to her after my death. Signed Anne Trail, William Trail signed permission.

N:307. Manumission from John Riggs to Nelly. Recorded 25 July 1807. Manumit my mulatto girl named Nell about 22 years of age. Signed John Riggs before Rick Green, Saml Riggs, Thos Davis.

N:307-310. Robert D. Dawson recorded deed 29 July 1807 from Richard Thomas and William Thomas, sons of Richard Thomas late deceased, of Montgomery County for $1522.50 tracts *Promise Fulfilled,* also part of *Resurvey on Mitchell's Range,* on south side of Seneca, three parts, one as deeded by Edward Gaither to Richard Thomas 1 July 1767, in all 217 ½ acres. Signed and acknowledged; Deborah, wife of Richard and Martha wife of William Thomas released dower.

N:310-311. Adam Robb recorded bill of sale 29 July 1807 from James Suter one Negro girl named Rachel about 12 years old. Provided nevertheless that if sum of £22.12 shillings paid on or before 10th December next, bill of sale is void.

N:311-313. Charles Willson recorded deed 30 July 1807, from Richard Jones for $1269 part of *Eleven Brothers,* containing 70 1/4 acres on first line of Carlton Belt and Elizabeth, his wifes' part of the tract. Elizabeth Jones released dower.

N:313-314. Charles Willson recorded deed 30 July 1807 from Carlton Belt and Elizabeth Belt his wife for $1269, part of *Eleven Brothers,* 86 1/4 acres.

N:315-316. Charles Gassaway recorded deed 31 July 1807, from Leonard Boswell for $378 sells 76 1/4 acres, part of tract *Mitchell's Range,* to first line of a tract called *Promise.* Reane Ann Boswell released dower rights.

N:316-317. Benjamin Berry recorded bill of sale 3 August 1807 from Robert Brooke Beall for $2000 sells Negro slaves: man named Peter and man named Jacob, one man named David and one woman named Bea and her children Sal, Sin and Peg; one Negro woman named Arry and her children Arch, Abel, Beck and Lucy; one Negro woman named Jane and her children Dick, Jane, Nance, Mariah and Acilton, likewise stock of horses, black cattle and hogs with all my household furniture. Receipt for $2000. Signed before Thos Simpson.

N:317. Edward House recorded bond 4 August 1807, to perform duties as constable. Signed with Solomon Holland.

N:317-318. Edward Burgess recorded bill of sale recorded 4 August 1807 from John Flemming. for £750 sells one Negro man Joe, 20 years; boy Harry 15years old; boy Patrick 12 years old; boy Vachel 11 years; boy Will 7 years old; Negro woman Henny 30years old and her child; Negro woman Lydda 40 years and her child; Negro woman named Nan, 55 years old; Negro woman Jenny 57 years old; to Edward Burgess Senior. Signed before Ben Ray Jr., Edw Burgess Jr.

N:318-319. Bennett Clements recorded bond 4 August 1807, to perform constable's duties with John Candler and William Darne, Jr.

N:319. Thomas West recorded bill of sale 6 Aug. 1807, from Rebecca English for $38, 3 feather beds and furniture, plates, crockery, other household items. Signed by mark before Jesse Leach.

N:319-321. Nathan White recorded deed 6 August 1807, from Leonard Howard for £10 part of *Hopewell,* containing 8 7/8 acres. Ann Howard released dower.

N:321. John Austin recorded bill of sale 8 August 1807 from Moses Stephens for £45 sells to John Austin Junr., John Ward Junr., and Ashford Trail, one black mare; one black colt and one bay colt; 2 cows and 2 yearlings.

N:321-324. Bernard Gilpin recorded deed 11 August 1807, from Richard Thomas and William Thomas for $5 assigns part of *Thomas's Discovery,* on 7th line of tract conveyed to Thomas and Sarah Robertson, adjacent to *Seneca Fork,* containing 343 acres; 2nd part begins at *Resurvey on Gravelly Ridge,* contains 123 acres.. Deborah wife of Richard and Martha wife of William Thomas released dower.

N:324-325. Robert P. Magruder records deed of trust 11 August 1807, from Thomas Pollard Junr., grants one Negro man, Nero; one woman slave by name of Moll; one other woman slave by the name of Beck; one mulatto girl slave by name of Sarah, and a Negro boy child by the name of Robert; four feather beds and furniture, 4 head of horses, one mahogany desk, one mans and woman's saddle, and bridle, one cart and gears, 2 shot guns, 3 ploughs and gears, 4 axes, other items. To secure to him for an account of the said Thomas Pollard and a debt due James Groomes. Signed before G. Howard, Benjamin Gaither.

N:325-326. Jeremiah Ducker recorded bill of sale 17 August 1807 from Benjamin Ray made 1 May 1806 by a certain Thomas Pitt Hays and Elizabeth his wife five Negro slaves two wit: Moses, Sam, and Lott and Lott's two children: Jane and John, which is recorded in records of Montgomery County, and since that time, Negro Jane died, and the said Negro woman Lott has had another female child whose name is Milly. Whereas the intention was that Benjamin Ray would hold the slaves for the sole use and separate benefit of Elizabeth Hays, and in no manner liable to the debts or contracts of her husband; for the premises above, and for five shillings paid by Jeremiah Ducker the brother of the said Elizabeth Hays, rents the said Negro slaves, Moses, Jane, Lott and the two children John and Milly. Signed Ben Ray Jr.

N:326-327. Jacob Smith recorded deed 25 August 1807 from Jesse Hyatt for £6, two lots #18 and #75, in Hyattstown, to pay annual rent of 5 shillings per lot. Signed & acknowledged.

N:327-328. Solomon Holland recorded deed 26 August 1807 from Honore Martin for £310 three lots in the town of Rockville on the southwest corner of Jefferson and Washington Sts. Sarah Martin wife of Honore Martin released dower rights.

N:328-329. John Bonifant recorded bond 26 August 1807 as constable.

N:329-331. Elizabeth Carroll recorded deed 3 September 1807 between the right reverend John Carroll of Baltimore and Robert Brent of the District of Columbia, surviving executors of Daniel Carroll Senior deceased, in consideration of will of Daniel Carroll, and distribution to grandchildren, for $1 assigns part of *Josephs Park*. As laid off by William Smith, surveyor, in 1804, adjacent to part sold by Daniel Carroll to Benjamin Becraft, to line of lot #3, held by Daniel Lee and conveyed to him by Joseph Simon, to the church lot of two acres, containing 198 2/10 acres.

N:331-333. Ann Carroll (one of the grandchildren of the deceased) recorded deed 3 September 1807, from the right reverend John Carroll of Baltimore and Robert Brent of the District of Columbia, surviving executors of Daniel Carroll Senior deceased, for 5 shillings, and in compliance with will, assigns part of *Josephs Park* as laid off by William Smith, surveyor, 19 June 1804 as lot no. 6 on said survey, beginning at 500 perches on 2nd line of *Joseph's Park,* containing 106 acres. Before Dan'l Brent, Robt Y Brent, acknowledged before Wm Culver, Thos Simpson.

N:333-336. William Carroll (one of the grandchildren of the deceased) recorded deed 3 September 1807 from the right reverend John Carroll of Baltimore and Robert Brent of the District of Columbia, surviving executors of Daniel Carroll Senior deceased , for 5 shillings, and in compliance with will, assigns part of *Josephs Park* as laid off by William Smith, surveyor, 19 June 1804 as lot nos. 8 & 9, beginning at part conveyed to Hugh Conn, and part that became the property of Clement Beall, to part conveyed to Thomas Cramphin, containing 216 3/4 acres. Deed delivery was delayed to allow parties to make arrangements with regard to a debt due from the estate of Daniel Carroll to Charles Carroll of Carrollton, and a debt likewise to from Patrick Sims (for whose benefit part of lot #9 was always intended) to the within mentioned Robert Brent, by the parties. It was agreed that the said William Carroll shall pay, or secure to be paid $1000 on account. Signed 7 April 1807 by Wm Carroll.

N:336-338. Elizabeth Carroll of the City of Washington, D.C. recorded deed 3 September 1807 from William Carroll for $1. Sells and assigns to her a lot of land conveyed to him by the executors of Daniel Carroll Sen. Out of a larger tract of land called *Joseph's Park*, part adjacent to Benjamin Becraft's part, containing 19 acres. Signed and acknowledged before Walt B Beall, Thos Simpson.

N:338-340. John Carroll, Bishop of Baltimore, and Robert Brent recorded bond 5 September 1807 from William Carroll of the City of Washington; whereas they have sold to Elizabeth Carroll a certain part of *Josephs Park* which includes within the lines thereof the old mansion house and former residence of Mrs. Eleanor Carroll deceased. William Carroll is to provide the educational support of his brother George Carroll until he arrives at the age of 21 years, and the balance remaining unapplied to be then paid over to the said George Carroll his heirs or assigns, and as Joint heir of his father Daniel Carroll Junr. Estate; he is also to pay remaining debts of estate of Daniel Carroll Sr. Daniel Carroll Junr. Dec'd 1798 June 28 to Wm Deakins executors $198.98Thos Cramphin, pd. Him 19.0. 3; Richard Ponsonby on acct., Findley Banadyne $700. Doctor Stuarts bond & interest 338.13.4; Doctor Stuarts account 64.0.6; Total: £760.19.11 1/4.

N:341. John Kelly recorded bill of sale 18 August 1807 from Jacob Howard for $200 sells and assigns one dark bay mare and colt; other livestock, housewares and furniture.

N:341-344. Doctr John Bowie recorded trust deed 26 August 1807 from Daniel Lee. Whereas Daniel Lee by his obligation to Thomas Cramphin, dated 6 April 1807, for £500, and Daniel Lee had purchased of Joseph Sim of Prince George's County, part of *Joseph's Park* containing 211 acres, assigns same to b e sold at public sale.

N:344-345. Peter Kemp recorded deed 26 August 1807 from Dorothea Edmonston of Montgomery County, and Edward Edmonston late of Prince Georges County; for $243 part of *Bear Garden Enlarged,* beginning at part formerly conveyed by Archibald Beall to Joseph Perry, containing 8 1/10 acres, Signed before Wm Culver, Walt B. Beall.

N:345. Thomas C. Nicholls recorded bond 26 August 1807 for constable with John Buxton, Jr.

N:345-349. William N. Silver recorded deed 31 August 1807, made 19 June 1807 between John M. Beatty, and Charles A. Beatty son of Col. Charles Beatty, late of the District of Columbia, Deceased; and William Norris Silver of Montgomery County, son of the said William Norris, the father, now deceased, with condition the sum of £63..15 a part of tract of land, called *That's It Resurveyed,* bearing date 10 April 1789.

N:349-350. Leonard Hays recorded deed 4 September 1807 from Alexander Reid for $324 assigns part of *Friendship,* to the 4th line of part laid out for Robert Sollers for 30 acres; containing 54 acres. Signed before Laurence O'Neale, Richard Beall. Mintie Reid released dower rights.

N:350-351. Solomon Holland recorded bond 5 September 1807, as Collector of the Tax for Montgomery County with Honore Martin and Lawrence O'Holt.

N:351-352. Benjamin Stoddard of Georgetown, recorded deed 9 September 1807 from John P. Vanness and Marcia his wife of the City of Washington, for $1 part of *Magruder's Purchase,* and *Addition to Magruder's Purchase,* but lately called *Flint Hills,* containing by estimation 295 ½ acres. Signed and acknowledged before J.P's of Baltimore, Theophilus Doughterty, John Bankson.

N:352-353. Aquila Beall of Prince George's County, recorded deed 9 September 1807, from William Campbell for £200,, tract called *Montrose* adjoining lands of Col Archibald Orme and Aquila Beall, 100 acres. Signed and acknowledged.

N:353-355. Zachariah Thompson recorded deed 16 September 1807 from Samuel Phillips of Prince George's County for $600, part of tracts *Hope Improved, Ray's Adventure,* and *Trouble Enough,* adjacent to line of deed conveyed by James Perry to Wm Gatrell for 25 acres; containing 135 1/4 acres.. Elener Phillips wife of Samuel released dower rights.

N:355-357. Sabrina Beall and others recorded deed 18 September 1807 from Philip B. Key. Whereas Colonel George Plater formerly of Saint Mary's County, now deceased, was in his lifetime seized in fee of a tract called *Bradford's Rest*, and sold part of it by his agent Joseph Sprigg Belt to Jeremiah Beall, and Jeremiah Beall, on 20 October 1801 made and published his last will, and devised a life estate to his wife Sabrina Beall, and after her death this same to be equally divided among his nine children: Daniel Beall, James Beall, Henrietta Beall, Elizabeth Beall, Sabra Ford wife of James Ford, Margaret Beall, wife of James E. Beall; Mary wife of John B. Magruder and Martha wife of Nathan Holland; and that Martha Holland aforesaid has since the death of her father, also departed this life, leaving her husband in full life and four infant children: Elias Holland, Sarah Holland, Mary Ann Holland and Eliza Holland, and leaving them entitled as tenants in common to one ninth part of land so devised by the will of their grandfather. Tract *Bradford's Rest,* containing 271 ½ acres. Anne Key wife of Philip Barton Key released dower rights.

N:357-360. George Washington Haymond recorded deed 19 September 1807 from Jane Threlkeld and Nancy Threlkeld of Shepherds Town, Berkeley County, Virginia for $1565 sells two parcels, parts of *Ebenezer* and *Paris*, beginning at tract called *Lucas's Adventure,* to part sold by Archibald Orme to Jane Threlkeld, 78 1/4 acres. Signed before Solomon Holland, James Perry

N:360-363. Harriet Williams, Leonard H. Johns and John K. Smith, executors of an estate of Elisha Williams, late of Georgetown, Washington, D.C. recorded deed 19 September 1807, from Thomas O. Williams. Whereas Thomas P. Williams on 8 October 1794 conveyed to Thomas O. Williams and Elisha O. Williams, tract called *Exchange and New Exchange Enlarged,* metes and bounds given adjacent to Rockville boundary, and up to the courthouse lot containing 148 acres; this deed assigns 67 ½ acre part for $1. Mary Clagett wife of Thomas Owen Williams released dower.

N:362-365. Charles Courts Jones recorded deed 19 September 1807, from Clement Smith of Washington, D.C. Whereas Charles Courts Jones by deed 26 November 1804 and sums deposited at the Bank of Columbia, bought part of a *Resurvey on Clean Drinking*.

N:365-367. Doctor John Bowie recorded deed 19 September 1807 from Charles C. Jones, indebted to Thomas Cramphin for $5800 with interest at end of six months from date of indenture (14 August 1807) secured with property, part of *Clean Drinking,* including the dwelling house of said Charles C. Jones, about 600 acres, except for 100 acres sold Thomas Cramphin. Signed before Thos Simpson, Walt B. Beall.

N:367-368. William Willson of John recorded deed 21 September 1807, from James Day, executor of Josias Harrison late of said county, for £225..9, lot #3, part of *Resurvey on Elizabeth,* adjacent to part of deed from Henry Griffith to Josias Harrison, for part of *Cow Pasture,* containing 133 5/8 acres. Signed and acknowledged before G. Howard, M. Browning.

N:368-369. James Hawkins recorded deed 21 September 1807 from William Willson of John for £225..9, lot #3 at end of last line of *Locust Bottom.* Sarah Willson released dower rights.

N:369-370. John Barber Junr. recorded 24 September 1807 the deposition of Edward King Senr., that on the 11th March last he was at the house of John Barber Junr. And he called this deponent and Elisha Walker to take notice that it was his will and desire that his daughter Nancy, should have a Negro girl named Matilda, one feather bed and furniture, and equal division of his estate with the rest of his children. Sworn 22 September 1807. Deposition of Elisha Walker, stated same. To Nancy Barber, depositions before Edward Burgess Jr.

N:370-372. William O'Neale Sr., recorded deed 24 September 1807 from Thomas Garrett and Elizabeth Garrett his wife for £102, one undivided half part of *Adamson's Choice* which fell to them by the decease of Eli Fee Haymond, who inherited tract under the will of William Fee.

N:372-374. Lewis Bealmear recorded deed 26 September 1807, from Samuel Bealmear for £1550, four parcel, two pieces of *Valentines Garden Enlarged,* a part of *Hobson's Choice,* and part of *Two Brothers,* in the whole 214 acres. Priscilla Bealmear wife of Samuel released dower.

N:374-377. Samuel Bealmear recorded mortgage 26 September 1807, from Lewis Bealmear. Sums of £350 pounds to be paid before the 25 March 1808, £350 before 25 March 1809 and £350 before 25 March 1810, to secure payment of same, mortgage for four tracts conveyed above. Elizabeth wife of Lewis Bealmear released dower rights.

N:377-378. Richard Freeman recorded bill of sale 26 September 1807 from Samuel Hepburn Esquire late of the town of Upper Marlborugh in Prince George's County, did in his life time some years ago sell his Negro woman slave called Dinah and her child Jacob to a free Negro man called Richard Freeman, the husband of said Dinah, and received full payment. In consideration of the premises I Samuel Judson Coolidge, administrator make over and convey the said Negro woman Dinah and her son Jacob to the said Richard Freeman. Signed 12 September 1807.

N:378-379. Honore Martin recorded deed 1 October 1807, made 20 June 1807 from John Shook for $80, part of *Brandy Hall,* adjacent to the *Pines,* containing 2 ½ acres. Dorcas Shook released dower rights.

N:379-380. William Holland recorded deed 2 October 1807 from Samuel Brooke for $125, tract called *Charlotte,* patented by Peter Cassanave, 15 October 1775, on 12th line of *Friendship,* to 17th line of *Charles and Benjamin,* and *George the Third,* containing 10 1/4 acres.

N:380-381. Asa Holland recorded deed 7 October 1807, from Michael McLewain and Amelia Mclewain for $200. 1/5 part of undivided tracts known as part of *Painter's Range, Cow Pasture,* and *Conclusion.*

N:381-382. William O'Neale Jr. recorded deed 10 October 1807, From John O'Neale for lot #3, part of *Wheel of Fortune,* 56 ½ acres. (signed by mark). Mary O'Neale released dower.

N:382-383. Richard Gott recorded deed 13 October 1807 from John Belt for £253..19..4, part of *Resurvey on Friend's Advise,* containing 96 3/4 acres. Signed, no dower release.

N:384. Robert Soper recorded certificate 13 October 1807, to qualify as Deputy Sheriff before Jesse Leach.

N:384. Joseph Forrest recorded bill of sale 13 October 1807 from John Chambers of Henry for £15 one grey mare, crop of corn and wheat and rye and oats. Signed before Nathan Holland Jr.

N:384-386. George Wolfe recorded deed 15 October 1807, from John H. Smith, guardian on behalf of Meshook, Susanna and William Richards, appointed by court to transfer parcells called *Ivy Reach, Hard Struggle* and *Resurvey on Discovery.* Lands formerly conveyed by Jesse Hyatt to William Richards containing 20 acres.

N:386-387. George Wolfe recorded deed 15 October 1807, from Ely Hyatt and Jesse Hyatt, for 5 shillings, same three tracts as above containing 20 acres

N:387-388. William W. King recorded deed 20 October 1807, from Arnold Warfield, for $100, part of lot #10, in Clarksburgh. Margaret Warfield released dower rights.

N:389-390. Thomas Windsor recorded deed 20 October 1807 from Nathan Burdett for $250. Part of tract called *Cow Pasture* at third line of *Hope Improved.* Mary Burdette released dower rights.

N:390-391. James Offutt of William recorded 24 October 1807, between James D. Offutt and Mary Offutt his wife now residents of the state of Kentucky, for $95. Part of *Fair Dealing,* that fell to Mary Offutt by her brother Zadock Offutt.

N:391-392 George Riley deed 24 October 1807 from William Clements, Edward H. Clements of Montgomery County for $800 all their right to tract called *Dann.* Ann wife of William Clements and Minty wife of Edward H. Clements released dower rights.

N:392. Leonard Watkins recorded qualification certificate 24 October 1807 as Justice of the Peace.

N:392-394. John B. Medley and others recorded power of attorney 26 October 1807. We Azaraiah Sanders of Nelson County, Kentucky and Zephorah his wife, for diverse good causes appoint John B. Medley attorney to affix names to deed to Thomas B. Beall. John Hobbs justice for Nelson County, affixed his name.

N:394-396. John Poole Jr. Recorded deed 26 October 1807 from Azariah Weaver Sanders and Zephorah Sanders his wife of Nelson County, and John Poole Jr. Assignee to Thomas B. Beall. Deed signed by John B. Medley, their attorney. Whereas Azariah W. Sanders made bond 23 October 1793 to Thomas B Beall, deed made for tract *Widow's Lot,* containing 27 acres.

N:396-397. James Suter recorded deed 27 October 1807, from Zadock Dickerson. Whereas He held certain estate in trust for separate use of Ruth Suter, who is now dead, leaving her husband in full life, he has become entitled to have real estate reconveyed to him, for sum of five shillings.

397-398. Laurence O. Holt recorded bill of sale from Alexander Suter, for £17..7 sells one dark bay gelding, one bright bay mare.

N:398-399. Benjamin King of Anne Arundel County, recorded deed 31 October 1807 from John M. Penn, crop of wheat and rye, plantation utensils and household furniture, livestock. Signed before Edw Burgess Jr.

N:399-400. Greenbury Griffith recorded deed 2 November 1807 from Benjamin Ray Jr. Late sheriff, on matter of Adam Robb by judgment against the estate of Thomas Orme, late of Montgomery County for £40 debt with interest plus costs. Tracts called *Hispaniola* and *Hold Fast*.

N:400-401. Lewis Tabler recorded deed 2 November 1807, from George Davis of Frederick County for $225, lots #3 and #57, in Hyattstown. Elizabeth Davis wife of George released dower.

N:401-403. Hamon Duvall recorded deed 2 November 1807 from George Culp of Montgomery County for $200 part of *Richardson's Range,* and part of *Owen's Resurvey,* metes and bounds for 168 acres. Signed by mark.

N:403-405. Thomas Jones recorded deed 2 November 1807 from Jeremiah Fowler of Montgomery County for £21 assigns *Fowlers Adventure*, beginning at *John's Delight,* resurveyed by John Harris, 2 June 1769, containing 3 3/4 acres. Lydia Fowler released dower rights.

N:405-406. Adam Robb recorded bill of sale 2 November 1807, for $132. Personal property. Ammishaddi O'Hagan. Witness Daniel Leach.

N:406-407. Paul Summers recorded deed 3 November 1807, from Bernard Gilpin, *Resurvey on Mount Radner* 97 ½ acres and 2nd part begins at 1st line of *Henry and Elizabeth Enlarged,* 4 acres. Signed and acknowledged before Richard Green, John Adamson.

N:407-409. Nicholas Hall son of Joseph, recorded deed 3 November 1807 from Jacob Steirs Jr. For $500 part of *Mount Zion,* on road leading from Monocacy to Greens Bridge. Sarah Steirs released dower rights.

N:409-411. Benjamin Watson of Pennsylvania, recorded deed 5 November 1807, from Richard Young for £381..15 tract lying in Frederick, Montgomery and Anne Arundel Counties. *Resurvey on Hobb's Purchase,* part of *Hazard* and *Never Fear,* 254 ½ acres, beginning at *Bush Creek Hills,* to 9th line of Charles Hobbs part of *Hazard* and *Never Fear*. Rebecca Young released dower.

N:411-412. John Buxton Senr. Recorded bill of sale 7 November 1807 from Brooke Buxton for $1000 sells and delivers to him, livestock, plantation utensils; weavers loom and gears and one copper still, crops of corn, wheat rye and tobacco, plantation utensils.

N:412. William Clements recorded power of attorney from Thomas Blacklock of Nelson County, Kentucky, to ask and demand and recover from a certain Camden Riley of Montgomery County, a debt due me. Signed 10 August 1805.

N:413. James H. Rawlins and Benjamin Bonifant recorded bill of sale 9 November 1807 from Horatio Beall for £180 sells one Negro man named Dick about 21 years old, nine head of cattle.

N:413-414. Thomas Garrett recorded release 12 November 1807 from Solomon Holland, for 5 shillings, mulatto woman Polly about 17 years old, conveyed to me by bill of sale 10 April 1807.

N:414-415. William Scott recorded bill of sale from Amos Scott, 12 November 1807 for £52, one old Negro woman by name of Grace; one bay gelding, 3 feather beds and furniture, one red cow, six winsor chairs, 2 walnut tables, one trunk, one cupboard.

N:415-416. James P. Soper of Anne Arundel County, recorded deed 14 November 1807 from Samuel Ridout of Annapolis, for $262.75 tract called *White Marsh,* adjacent to road leading to Bladensburgh containing 162 ½ acres.

N:416-417. John Etchison recorded deed 16 November 1807, from Bernard Gilpin for $100 part of *Mount Radnor,* beginning at 2nd line of *Henry and Elizabeth,* containing 93 acres. Signed & ack.

N:417-419. Elisha Etchison recorded deed 16 November 1807, from Bernard Gilpin for $100 part of *Mount Radnor,* beginning on the 3rd line of *Henry and Elizabeth,* containing 53 1/4 acres, and a 2nd part of SE corner of part of *Mount Radnor,* to Jonathan Fry's lot, containing 10 acres.

N:419-420. Mary Howard of Frederick County recorded deed 16 November 1807 from Samuel Thomas Junior, Sarah Thomas, Henrietta Thomas and Elizabeth Thomas of Montgomery County for £10 part of *Addition to Charley Forrest,* 225 acres, part of divided tract. Signed by Samuel Thomas Jr., Sarah Thomas, Henrietta Thomas, and Elizabeth Thomas. Mary, wife of Samuel Thomas Jr., released dower.

N:420-421. Samuel Thomas Junior, Sarah Thomas, Henrietta Thomas and Elizabeth Thomas of Montgomery County recorded deed 16 November 1807 from Joseph Howard and Mary his wife, of Frederick County for £10 part of *Addition to Charley Forrest,* 121 acres, part of divided tract.

N:421-422. Burgess Willett recorded deed 19 November 1807 from Catharine Jones, Jesse Leach and Sarah Leach his wife; and Polly Willett all of Montgomery County, children and heirs of Ninian Willett who died intestate, possessed of *Jones Inheritance,* and are entitled to undivided shares of real estate.

N:423-427. Leonard Hays recorded deed 19 November 1807 from Charles A. Beatty heirs. Whereas Charles Beatty gave bond to William Jarrett for property who passed his bond to Leonard Hays 12 January 1799, now known as *Resurvey on that's It Resurveyed,* 49 ½ acres, deed from heirs of Charles Beatty to Leonard Hays made. . Letty Beatty wife of John M. Beatty and Eunice Beatty wife of Charles A. Beatty released dower rights

N:427-429. John Adamson recorded mortgage 21 November 1807, from Watson Beckwith, whereas by bond of obligation for $240 dated 14 July 1807, secures with tract *Paradise Enlarged.*

N:429-430. John Spohn recorded deed 23 November 1807, from Laurence Snyder for £225, part of *Moneysworth,* adjacent to lot formerly the property of George Harris on NE side of the Great Road. Eave Snyder, wife of Laurence Snyder released dower.

N:430-432. Daniel Smith Senr. recorded bill of sale 23 November 1807 from Daniel Smith Jr. for £308/13 sells Negro man called Ralph; Negro boy called Basil and one called Jim, one old Negro woman called Phillis and one Negro girl called Hannah, all my household furniture, an old wagon and gears, four horses, two colts, 22 head of cattle, 5 head of sheep, 19 hogs and 25 pigs; a parcel of old tobacco and my present crop of tobacco in the house, all my wheat, rye and oats.

N:432. Thomas Perry recorded bill of sale 24 November 1807 from Francis Perry for $60. One Negro girl named Nell about two years old. Signed before Edward Burgess Junior.

N:432-434. John R. Campbell recorded deed 26 November 1807, from Joseph D. West of the District of Columbia for $300 part of *Exchange and New Exchange Enlarged,* conveyed to him by William Magrath, 8 June 1797, adjacent to courthouse lot in Rockville. Signed and acknowledged.

N:434-435. Joseph D. West recorded deed of mortgage 26 November 1807, from John R. Campbell for $250, lot #39, agreeable to plat of Williamsburg, now called Rockville. Signed & acknowledged.

N:435-437. Barton Duley recorded deed 28 November 1807 from James D. Offutt and Mary his wife, of Kentucky, for £100 all their interest in 20 acres and a mill on the same land that James Offutt devised to his daughters.

N:437-438. Mary Howard recorded deed 30 November 1807 from Richard Thomas and William Thomas, sons of Richard Thomas deceased for $5 assigns part of *Snowden's Manor Enlarged,* containing 27 Acres. Deborah Thomas and Martha Thomas released dower.

N:438-439. Hezekiah Veirs from George Clarke of Baltimore County, power of attorney recorded 2 December 1807 directed to sell, lease or let tract *Harrymone Outlet* containing 200 acres.

N:439-440. James Bayley recorded bill of sale 2 December 1807 from Jacob Lizear for $200 sells crops and household furniture, black cattle, and plantation utensils.

N:440. Robert W. Fleming recorded qualification certificate as Justice of the Peace, 5 Dec. 1807.

N:440-441. Thomas Peter and others recorded bill of sale 7 December 1807 from Isabell Grant of Montgomery County for 7593 pounds crop tobacco and £5..3 sells to Thomas Peter, Robert Peter, David Peter, George Peter and James Dunlap executors of the will of Robert Peter deceased and James Peter of Washington, D.C. all my tobacco; some packed and some hanging in the house, two horses, and a colt; four cows and 3 yearlings, 10 head of sheep, furniture and plantation utensils named. Signed by mark before Nathan Holland, Wm Smith.

N:441-443. Lewis Beall recorded deed 5 December 1807, from Alexander Adams. Whereas Benjamin Adams late of Frederick County, deceased, did by his will 5 October 1764, give to Sarah his wife, land on north side of the road commonly known as the Falls Road during her life, and after her deceased to son Alexander for $1500 he conveys part of *Exchange and New Exchange Enlarged,* containing 157 acres, whereon William O'Neale, Sr., lately resided.

N:443. William Buxton of Thomas recorded list 8 December 1807, late of Clarke County, Kentucky, viz: Negro Jenny about 42 years; Negro Harriett 5 years; Negro Dingo 2 years old, property of the subscribers.

N:444. Bond to State of Maryland by John Fleming, as sheriff, recorded 9 December 1807, with Henry O'Neale, Saml Lane, Thomas Fletchall, Nathaniel Beall, Van Swearingen, William Benson.

N:444-445. Elizabeth Robinson recorded bill of sale 9 December 1807 from Benjamin G. Orr, for value received in certain service performed by Elizabeth Robinson, her sons Wm, Robert and Olly and her daughters, Esther, Lizzy and Hannah, conformably to certain articles of agreement made in February 1803, I hereby assign to Elizabeth Robinson and her heirs, all my right title and estate in a certain Negro man named John Lee. Signed Benj. G. Orr before John Adamson.

N:445-446. Adamson Waters recorded bill of sale 10 December 1807. I Nacy Waters of Montgomery County for $700 sell and assign all the goods, household stuff, Negroes, stock and crop implements and furniture particularly mentioned in the following schedule, to wit: one Negro man named Solomon, one boy named Lewis, 6 head of hogs, one cow, 2 horses, three feather beds and furniture, 6 Windsor chairs, one desk, one cupboard, one dozen Chaney cups and saucers, half dozen plates, all my crop of tobacco raised in the last summer, etc. Signed Nacy Waters before Jesse Leach.

N:446-447. William Lee, a Negro recorded manumission 11 December 1807. I Betty Robinson[4] of Montgomery County for diverse good causes and the further consideration of $82. Release from slavery and set free my son, William Lee, a Negro man, being of the age of 22 years the 23 February last and able to work and gain a sufficient livelihood. Signed Betty Robertson by mark before Jesse Leach, John Braddock.

N:447-448. Upton Beall recorded deed 11 December 1807 from Lewis Beall for $50 part of tract, *Exchange and New Exchange Enlarged,* beginning at 8th line of tract, to the main road leading to Frederick Town from Rockville, to part of tract conveyed formerly by Arthur Nelson to Thomas Johnson, containing 72 sq. perches. Signed before Nathan Holland Jr., John Adamson.

N:448. Walter B. Beall recorded bill of sale 17 December 1807 from Zachariah Willson, for $100 assigns one black mare 8 years old, and one black colt about 6 months old.

N:449-452. Hezekiah Harris et.al (Charles Hay Harris, Ann Harris and Rebecca Harris, all sons and daughters of Nathan Harris, late of Montgomery County) recorded deed 18 December 1807, from John M. Beatty and Charles A. Beatty, sons and devisees of Charles Beatty of Washington, D.C. deceased. Whereas Charles Beatty made and executed his bond in writing 10 April 1789 for £240 to Nathan Harris, now deceased, to convey land being resurveyed about 75 acres, on paying sum of £112..10 paid in his lifetime with interest, deed made for *That's It Resurveyed,* adjacent to part formerly conveyed to William Norris son of George, containing 63 1/8 acres. Letty Beatty wife of John M. Beatty and Eunice Beatty wife of Charles A. Beatty released dower.

N:452-453. Elizabeth Beall from Sabrina Beall, bill of sale for £18..15 sells my Negro girl Milly, aged 4 years 2nd February last, to serve until she arrives to the age of 25 years.

N:453-454. Rachell Beall recorded bill of sale 21 December 1807 from Sabrina Beall to her daughter, for £10 my bay mare colt, Bonny 3 years old. Signed before Nathan Holland.

---

[4]Betty Robinson, aka Elizabeth Robinson (see two deeds earlier) may be Betsy Lee age 80 on 1832 Free Black Census, along with John Lee, age 80. Others in that group included Esther Robinson 40, Betsy Lee 37 and Hannah Lee 31.

N:454. Henrietta Beall recorded 21 December 1807 from Sabrina Beall, bill of sale for £15 for my Negro girl, Amy, aged 2 years 12 March last past, she to serve until she arrives at the age of 25 years. Signed by Sabrina Beall.

N:454-455. Schedule of Mordecai Mobley, an insolvent debtor, received 23 December 1807 listed some shoemakers tools, some old barrels, 1 powdering tub, two hoes, one razor, one flax brush, some straw and some fodder before Jesse Leach, Richard West.

N:455. Schedule of Samuel Moore, insolvent debtor made 25 December 1807, listed some shoemakers tools, 1 piggin, 1 boot, 1 mans saddle, some old barrels, 1 keg, 1 jug, 1 razor.

N:455-456. John Beall of Levin recorded list of slaves recorded 23 December 1807. Negro Lydia about 35 years; Rachel about 9 years old; property of subscriber by deed of gift made by the late Col. George Beall of Prince George's County

N:456-458. Charles Gassaway recorded agreement 24 December 1807 with Ezekiel Linthicum, Thomas Hickman and Thomas Fletchall on behalf of his sister, Elizabeth Hickman. Whereas Ezekial Linthicum and Thomas Hickman, part of a tract called *Preston's March,* and the said Linthicum holds in fee simple part of a tract called *Cider and Ginger,* adjacent to *Preston's March;* and the said Charles Gassaway holds in fee simple a tract called *Refusal,* adjoining to the aforesaid, and above and controversies have arisen between the said Ezekkial Linthicum, Thomas Hickman, Elizabeth Hickman, and Charles Gassaway respecting the variation of the compass lines of *Preston's March,* they have come to an agreement, to fix boundaries.

N:458. Charles Soper recorded schedule 24 December 1807, an insolvent debtor listed one saddle and bridle, and one silver watch, before Jesse Leach, Nathan Holland Jr.

N:458-460 Josiah Jones recorded deed 24 December 1807, made 16 November 1807 between Eden Edmonston for $750, part of tract devised to me by Thomas Edmonston, part of *Deer Park Enlarged,* to second line of division between Roger Edmonston and Thomas Edmonston. Receipt. Acknowledgment. No dower release.

N:460. William O'Neale of John recorded schedule 28 December 1807, an insolvent debtor listed a parcel of dung hill fowls, 1 iron pot, 3 old barrels, ½ dozen knives and forks. Signed before Nathan Holland, Jr.; Richard West.

N:460-462. Lewis Beall recorded deed 28 December 1807 from George Washington Haymond for $76, assigns parcel that was conveyed from him to Samuel Willson, 24 March 1806, leased by him to a certain Will Carroll, and afterwards released to him, being part of *Willaims Meadows,* Signed before John Adamson, Jesse Leach. Mary Haymond released dower rights.

END OF LIBER N

INDEX

113

114

116

119

121

125

126

131

133

135

Index to Town Lots & Other Place Names

INDEX TO LAND TRACT NAMES

138

139

www.ingramcontent.com/pod-product-compliance
Lightning Source LLC
Chambersburg PA
CBHW080616270326
41928CB00016B/3084